Christ Church Papers No. 1

CHRIST CHURCH AND REFORM
1850–1867

THOMAS JONES PROUT
'The Man who Slew the Canons'

CHRIST CHURCH AND REFORM 1850–1867

E. G. W. BILL
AND
J. F. A. MASON

OXFORD
AT THE CLARENDON PRESS
1970

Oxford University Press, Ely House, London W. 1
GLASGOW NEW YORK TORONTO MELBOURNE WELLINGTON
CAPE TOWN SALISBURY IBADAN NAIROBI DAR ES SALAAM LUSAKA ADDIS ABABA
BOMBAY CALCUTTA MADRAS KARACHI LAHORE DACCA
KUALA LUMPUR SINGAPORE HONG KONG TOKYO

PRINTED IN GREAT BRITAIN

FOREWORD

SINCE 1929 much work has been done on the contents of Christ Church Library, and since 1950 even more on the Archives of the House. As a result a very large amount of material on the history of Christ Church and its possessions has come to light. The House hopes to issue at irregular intervals monographs and editions by various hands which will make some of this material available in print.

HENRY CHADWICK
DEAN OF CHRIST CHURCH

18 October 1969

PREFACE

WE were led to produce this study of constitutional change in an Oxford college by the imminence of the centenary of the Christ Church, Oxford, Act of 1867; though in the event it was not possible to publish it in the centenary year. We have written at what some may think excessive length; but Christ Church is a unique institution, the events which led to the Act of 1867 have no parallel in any other Oxford or Cambridge college, and the transition to modern Oxford was beset by special difficulties in the House.

These events have not been related before in any detail, though H. L. Thompson, who took part in them, left succinct summaries in his excellent books on Dean Liddell (1899) and on Christ Church itself in the College Histories series (1900), as did Arthur Hassall, who knew several of those who took part, in his commemorative volume of 1911; we have found their works most helpful. But resident senior members of Christ Church have, on the whole, been little prone to reminisce in print; as a result much of this book is necessarily based on unprinted sources whose nature has not always enabled us to describe the personalities of our story as fully as we would have liked.

Although the records of Christ Church, notably the Chapter Act Books, amply show the pre-1867 administration of the college at work, the Dean and Chapter (being the party under attack) made no attempt to keep an official record of the events of 1858 and 1867; accordingly we have been much dependent on the invaluable private collections of correspondence made by Dean Liddell and T. J. Prout now in the archives of Christ Church (MS. Estates 117, ff. 1–90, 91–207), and on MS. 449 (the minute book kept by Prout's colleague, T. V. Bayne) in Christ Church Library. (Unfortunately, Bayne's extant diaries, also in Christ Church Library, begin much too late to be of use.) The

Longley, Palmer, Wordsworth, and Tait Collections in Lambeth Palace Library, portions of the Gladstone Papers in the British Museum, the papers of the Executive Commissioners appointed in 1854 in the Public Record Office, and Mountague Bernard's papers in the Bodleian Library, particularly the two last, are other foundations of our account.

For light on the views of those hostile to the changes of 1867 we are grateful to the Principal and Librarians of Pusey House (for access to the papers of Dr. Pusey) and to the Warden of Liddon House (for access to the manuscript diary of H. P. Liddon). We were not able to trace the papers of two of the five Referees whose Award was the basis of the 1867 Act, but we are grateful to Lord Coleridge and Lady Page Wood for their attempts to enable us to find those of Sir J. T. Coleridge and of Lord Hatherley. Lord Saye and Sele made available the papers of Edward Twisleton, and we are most grateful for his generous hospitality. Lord Harrowby kindly provided a copy of a letter to his grand-uncle, and the Warden of St. Edward's School a copy of an extract from A. B. Simeon's manuscript autobiography; Mr. R. F. Cox of Messrs. Begbie, Robinson & Co. provided a copy of the Report on the accounts of Christ Church in 1865. Mr. P. Jaques has also assisted us. One gap in our sources should, however, be mentioned; the full papers of Dean Liddell himself, if they exist, have not yet been traced.

The late Mr. John Walter kindly answered questions; Mr. Roger Lancelyn Green assisted us by checking that the letters of C. L. Dodgson then known to him (March 1967) contained no reference to our subject. (Dodgson himself once meditated an account of the negotiations of 1865–7. In his diary for 17 March 1882 he wrote: 'In the evening took to Prout's room the MS. book Payne [*rectius* Bayne] has lent me (record of meetings of Students etc., in the days when we negotiated with the Chapter etc., about our position) and we looked through letters he [i.e. Prout] had on the subject. I contemplate printing, for private circulation, a history of the whole affair' (*Carroll Diaries*, ii. 405). So far as is known. Dodgson never wrote, let alone printed, the proposed account. He certainly intended to use the essential sources: the book lent him by Bayne was Christ Church Library MS. 449; the letters in Prout's possession were those now in Christ Church Archives, MS. Estates 117.)

We must mention with particular pleasure our conversations with the Reverend R. F. McNeile, the senior ex-Student of Christ Church, whose recollections of the survivors of the Christ Church of the 1860s whom he knew nearly seventy years ago were vivid and helpful.

Members of the staff of the Library, the Treasury, and the College Office of Christ Church have all smoothed our path in various ways.

Finally we are grateful to the Dean of Christ Church, to Dr. J. N. L. Myres (collateral descendant of Dr. Heurtley), to Mr. R. N. W. Blake, and to Mr. W. E. S. Thomas for reading our text and for their valuable comments. Professor W. R. Ward performed the same kindly office for Part I. They are not responsible for the imperfections and infelicities of our account.

In one sense we have been presumptuous; for we are both non-gremial members of Christ Church, and in the abusive word of an earlier day are therefore 'squills'. Nevertheless, we hope we have interpreted with understanding the motives and actions of the Dean, Canons, and Senior Students of the House who, in their different ways and from their different standpoints, sought a century ago to fashion Christ Church to its own best advantage as a place of religion, learning, and education.

E. G. W. B.
Archivist

J. F. A. M.
Librarian

Christ Church
St. Frideswide's Day, 1968

CONTENTS

APPENDICES

LIST OF PLATES

I

The Old Christ Church

FOR more than a century Oxford has endured the steady and unremitting tramp of reformers, and seldom can any institution have submitted so patiently to the attentions of the well-intentioned. University reform is a subject on which any man may have an opinion, and indeed most have, and were it possible to muster simultaneously all those who have obliged the University in this respect, they would undoubtedly stretch, if not from Land's End to John o' Groats, most certainly from Paddington Station to Worcester College. Of all reforms which took place in this period, the most momentous were those which occurred in the middle years of the nineteenth century, for they, more than any other, transformed the nature of the University. Two theories of the purpose of a university education were in conflict. For centuries Oxford had been the cradle of the Church of England. Education was in the hands of its clergy, who held almost all Fellowships and generally looked to a career in the Church on leaving the University, and admission was restricted to Anglicans. In such a system, education was not vocational, except for the clergy, and more attention was paid to the training of judgement and to the inculcation of Christian morals than to the advancement of learning. Yet within a few years the monopoly of the Church of England had been fatally breached, and by a succession of Acts of Parliament, commencing with the Oxford Act of 1854, the University was liberalized, ancient restrictions removed, and the principle of free competition established. The University became increasingly secular in character, the gradual abolition of tests and oaths opened it to those sections of the community previously excluded, and learning was stimulated by opening Fellowships and increasing the professoriate.

It is frequently a prior condition of reform that it should, not necessarily with a pious regard for truth, discredit the system which it seeks to replace, and unreformed Oxford has suffered many unjust criticisms and calumnies, some of which have remained unchallenged. The University was represented as sunk in sloth and corruption, fettered by medieval customs and obsolete practices and hostile to the morning breath of reformation. It was a picture in which the warts obscured the features. One of the principal sources for this view of Oxford was the Report of the Royal Commission published in 1852, but it is sometimes forgotten that while many desirable and necessary proposals were there put forward, the main intention of the authors of the report was nothing less than to revolutionize the University by transferring power to the hands of the Professors. As a cure for the undoubted ailments of Oxford it was comparable with the surgeon who cured his patient of tonsilitis by cutting his throat. Acceptance of the criticisms of Oxford without due allowance for the motives and purposes of those who made them, has obscured the fact that the evils from which the University suffered were to a large extent of recent origin, and that they varied greatly between one college and another. The case of Christ Church, which, having had no statutes at all for over 300 years, received two sets within less than a decade is of particular interest in this connection. It was not only the largest and wealthiest college, but it had never suffered from the torpor of which Gibbon complained in the eighteenth century, and in the first quarter of the nineteenth century it had led the University in academic distinction. In the years that followed, the tutorial system developed symptoms of strain, and an important cause, as in other colleges, was the unforeseen effect of the public examination system. But at Christ Church other causes were also at work which were peculiar to the college, and causes which were perhaps prevalent in other colleges were non-existent at Christ Church. The principal defects of Christ Church in this period flowed not from the University but from the social and educational condition of society as a whole. As in all institutions there were some opposed to all reform, but at Christ Church their number, except perhaps in the Chapter, was small. The most senior of the Tutors gave their support to the Tutors' Association of 1852–4, which stood for moderate reform and in particular for reform of the tutorial system, and the Senior Censor, Osborne Gordon, was an influential voice in mustering support for the extension of studies in the University introduced by the statute of 1850.[1] Given the temper of the Tutors of Christ Church and the absence of many of the obstacles to reform which existed in other colleges, it may be asked why the introduction of reform was the cause of prolonged and sometimes acrimonious debate. The answer is to be found in the constitutional arrangements at Christ Church, which were such that what in other colleges was an argument about education became, at Christ Church, an argument about power. If the Royal Commission failed to diagnose the true causes of the decline of Christ Church, it would be unreasonable to expect the solutions offered by the legislature to meet the case, without adopting an exhilarating view of the wisdom of Parliament.

Thus it was that the Ordinance of 1858, which was the product of the Oxford Act of four years earlier, failed utterly to solve the problems of Christ Church, and threw the college into a state of confusion for almost ten years until a body of statutes, drawn up by mainly lay referees, was embodied in the Christ Church, Oxford, Act of 1867.

For the colleges, their statutes were at the heart of reform. They were the instrument through which power was distributed and exercised, and their function was well described by the Royal Commission in 1852. 'No Statutes

[1] O. Gordon, *Considerations on the Improvement of the Present Examination Statute* (1847).

are really required', it remarked, 'except those which define its [i.e. a college's] constitution and government, the rights and duties of its members and officers, the mode in which vacancies are to be filled up, and the causes which are to produce such vacancies.'[1] Christ Church was alone amongst Oxford colleges in having no statutes, and although there is good evidence that statutes would have been granted but for Henry VIII's death early in 1547, the foundation was of such a nature that from its commencement the college was well able to function without them. In the Dean and Chapter, who were stated by the foundation charter of 1546 to be the legal corporation of Christ Church and in whom the endowments were vested, there existed a body familiar in English law and imbued with known powers and attributes, and since no serious attempt was made in the years following the foundation to provide statutes, it may reasonably be assumed that from the beginning the Governing Body was intended to be the Dean and Chapter. The usual functions of college statutes did not in these circumstances require definition, for the members of the Governing Body were appointed by the Crown and not by election or co-option and they possessed the power ordinarily exercised by any capitular body. They stated a historical fact when they informed Lord Palmerston in 1854 that 'the Dean and Chapter are the Corporation'.[2] Despite its dual nature as cathedral and college, Christ Church was united in its Governing Body as a single foundation, 'a house of education', as Dean Gaisford put it, 'within the University, just as are the other colleges'.[3]

By the same token, Christ Church was, as Gaisford informed the Archbishop of Canterbury in 1854, 'totally and fundamentally different from every other cathedral in the kingdom'.[4] Almost the only diocesan duty it discharged

[1] *Report of the Oxford University Commission* (1852), p. 147.

[2] *Second Memorial of the Dean and Chapter of Christ Church to H.M. Secretary of State for the Home Department* [1854].

[3] *Report of the Cathedrals Commission* (1854), p. 769.

[4] Ibid.

was the election of the Bishop of Oxford and the Cathedral itself was primarily a college chapel. In other cathedrals the Bishop was the Visitor, but at Christ Church this office was exercised by the Crown. In other cathedrals the grants of canonries by the Crown were presented to the Bishop who instituted and issued his own mandate for installation, but at Christ Church the grants were not presented to the Bishop and he did not institute. Perhaps the most striking difference lay in the number of Canonries appropriated to Professorships. At the foundation eight Canonries of Christ Church were created, but none of the three Regius Chairs of Divinity, Hebrew, and Greek then established in the college was attached to a Canonry. It was not until 1604 that a Canonry was appropriated to the Professorship of Divinity, and the Professor of Hebrew had to wait until 1630 for a similar provision. There thus remained as many as six Canonries not attached to Professorships. This position continued unchanged for over 200 years, until between 1840 and 1858 three more canonries became attached to Professorships, and another to the Archdeaconry of Oxford. Christ Church was thus charged with Professorships to a much greater extent than any other college.

The power and prestige of the Dean and Chapter were very great both inside and outside the walls of Christ Church. They administered the vast estates of the college and distributed amongst themselves, as they were entitled to do, about two-thirds of its annual income; they controlled the internal economy; they exercised an immense ecclesiastical patronage, not only appointing to Studentships of Christ Church but presenting to the ninety college livings. Within the College the eight Canons of Christ Church were declared by Lord Hardwicke in 1736 to be 'in the nature of coadjutors of the Dean', and within the University they had the standing of Heads of Houses at a time when the head of a college was a much more powerful figure than he is today. It is no wonder that Dr. Johnson considered it a great thing to dine with the Canons of Christ Church. Powerful though they were, the most powerful person of all was the Dean. The Canons could act only intermittently through the Chapter but the Dean exercised a continuous and all-embracing authority inside and outside the Chapter. The Canons were often non-resident, though the professorial canons were required to reside for the delivery of their statutory lectures, and it was said of one nineteenth-century canon that he was so unfamiliar with his stall that on one of his rare visits to Christ Church he was obliged to inquire of the porter where his lodgings were situated. The Dean, on the other hand, was constantly resident in term. His authority was decisive in the academic activities of the college, where he acted with the Senior and Junior Censors, both of whom were Students, and not, except in elections, with the Chapter; he admitted undergraduates; he wielded the important privilege of appointing Tutors; he appointed Servitors and exercised a vigilant supervision of appointments to Exhibitions. In short, he was the bridge between Canons and Students, Chapter and College. The character and reputation of the college depended to a large degree upon his personality. Cyril Jackson, who was Dean from 1783 to 1809, left such a deep imprint on his contemporaries that both his immediate successors as well as several of the Canons imitated his manners and mannerisms for many years afterwards, albeit with but indifferent success. Gaisford, whose misfortune it is to be remembered chiefly as the butt of some largely apocryphal anecdotes, was a firm and authoritarian Dean who exerted himself to uphold the dignity and traditions of the college. Pusey said of him that he was 'a representative of the best in the past which has been passing away, and respect for him was a check to revolution in many institutions'.[1] He applied himself attentively to the details of college administration, including its financial business, and in academic matters

[1] B.M. Add. MS. 44281, f. 181.

he was a shrewd judge of ability. His personal rule was all-pervasive.

The government of Christ Church by the Dean and Chapter worked well for more than 300 years. They governed largely by precedents of their own making, which in the course of time assumed the authority of statutes but could always be abrogated when the need arose. The absence of unalterable statutes not only allowed great flexibility in the government of the College but relieved it of many of the enervating features of other colleges. Christ Church was not hampered by considerations of founders' kin or by the appropriation of places on the foundation to particular localities, and the recruitment of the Chapter itself depended not on election or co-option, with the evils of seniority and faction which often attended such methods, but on the Crown, and although there were occasions when Crown patronage was exercised from political motives it seldom became an abuse. Such a body, small in size, composed of men of learning and experience, without hope of great personal advancement in the college, unrestricted by the dead hand of the founder, possessed many advantages. Above all, it was able to reform itself, and it is an irony that most of the reforms introduced in the middle of the nineteenth century by Parliament, such as the increase in Students' stipends and the opening of Studentships to general competition, were within the power of the Dean and Chapter to accomplish unaided.

The monopoly of power exercised by the Dean and Chapter entirely excluded the Students, who corresponded in a general way to the Fellows of other colleges, from any share in the government of Christ Church. Despite the inferiority of their position compared with that of Fellows elsewhere, their relationship with the Chapter was in general friendly and harmonious. This may be attributed to two factors. Firstly, the Students and many of the Canons shared a common experience in having started their academic careers as undergraduates of the House, and an immensely strong Christ Church sentiment was created by the fact that many of the Canons had once been Students themselves and some of the Students could hope to succeed to the Canonries as they became vacant. The strength of this sentiment narrowed the gulf between the governors and the governed. Secondly, there was the force of custom in regulating the rights and duties of the Students. Since they were unprotected by written statutes and had no voice in the Governing Body, the importance of custom can hardly be exaggerated, the more so as it was possible to question whether the Students were legally members of the foundation at all. Their claim so to be considered rested on a paper in the Augmentation Office dated 1 October 1546.[1] This document is loosely framed in the form of a memorandum and was no doubt intended to serve as the basis for statutes which in the event were never granted. It describes the college as consisting of a Dean and Chapter, three public Professors of Divinity, Hebrew, and Greek, 100 Students, 24 servants and officers, and an equal number of almsmen. When its authority was tested in 1737, Lord Hardwicke ruled that it had no legal validity, but in practice the number, status, and emoluments of the Students were derived from it until well into the nineteenth century. The harmonious relationship existing between Students and Chapter thus depended to a large extent on the confidence of the Students in the Chapter, and in particular their confidence in those members of it who had formerly been Students themselves.

During the 1840s and 1850s this confidence was gradually eroded and the bond of community relaxed. The Canonries attached to the Chairs of Divinity and Hebrew had for long been held more often than not by men brought in from outside, but the remaining Canonries had generally, though not invariably, been held by Christ Church men. For a brief period between 1830 and 1836, not only five of the six non-professorial Canonries but also both professorial

[1] Public Record Office, particulars of grants no. 827.

Canonries were held by Christ Church men. This now changed. In 1839 there was agitation in the University for an increase in the professoriate and even Robert Hussey, then Censor and by no stretch of the imagination an ardent reformer, wrote a pamphlet in favour of it. Before interest in University reform was temporarily extinguished by the violent climax of the Tractarian Movement, Parliament in 1840 provided for two new Professorships to be attached to Canonries at Christ Church, as and when vacancies occurred, attached a further Canonry to the Lady Margaret Professorship of Divinity, and, perhaps to assuage feeling on the inflammatory subject of state interference with the Church, yet another Canonry to the Archdeaconry of Oxford.[1] Two years later the Crown created and filled the Chairs of Ecclesiastical History and Pastoral Theology.

The effect of these legislative measures was not only to increase the number of professorial Canons, albeit prospectively, from two to five, but progressively to increase the number of Canonries held by men who had no previous connection with Christ Church. Between 1840, when Godfrey Faussett, a Fellow of Magdalen and Lady Margaret Professor of Divinity, succeeded to the Canonry vacated by Dr. Woodcock, and 1853, when he was himself succeeded by C. A. Heurtley, a former Fellow of Corpus, no indigenous member of Christ Church succeeded to a Canonry, apart from C. C. Clerke, who succeeded to that provided for the Archdeaconry. Whereas in 1830, seven out of eight Canonries had been held by Christ Church men, in 1853 the number had fallen to five, and the trend of professorial appointments suggested forcibly that it would diminish still further. It is at first sight curious that the Students of Christ Church should have been so signally unsuccessful in obtaining appointments to these professorships during these years. The exception was Robert Hussey,

[1] 3 & 4 Vict. cap. CXIII (L. L. Shadwell, *Enactments in Parliament Specially Concerning the Universities of Oxford and Cambridge* (Oxford Historical Society), iii (1912), 87–9).

whose timely pamphlet on the professorial system no doubt materially assisted his elevation to the Regius Chair of Ecclesiastical History, but exception he remained. There were many reasons for their lack of success. There was a shortage of suitable candidates owing to a crisis in the supply of Tutors; there were doubts about the need for a Chair in Pastoral Theology at all. Perhaps above all, the dominance of the college system and the close hegemony of the Tutors were inimical to the professorial system. The very nature of this system was in a state of uncertainty and a constant subject for debate. Before the creation of the new Schools in 1850, most Professorships were remote from the labour of teaching undergraduates, and in many instances equally remote from any other kind of labour too, and a chair was not the inevitable climax of a Tutor's ambition. If the function of a Professorship within the University was in dispute, its relevance to learning outside the University was sometimes barely credible. We are told, for example, that Dr. Daubeny's experiments invariably went wrong,[1] and the ancient problem of squaring the circle was as nothing compared with Dr. Buckland's efforts to square his account of the Deluge with orthodoxy.

In the case of the Lady Margaret Professorship, a special obstacle blocked the way of the Students. Election to the chair was during this period vested solely in those members of Convocation who were graduates in Divinity, and it has been said that 'this provision practically gave a great advantage to members of colleges whose Fellows were obliged by their Statutes to proceed to degrees in Divinity—Corpus, Magdalen and St. John's'.[2] Only one of the six Lady Margaret Professors elected between 1715 and 1853 had not been a member of one of these colleges, and in 1853, of the four candidates three, including the successful one Heurtley, came from the three favoured colleges. No member of Christ Church stood a good chance of election.

[1] W. Tuckwell, *Reminiscences of Oxford* (1900), p. 32.

[2] C. A. Heurtley, *Wholesome Words*, ed. W. Ince (1896), p. xxxv.

These changes in the composition of the Governing Body of Christ Church involved serious consequences for the Students, or seemed to them to do so. Not only were the prospects of preferment to a Canonry reduced, but the increasing number of Canons appointed from other colleges threatened to disrupt the delicate balance of custom and tradition between Chapter and Students by introducing an element hostile or indifferent to it. An element of uncertainty and therefore of insecurity was injected. Other disquieting problems loomed, and contained the threat of worse to some. Two Canonries still remained unappropriated to Professorships, but for how long? How would the office of Treasurer, always in the past held by a Christ Church man, be discharged when Dr. John Bull, who had held it since 1832, died and his Canonry devolved on the Regius Professor of Ecclesiastical History? More important still, how would the office of Sub-Dean, also always held by a Christ Church man, continue to be exercised? The Sub-Dean was the Dean's deputy, and before 1858 the only Canon closely and directly involved in the educational work of the House, and particularly in the conduct of Collections and as Censor Theologiae in the instruction of the Bachelors. The impact of these changes, actual and potential, proved to be a potent factor in the discussions on reform about to take place, and gave them a peculiar flavour distinctive to Christ Church.

In any account of the progress of reform at Christ Church, some consideration of the method of appointing Students and of the regulations governing their tenure is necessary. From the earliest days of the college, the 100 Studentships, to which a further Studentship was added by private benefaction at the Restoration, were divided into three groups or classes. The twenty Seniors were known as Theologi and were required to be in Holy Orders. Below them were forty Philosophi, who were either Masters or Bachelors, depending on their length of residence, and were only occasionally in Orders, and below them again were forty Discipuli or undergraduate Students. The first four Philosophi were termed Faculty Students. The Studentships differed from the Fellowships of other colleges in several ways. Most importantly, as we have seen, they did not entitle their holders to participate in the government of the college, and unlike Fellowships in most other colleges they were tenable by undergraduates. Very few Studentships were closed. None was reserved for founder's kin or indeed for the kin of the many benefactors of Christ Church, and none was reserved for a particular locality. There were, it is true, Exhibitions tenable at Christ Church which were reserved for particular places, but none of these entitled its holder to a Studentship. Three Studentships a year were required by legislation of Elizabeth I to be elected annually from Westminster School, and one was nominated as a vacancy occurred by Lord Vernon under the terms of an award made in 1599. With these exceptions, all Studentships were open to all members of Christ Church, except Servitors. Many of the objections levelled against the Fellowships of other colleges did not in these circumstances apply to the Studentships of Christ Church, and criticism tended to concentrate on the manner of their appointment.

The election of Students took place annually in December, and during the first half of the nineteenth century the number of vacancies, in addition to the Westminsters, varied from none at all to as many as a dozen, averaging seven or eight. Students not from Westminster were known as Canoneers. To describe a Canoneer Student as 'elected' accurately describes the formal procedure of the Chapter and is the word used by the Canons in recording their actions, but in fact the Students were appointed by the nomination of the Dean and Canons in rotation, the Dean having two turns and each of the Canons one, and were not elected in the ordinary sense of the word. A College Roll was kept on which young men were nominated by the Dean and Canons as their turns came round, and such nominations were from time to time made before the Student-elect had even matriculated. In the absence of a system of selection by examination or by founder's kin or by local preference some method of this kind was inevitable, but it was one which was manifestly liable to abuse, and its critics claimed that it treated Studentships as ecclesiastical patronage and that it led to widespread nepotism. The Royal Commission of 1852, which took the view that Fellowships should be awarded solely for merit established in open competition, considered the manner of nominating Students a principal cause of the decline of Christ Church in the 1830s and 1840s.

In 1854 the Dean and Chapter explained and defended at length the principles on which they claimed to act in a letter to Lord Palmerston.[1] In it they declared that other considerations than 'mere intellectual merit' should be taken into account.

It seems plain [they said], that the main intention of Founders and Benefactors was *not* to institute *prizes*, but to furnish *aids* to those who, without assistance, would be unable to avail themselves of an Academical education. And as the mass of mankind are of average ability, it would be extremely hard, if any of those for whom these aids were meant by the Donors, should be deprived of all share in them.

They had, they continued, sought to combine with rewards for intellectual superiority, encouragement 'to the patient industry and good behaviour of young men, less highly gifted perhaps in point of talent, but qualified by sound principles and a sober mind to fill those numerous departments in the Body Politic, on the proper conduct of which the Lay as well as the Clerical institutions of the nation mainly depend'. Open competition for Studentships was dismissed because 'it is of the utmost importance that the *morale* of all Candidates should be well ascertained before

[1] *The Dean and Chapter of Christ Church, Oxford, to Viscount Palmerston* [1854].

their Election; and this is the more necessary at Christ Church, since, when once admitted, the Students have no probationary year', and residence was therefore insisted on prior to election. A similar point of view was expressed by the leading Student of his day, Osborne Gordon, then Senior Censor, in a letter to Gladstone in 1854.

> We have no right [he wrote], to expect all first rate men. We hold a great number of poor livings, and if we are enabled to bring up good clergymen to succeed to them, and can give some assistance to students working their way at the bar and in other walks of life, we must be content though they are but men of moderate abilities.[1]

In defending the manner in which they appointed Students, the Dean and Chapter were not unmindful that they were also defending their own right of patronage, which appointment by examination would have destroyed, but Gordon, who shared their views, had no such motive, and the system survived principally from reasons of choice and necessity. It represented the belief that the purpose of the University was to provide education rather than learning. In appointing Students, the Dean and Chapter followed the ancient tradition that places on the foundation should be given to those who needed them, and the assessment of need had never been settled in the examination room. Although by the nineteenth century the financial value of such places had ceased, in the majority of cases, to be an important consideration, the idea that they should be given as aids and not as prizes remained. A belief in the examination system as a means of rewarding merit was a slow and sporadic growth in the nineteenth century, and only gradually gained acceptance. Even at Oriel and Balliol, which had opened their Fellowships to competitive examination, the results were not uniformly successful. At Oriel the hostility between Newman and Provost Hawkins

[1] P.R.O., H.O. 73/44, undated letter written in 1854.

contributed to many inferior appointments between 1830 and 1840, and at Balliol the examinations were considered by Mark Pattison to have little effect on the result of an election.[1]

At Christ Church there were several reasons why the old system was particularly tenacious. In some small colleges endowments were undoubtedly abused, but Christ Church was free from the evils of founder's kin and the claims of particular localities, and its mere size afforded an important safeguard in providing the electors at all times with a wide choice of candidates. Then again, Studentships, unlike most Fellowships, were awarded to undergraduates and it may be doubted whether in the absence of a university matriculation examination the general level of scholastic attainment in the schools was high enough to allow appointments to be made by examination, at least until the reforms of Arnold at Rugby and Butler at Shrewsbury had penetrated the leaven. This explains the insistence of the Dean and Chapter on residence prior to election, and if residence was insisted on it was clearly not possible to combine it with the opening of Studentships to general competition. The requirement of residence dispensed with the need for a probationary year once a Student had been elected and this created a further difficulty in the way of opening Studentships to general competition. It may, however, be asked why, since the powers of the Dean and Chapter were so wide, they did not provide a probationary year. The answer is to be found in the peculiar constitution of Christ Church. Such a measure would have been fraught with difficulty, for it would have struck at the roots of the independence of the Students, who were excluded from the Governing Body, if the Dean and Chapter had claimed to be able to remove them, not for a breach of the regulations of college or University, but because they judged a man unsuitable to remain a Student. When eventually, in order to forestall reform from outside, the Dean and Chapter abandoned

[1] Mark Pattison, *Memoirs* (1885), p. 178.

their patronage in 1854 and opened Studentships to competitive examination by men 'of irreproachable moral conduct as well as competent learning',[1] they confined the competition to undergraduates of Christ Church of one year's standing. The only Student to be appointed by this decree was J. H. Ramsay in 1854. Ramsay took a double First and stood unsuccessfully for a Fellowship at Oriel, which was awarded to a native of Gloucestershire, since there was a preference in favour of that county.

Although Canoneer Studentships were not awarded by examination until 1854, it should not be concluded that intellectual ability had previously counted for little or that men of real ability were not appointed, for Christ Church was as concerned as any other college to attract men of distinction. The unfortunate reference in the letter to Palmerston to 'mere intellectual merit' was gleefully seized upon by critics, and is the probable source for the story in Tuckwell's *Reminiscences* that Dr. Barnes, the most ancient of the Canons and known ironically in the college as 'Brains', ruminating on his own nominations, remarked, 'I don't know what we're coming to. I've given Studentships to my sons, and to my nephews, and to my nephews' children, and there are no more of my family left. I shall have to give them by merit one of these days.'[2] Nepotism is a charge more easily made than refuted. Certainly there were instances of Canons nominating relatives, and it would have been remarkable had it been otherwise, bearing in mind the determination of the Dean and Chapter to award places as aids rather than as prizes. If ability be taken as the test, there appears to be no obvious reason for believing the sons of Canons to be more stupid than the sons of less-favoured mortals. At all events, the practice of appointing close relatives was not on a sufficient scale to become a serious abuse, and the academic requirements for progression from one class of Student to the next[3] provided a

[1] Chapter Act Book, 22 Feb. 1854.

[2] W. Tuckwell, *Reminiscences*, p. 134.

[3] *Supra*, pp. 11–12.

salutary check on the appointment of unsuitable candidates. Osborne Gordon informed Gladstone, who was well able to verify the truth of the statement, that of the 60 graduate Students in 1854, 20 were Westminsters, 22 elected solely by merit, and 18 were friends or relatives of Canons, and of the latter 'several of them [were] such as might have been recommended if they had not been so'.[1] Dr. Jelf told Gladstone at the same time that 'nepotism has been for the last 20 years the exception and not the rule'.[2] There is good evidence that despite the principle of election which the Dean and Chapter claimed in their letter to Palmerston to follow, a considerable proportion of Studentships were awarded for merit. In his evidence to the Committee set up by the Hebdomadal Board in 1853 Robert Hussey, the Regius Professor of Ecclesiastical History and a former Student, listed the names of thirty-seven men of public distinction, including Gladstone, C. J. Canning, Cornewall Lewis, and H. G. Liddell, who had been appointed between 1823 and 1846.[3] There were, as will be shown, serious difficulties in recruiting sufficient Tutors at Christ Church during this period, but the cause of these difficulties did not rest primarily in the manner in which the Dean and Chapter exercised their patronage.

Once appointed, a Student enjoyed a large measure of independence and could hold his Studentship for life if he chose to avoid the few grounds for its forfeiture. There were many more Studentships than were required for the teaching work of the college, and the question arises of the purpose of a Studentship when its possessor had taken his B.A. and M.A. degrees, which he was required to do within the statutory times. A Studentship without teaching duties would today normally carry with it the obligation to pursue some field of research in the University, but in the first half of the nineteenth century this was not the case, though

1 B.M. Add. MS. 44378, f. 217^{v}. 2 B.M. Add. MS. 44381, f. 36.

3 *Report and Evidence ... Presented to the Board of Heads of Houses ...* (1853), p. 248.

there were individuals who remained at Oxford for the purpose. Critics of the old system, seeing the foundations of colleges full of Fellows who did not teach and made no contribution to scholarship, condemned Fellowships as sinecures. There was some truth in the charge, but it was not the whole truth. As the Dean and Chapter had informed Lord Palmerston, a Studentship at Christ Church was intended not only to enable the Student to take his degree but to assist him to prepare himself for a career in the Church or the lay professions. In this respect the Ordinance made a profound difference in the nature of a Studentship.

Whether a Student entered the Church or a lay profession he was compelled to take Orders on entering the ranks of the Theologi or to surrender his Studentship. If he entered the Church he would normally take Orders on reaching the canonical age, but it was possible for him as for the Student destined for the law or for medicine to hold his Studentship for six or seven years without taking Orders. It is sometimes assumed that in pre-reform Oxford Fellowships were tenable only by clerics. This is not entirely true, for at many colleges the position was similar to that at Christ Church, and it was common for Fellowships to be held by B.A.s until the period prescribed for taking Orders arrived. Many colleges also possessed Faculty Fellowships similar to the four Faculty Studentships at Christ Church, which were tenable by laymen. When Christ Church was founded almost the only career open to a Student was the Church. After taking his Master's degree he was expected to study theology until accepting a living, and it was for this purpose that the college was endowed with so many livings. By the nineteenth century the Church, although still the principal vocation for a Student, was by no means the only one, and the secular professions, particularly the law, attracted an increasing number. Of the Canoneer Students appointed between 1838 and 1856, whose subsequent careers can be traced, some forty-eight entered the Church and thirty-three the secular professions. Those who entered the law or medicine were obliged to pursue their studies outside Oxford, and the emoluments of their Studentships assisted them to do so. During this time it would be unreasonable to describe a Studentship as a sinecure. When professional training had been completed, it was a charge which could be levelled with justification, but at this point, as we shall see, the custom of the college prevented abuse. If a Student, on the other hand, decided to enter the Church, he was under a strong motive to do so at an early opportunity, a fact which caused Pusey to lament the decline in the study of theology, for although the cost of living at Christ Church was remarkably low compared with other colleges, stipends were inadequate to enable him to remain in residence without other means of support. The emoluments of Students had been laid down in 1547 and remained unaltered until 1858, apart from the increment secured by the Corn Rent Act of 18 Elizabeth I Cap. 6. The Report of the University Commission in 1852 stated that the 41 Junior Students received about £25 a year, the next 40 about £30 and the senior 20 about £45 plus the proceeds of Bishop Wood's estate[1] which raised the income of this last group to about £80. In 1854 the figures, according to Osborne Gordon, were £37, £44, and £61 respectively, and the income of Bishop Wood was believed to average £600 a year, or £30 to each beneficiary.[2] Whichever figures are accepted, the Studentships of Christ Church were financially of much less value than the Fellowships of most if not of all other colleges. Against these paltry sums a Canonry in 1856 was worth £1,319. The Censors, who with the Dean and Sub-Dean were responsible for the tuition and discipline of the college, and the college officers (all appointed by the Dean and Chapter) received in addition to the emoluments of their Studentships a small annual fee.

[1] An estate at Chatteris, Cambs., bequeathed by Thomas Wood, Bishop of Lichfield and Coventry, in 1692 'in trust for all Senior Masters of Christ Church being Students'.

[2] *Letter to the Rt. Hon. W. E. Gladstone* (1854), p. 4.

Tutors were able to increase their income by taking pupils, but the duties of Censor and Tutor pulled in opposite directions, and Vere Bayne, who became a Tutor in 1856, wrote in the following year that 'At present the Censorships being only nominally endowed are rendered valuable by having a larger number of pupils assigned, and not to neglect these the time and energies of the Censors are taxed to a far greater extent than is reasonable.'[1]

'It is obvious', wrote Osborne Gordon, 'that there are no splendid prizes here—nothing to make the fortunate possessor of one of them feel that he has nothing more to do in life.'[2] A Studentship was an office without power and for the most part without occupation or adequate stipend, and in consequence non-residence was very prevalent. Non-residence was not in itself necessarily an evil consequence, for it not only assisted those Students, as we have seen, who wished to pursue their studies outside Oxford, but it was of positive benefit to the Church, and the staunchest advocate of residence can hardly have desired to see 101 Students constantly present in the college, for, apart from any other disadvantages, their occupation of rooms would have vastly reduced the accommodation for the generality of undergraduates, and for several decades before the erection of the Meadow Buildings the college was grossly overcrowded. On occasion, non-residence even proved of some considerable benefit to learning, and a reformer such as Liddell, who was not opposed to it in principle, defended it on these grounds, and advanced the case of Sir Charles Newton, the archaeologist, who held a Faculty Studentship at Christ Church.

He was [said Liddell] for many years in the archaeological department of the British Museum, and having by patient daily study acquired a degree of technical knowledge possessed by few, he obtained the post of Consul at Mitylene. There the sum added to his salary by his Faculty Studentship enables him to

[1] P.R.O., H.O. 73/44, 21 July 1857.

[2] *Letter to the Rt. Hon. W. E. Gladstone* (1854), p. 4.

pursue researches and make acquisitions which will at a future day greatly redound to the credit of Oxford. Without his Studentship he could afford to live, but would have no funds at his command; and those opportunities of which he is so peculiarly qualified to take advantage would be lost.[1]

Since Studentships were awarded for life, non-residence, despite its advantages, could and probably would have developed into a serious evil but for the regulations introduced by the Dean and Chapter over the centuries governing the forfeiture of Studentships. It is an irony that the first attempts to reform the University cured it of non-residence, but in so doing encouraged the Life-Fellow, who became a great abuse as readers of Sir Charles Oman's autobiography will recall. These regulations were designed to prevent Studentships from becoming sinecures, to promote a rapid turnover of Studentships, thereby increasing the number of places available, and to ensure that college Tutors were young men. In these aims they were undoubtedly successful, for the average tenure of a Studentship was ten or twelve years and the average age for vacating it, so Pusey tells us,[2] thirty or thirty-one. There were many grounds on which a Studentship had to be vacated. A Student forfeited his place if he failed to take his degrees at the prescribed times, if he took a Fellowship in another college, if he failed to take Orders on entering the class of Theologi, if he married or took a living. Of these, the three last were the most common.

Unlike marriage and the failure to take Orders at the requisite time, taking a living was not in itself automatically a cause of forfeiture. It was not a general disqualification, for not all livings were included in the prohibition and the two College librarians and the Cathedral precentor were exempt. The need of the college to obtain a reasonably rapid turnover of Studentships was balanced by its need to

[1] B.M. Add MS. 44236, f. 273.

[2] *Report and Evidence . . . Presented to the Board of Heads of Houses . . .* (1853), p. 129.

fill the college livings, if possible, with members of Christ Church. Of the ninety livings possessed by Christ Church, the greater part had been acquired at the foundation and were situated in areas where the college had property. In the eighteenth century a small number of relatively valuable livings were purchased on behalf of Trusts, but for the most part the foundation livings were small in value. It was the practice of the Dean and Chapter to offer vacant livings to the Students in order of seniority, and if refused by them to the Cathedral Chaplains. There is little evidence at Christ Church to support Roundell Palmer's complaint that men 'grew old, waiting for livings, and lounging about common-rooms'.[1] Even the best of the college livings did not equal many in other hands, and the most valuable were always claimed by the Censors and officers. By ancient custom curacies held by licence were tenable with Studentships, and owing to their poverty many of the foundation livings fell into this category. In the nineteenth century many curacies ceased to be revocable and the Bishop's licence had the effect of institution. To meet this new situation the Chapter ruled in 1841 that curacies traditionally held with Studentships should so continue, except where the college had been able greatly to augment their value. Poor curacies not in the gift of the college, an increasing number with the division of parishes by ecclesiastical districts, did not receive this protection. Thus by no means all Students who took livings were obliged to surrender their Studentships: taking a living in fact had much less disastrous consequences than taking a wife. As for the non-resident Student who lived in London reading law or medicine, so for the Student combining his Studentship with a parish, the emoluments of the Studentship were, in effect, a pension. To have altered the system would have impoverished still further many already poor parishes and at the same time reduced the number of Students willing to take them. By the operation of these

[1] R. Palmer, *Memorials Part I: Family and Personal 1766–1865*, ii (1896), 194.

customs regulating the causes of forfeiture of a Studentship, the potential evils of the non-resident life-Student were avoided, and the Dean and Chapter could claim with justice that 'there are therefore no idle residents, obstructing the work of the college, and setting examples of uselessness'.[1]

Thus although Christ Church had no statutes it had a constitution. At the summit were the Dean and Chapter, wielding great power but restrained by the powerful force of custom. Below them were the Students, holding offices without power and, except for those engaged in tuition, without occupation or adequate stipend, but bound by strong ties of sentiment and the hope of succession, yet ties which weakened as the nineteenth century advanced. The constitution functioned satisfactorily for more than 300 years, apart from occasional and temporary periods of tension between Dean and Chapter and Students, but the attempt by Parliament to reform the University, although principally educational in intent, provoked a constitutional struggle at Christ Church. Constitutional and educational issues were closely interwoven, but it is as a struggle for power rather than for the reform of education that the history of the Ordinance of 1858 and subsequently of the Statutes of 1867 is chiefly memorable.

[1] *The Dean and Chapter of Christ Church, Oxford, to Viscount Palmerston* [1854].

II

Christ Church and University Reform, 1850–1854

THE first signs of the approaching crisis developed in the field of education. There is evidence that as a place of education Christ Church in the 1840s and for some years previously was in a period of comparative decline. Accusations of educational decline, as of moral decline, are not easy to measure, but on one point there could be no dispute, namely the progressively disappointing performance of the college in the Schools. For many years there had been a steady decline from the dazzling achievements of Christ Church men in the early part of the century, and the Royal Commission showed that between 1821 and 1830 Balliol gained 11 Firsts and Christ Church 51, but between 1831 and 1840 the figures had changed to 22 Firsts at Balliol and 31 at Christ Church, and between 1841 and 1850 they were 22 and 13 respectively. Whether or not the number of Firsts be taken as an infallible yardstick of merit, and Mark Pattison, it is worth recalling, considered that at this period the number of second classes was better evidence of efficient tuition,[1] these figures clearly indicate some kind of change within the college, and in view of the relative sizes of Balliol and Christ Church at the time they are even more startling than at first sight. The Report claimed that the cause lay in the opening of Fellowships at Balliol, but this cannot be so for there was little change at Christ Church when Studentships were opened in 1858. Yet there is an element of truth in this analysis, for the Report did not recommend the opening of Fellowships from abstract principles but as a cure for specific defects in the tutorial

[1] Pattison, *Memoirs*, p. 26.

system, and some of these defects were certainly present at Christ Church.

In the University as a whole the unforeseen result of the reform of the examination system earlier in the century by the creation of Classes and the separation of the Classical and Mathematical Schools, had been the virtual breakdown of the tutorial system. The standard required for Honours, and to a much less extent for a Pass degree, had steadily risen. The examination had changed its character by becoming written instead of oral, and this had caused increased emphasis to be laid on philosophy and composition and correspondingly less on construing. The tutorial system had not everywhere adjusted to these altered circumstances. Many colleges, burdened with incompetent Fellows appointed from founder's kin or other closed foundations, had been unable to find enough tutors of the right quality. In consequence, tutors taught too many subjects, their classes were too large and were composed of the undifferentiated able and less able, and tutors themselves looked to a career in the Church rather than the University and were neither rewarded nor penalized by the success or failure of their pupils. The inadequacy of the collegiate system of instruction led to the phenomenal rise of the private tutor, whose assistance was sought by the great majority of undergraduates for an average of three terms. The Report hoped that the effect of opening Fellowships would be to sweep away inferior Fellows and closed Fellowships, and to increase the number and quality of tutors.

These defects in the tutorial system were felt more in the smaller colleges than in the large ones. At Christ Church there were no closed Studentships and the quality of appointments to tutorships was, on the whole, high. Whereas most colleges had difficulty in scraping together two or three tutors, and many were unable to provide any instruction in mathematics, Christ Church usually had six Tutors and a Mathematical Lecturer.[1] There was also a

[1] Mr. John Sparrow describes the system admirably in Chap. 3 of his

Praelector Rhetoricae and the office of Praelector Graecae was revived by Gaisford after lapsing for many years. There is also evidence at Christ Church that the size of classes was smaller than in some other colleges,[1] where classes of nineteen or twenty were not uncommon. Yet although conditions at Christ Church were better than in many colleges, there are indications that all was not well and that the tutorial system was under some strain. It is significant that undergraduates found it desirable to resort to private tutors. Gaisford forbade the practice, but Robert Lowe relates that throughout the time he was a private tutor 'one-half of my pupils came from Christ-church'.[2] Gaisford forbade the use of private tutors because he pursued a policy of active discouragement of competition for university honours. In his time even Students were not compelled to compete for honours. Since private tutors were often recruited from recent B.A.s and constituted a body of learned men from whose ranks college tutors might be appointed, the effect of Gaisford's policy was to deprive Christ Church of a valuable source of potential Tutors. In 1857 C. W. Sandford, the Reader in Greek and an experienced tutor, informed the University Commissioners that

> the dearth of Students eligible to the tutorial office, which at present seems to threaten us, has arisen partly from the . . . few inducements held out to those who would be willing to remain in residence after passing the examinations for the degree of Bachelor of Arts with a view to future employment in the college; from the uncertainty also which it used to be the policy of the chief authority of the college [i.e. Gaisford] to keep up as to whether an appointment to a tutorship would follow on continuance of residence.[3]

Mark Pattison and the Idea of a University (1967), p. 66; but the number of Tutors at Christ Church was at least twice that of 'three' which he attributes to the 'larger colleges'.

[1] H. L. Thompson, *Henry George Liddell* (1899), p. 27; Sir Algernon West, *Recollections* (1899), i. 64; lists of Tutors and pupils of various dates in Ch. Ch. Archives and Library.

[2] *Report of the Oxford University Commission* (1852), Evidence, p. 12.

[3] P.R.O., H.O. 73/44, 13 July 1857.

Perhaps the most important single factor in the crisis which affected the tutorial system at this period was the decline of Westminster School, for the Westminster Students had for generations supplied the House with the majority of its Tutors. For three centuries the school had sent many of its most able sons to Christ Church, but early in the nineteenth century it succumbed to rapid and protracted decay. It failed to absorb the lessons of Arnold's Rugby, its finances were weak, and successive cholera epidemics in London caused parents to prefer the salubrious conditions of the new schools rising in the country. The numbers fell dramatically, and with them the choice of suitable candidates for the obligatory Westminster Studentships. The school customarily presented as many as eight or nine candidates to the electors, but in 1829 the Master of Trinity College, Cambridge, who shared with Christ Church the obligation to take at least three, refused to accept more than the statutory minimum on the grounds that more able students were to be found elsewhere.[1] Christ Church, which had a closer link with Westminster than Trinity, adopted a laxer policy and for many years tended to take more than three, thereby allocating Studentships to men of manifestly inferior accomplishments. In 1857 the only Westminster Student to hold a Tutorship was T. J. Prout, and in the same year Osborne Gordon complained that in the three previous years ten Students had been elected from Westminster, to which 'the House has been very little indebted for the last 20 years',[2] leaving only two places for general competition within the college. In his evidence to the Public Schools Commission in 1862 Liddell, speaking as Dean of Christ Church and former Headmaster of Westminster, declared that 'In former days the Westminster boys supplied Christ Church with some of the best men on the student's list—almost all the tutors were Westminsters; but for many years past they have sent us

[1] Christ Church Archives, MS. Estates 142, f. 68.

[2] P.R.O., H.O. 73/44, 1 July 1857.

very few tutors. Indeed I believe we have only had two such within my memory, and now there are none, and very few in prospect.'[1] Sandford, who took a more sanguine view of the future than Liddell, contributed the startling information that 'the last first class in classics won by a Westminster student was in 1837; the last first class in mathematics was in 1834'.[2]

Westminster was an extreme case and illustrated the folly of excessive dependence on a single school, but some of the causes of its decay also affected, though not in equal degree, other traditional nurseries of Christ Church, such as Eton and Harrow, from which the mass of the undergraduates came. In 1838 E. K. Karslake, who had just matriculated at Christ Church, wrote to his old Headmaster, Christopher Wordsworth, that 'Harrow is at Oxford, so far as scholarship is concerned, at a very low ebb. Mr. Hussey is said . . . to have asked some freshman whence he came, and upon his replying from Harrow, to have said "O then, I must teach you Greek, Latin and English."'[3] The new Public Schools not only attracted men away from the older schools, but sent their best pupils to colleges other than Christ Church. 'I believe it to be the case', wrote Sandford, 'that the great prizes are not won now by Eton, but by such schools as Rugby and Marlborough.'[4] Few boys from either school came to Christ Church. The social élite came to Christ Church in great numbers, a fact recognized in 1859–60 by the brief and undistinguished residence of the heir apparent himself, but although many of them subsequently attained positions of eminence in public life, they rarely came for the sake of the academic advantages which the University had to offer, and, as the case of Osborne Gordon's pupil Lord Robert Cecil illustrates, it was not considered socially acceptable for them

[1] *Report of the Public Schools Commission* (1864), iii, Evidence, pt. 1, p. 393.

[2] Ibid. ii, Appendix, p. 11.

[3] Lambeth Palace Library, MS. 2141, f. 258v.

[4] *Report of the Public Schools Commission* (1864), ii, Appendix, p. 11.

to compete for honours. Gordon himself, who was reputed to be second to none in his love of a lord, probably over-valued those whose birth, in the words of an earlier Tutor of Christ Church, 'exempted them from a life of labour',[1] and he spoke gratefully of 'those members of the higher classes who have hitherto frequented Christ Church and to whom we have always been and still are endebted for a great part of the honours, and who so far from being the idlest and worst conducted of the community are very often the most industrious and exemplary'.[2] A perhaps shrewder and more realistic view was expressed by Sandford to the Public Schools Commission.

> The parents of the boys at Eton [he wrote, comparing that school with Rugby and Marlborough] are richer; their sons have not their own fortunes to make . . . It may be said that eldest sons come to Christ Church, and younger sons go to other colleges. The boys at the other schools, on the contrary, know that if they are to succeed they must work. The real advantage derived from Eton is less intellectual than social education. Eton is expected to make a boy a gentleman, and this expectation it fulfils.[3]

Consideration of the changes that have been described leads to the conclusion that in 1850 Christ Church as a place of education was in a condition of decline, but it also suggests that the decline was of fairly recent date. The public examination system had placed a new and heavy burden on the tutorial system of Christ Church, but it had been felt less than in smaller colleges partly because Christ Church enjoyed an appreciably larger number of Tutors and also because its Studentships were not encumbered with the obligations of founder's kin and local connections. Nevertheless, there was a shortage of Tutors, and the principal reasons for this were to be found in the decay of Westminster and the effect of Gaisford's deliberate policy

[1] Edmund Goodenough in 1815.

[2] P.R.O., H.O. 73/44, undated letter written to Gladstone in 1854.

[3] *Report of the Public Schools Commission* (1864), ii, Appendix, p. 11.

with regard to university honours. Both these factors had not begun to operate until the second quarter of the nineteenth century, when the decline of Christ Church in the public examinations first began. The Royal Commission was mistaken in attributing the decline of Christ Church to the exercise of their patronage by the Dean and Chapter, for it was the Westminster Studentships, which were not appointed by the Chapter, that were poorly filled, whereas the Canoneer Studentships, as we have seen from the evidence of Liddell and others, supplied the great majority of the Tutors. The temporary factors contributing to the state of the college might be thought eventually to pass away, and such was certainly the view of many of the most experienced Tutors at Christ Church—certainly Gaisford could be relied upon to do so, while in the case of Westminster the old connection was not to be fully renewed. But even if these temporary difficulties had been solved, it may be doubted whether Christ Church would have been able permanently to appoint a sufficient number of properly qualified Tutors from its own members, particularly after the extension of studies prescribed by the Statute of 1850, in view of the changing social pattern of its undergraduate members. The Royal Commissioners, it may be thought, therefore, were right to recommend the opening of Studentships to the University, though the reasons which prompted them to do so were not the only reasons, or even perhaps the most important reasons, which made such a course desirable at Christ Church.

Such was the state of Christ Church when Lord John Russell appointed the Royal Commission in 1850. The question of university reform had then been agitated for half a century. During this time the University had made some progress towards reforming itself by the introduction of classes into the Examination Schools and by establishing new disciplines, but the predominance of the colleges, entrenched (except for Christ Church) behind their statutes, made the University an ineffective organ of change. The

Tractarian Movement absorbed the energies of most men for over a decade, and reform, in the partisan words of Goldwin Smith, 'showed a tendency to recede when Tractarianism, having become dominant, betrayed its hostility to intellect and its determination to keep the endowments, consequently the tutorial staff, as close as possible to those whom it called *pauperes Christi*; in fact, to youths of inferior intellect and submissive character, such as ecclesiastical leadership requires'.[1] As the movement subsided after Newman's apostasy, interest in reform quickened. In a letter to Roundell Palmer in 1849 Goldwin Smith described the new temper in the University. 'The general state of men's minds here', he wrote, 'is what you might naturally expect after a long period of fierce controversy. Torpor and apathy prevail . . . The better sort of men are turning to practical matters, new examination statutes and University Reform.'[2] Russell's Commission made its report in 1852. To this justly famous work every historian of nineteenth-century Oxford owes a great debt. It abounds with ideas and information, and is well written and well constructed. The Commission, however, suffered from several initial disadvantages which had an effect on its work. Its terms of reference precluded consideration of the essential question of college finance. More important, it was a Royal and not a Parliamentary Commission, and thus had no power to command evidence. Some of the evidence it received was of a tendentious nature and none of it was sifted by interrogation of witnesses. No evidence was given by many who, although perhaps favourable to a measure of reform, were opposed to the methods chosen. In most Commissions the relationship between evidence and conclusions is more mystical than mathematical, and the evidence received by the Oxford Commission is used very selectively in its recommendations. In its proposals for the University, as opposed to the

[1] G. Smith, *Reminiscences* (1910), p. 100.
[2] Lambeth Palace Library, MS. 1877, f. 139.

colleges, the Commission was captured by what might be termed the advanced liberals, Jeune, Liddell, and Stanley, and Liddell in particular was profoundly influenced by Henry Halford Vaughan, the Regius Professor of Modern History, whose influence on the report was far-reaching.

The views of the Commission on many aspects of reform are outside the compass of this account. Their recommendations for the reform of the colleges, a subject in which A. C. Tait took a particular interest, are more to the point. The objectives of the Commission were educational. They sought to raise academic standards and to associate the University more actively with the lay professions, and they proposed to achieve these ends chiefly by improving the quality of Fellows and by encouraging new studies. They therefore proposed to open Fellowships to general competition, to raise their stipends, abolish undergraduate Fellows, limit the number of Fellows, and so far as possible relieve them of the obligation to take Orders. The effect of these measures, it was anticipated, would be the improvement of teaching in the colleges.

In considering Christ Church the Commissioners made specific proposals in accordance with their general principles, and many of their proposals were later incorporated into the Ordinance of 1858.

> The Dean and Canons [they declared] have only to surrender their patronage, and, invite the best scholars in England to contend for their Studentships. In this Society . . . the Studentships should be divided into two classes, corresponding to the Fellowships and Scholarships of Colleges. Means should be found to increase the value of the Studentships, especially the Senior Studentships, in order to enable that great Institution to compete fairly with other Colleges. It is not unreasonable to expect that something should be done by the Chapter, whose own income is very large; and if not while the present vested interests subsist, yet on the occurrence of vacancies. If the two stalls which are unconnected with Professorships are allowed to remain so, a considerable portion of their present emoluments might be applied to the

purpose of increasing the value of the senior Studentships . . . For the present it might be advantageous to suspend the election to twenty Studentships. The number of Westminster Scholars to be elected to Christchurch every year should be fixed at a fair amount, and a definite proportion of the junior Studentships should be set apart for persons educated in that School.[1]

Since the Commission received no formal evidence from Christ Church, it would be tempting to assume that these proposals were formulated by Liddell, the only Christ Church member of the Commission. In fact this does not seem to have been the case, and it is probable, to judge by parallel instances, that he was absent from a discussion in which he was to a considerable degree an interested party. In 1856 he stated emphatically that the recommendation for suppressing the two Canonries was made independently of his advice,[2] and during the discussions on the Ordinance his opinion on several important matters differed markedly from the views earlier expressed by the Commission.

Two years later, in 1854, the Oxford Act was passed.[3] Looking back many years later, Goldwin Smith summarized the achievements of this period of reform as sweeping away medieval statutes, opening Fellowships and Scholarships, transferring the University from clerical to academic hands, abrogating tests and enlarging studies.[4] The architect of the Act was Gladstone, then Member of Parliament for the University and a recent convert to the cause of university reform. From its first draft the Bill underwent considerable changes before it became law, partly as a result of Gladstone's enormous correspondence with interested parties and partly as a result of its passage through Parliament, where it was beset on the one side by a highly vocal group of radicals in alliance with extreme reformers outside Parliament headed

[1] *Report of the Oxford University Commission* (1852), p. 176.

[2] P.R.O., H.O. 73/44, 24 Apr. 1856.

[3] 17 & 18 Vict. cap. LXXXI (Shadwell, iii. 153 ff.). Cf. W. R. Ward, *Victorian Oxford* (1965), pp. 193–9.

[4] G. Smith, *Reminiscences*, p. 114.

by Liddell himself, whose demands would have wrecked it, and on the other hand by conservatives such as Roundell Palmer. The most important change lay in the manner in which the details of reform were to be introduced into the colleges. In its early stages the Bill proposed to settle such matters by direct legislation. This was a course much favoured by Jowett and powerfully argued by him, but Gladstone eventually decided to abandon it in favour of a small number of broad general principles which were to be interpreted by a body of Commissioners appointed by the Act. Reform by means of a Commission reduced the direct interference of Parliament to a minimum and was politically acceptable to those, such as Lord Derby (then Chancellor of the University), who viewed the encroachment of the legislature with repugnance.

The Commissioners appointed by the Act were the Earls of Ellesmere and Harrowby, C. T. Longley, Bishop of Ripon, Sir John Coleridge, G. H. S. Johnson, Dean of Wells and the only member of the original Royal Commission, Sir John Awdry, and Sir G. C. Lewis. All of them, except Coleridge and Johnson, were Christ Church men, and Longley had been Tutor and Censor as well. The enactments specifically relating to colleges which they were required to interpret were few in number. The Act required Fellowships to be awarded for merit, abolished undergraduate Fellowships, and the rights of preference to Fellowships, but not to scholarships, possessed by schools. The Commission was empowered to assist the colleges to draw up new statutes based on these principles, and if necessary actually to draw up college statutes, which must then be approved by two-thirds of the relevant Governing Body. It had wide discretionary powers, and its members, who were highly regarded in the University and sympathetic to its needs, acted, in Longley's words, in a spirit of 'Conservative Reform'.[1] The defect of all such bodies was diagnosed by Goldwin Smith, who described them as

[1] B.M. Add. MS. 44385, f. 171.

'better for deciding questions judicially than for constructing: they cannot *think*',[1] but it was hoped that by releasing colleges from their ancient statutes and by filling Fellowships with able men the Commission would make it possible for colleges to reform themselves in the future by adopting, for example, such measures as their particular circumstances dictated for college extension and for regulating the cost of education.

So far as Christ Church was concerned, the Act of 1854 was an unsatisfactory measure. Neither the Dean and Chapter nor the Students welcomed the destruction of the old Christ Church. It was a drastic remedy for ills which they believed to be of a temporary nature. Yet whatever the reception of the Act might have been, it contained a flaw which must eventually prove fatal. It gave the Students no share in the Governing Body of Christ Church and left the powers of the Dean and Chapter intact and undiminished. It provided for educational reforms which directly concerned the Students, but neither gave them any share in the preparation of the statutes which were to implement these reforms, nor, by excluding them from the Governing Body, any decisive voice in the subsequent administration of the statutes. It thus destroyed the traditions governing the composition and rights of the Student body, but failed to raise the Students to an equality with the Fellows of other colleges. These defects of the Act so far as Christ Church was concerned flowed from one central defect, namely the denial to the Commissioners of power to amend the constitution of the Governing Body. To have legislated on the powers of the Dean and Chapter was politically inexpedient, not least because the Cathedrals Commission was still sitting in 1854, but none the less the peculiar circumstances of Christ Church required a solution different to that appropriate for other colleges, and this the Act failed to provide. How far Gladstone appreciated this and how far he was the prisoner of circumstances is difficult to

[1] B.M. Add. MS. 44303, f. 127.

determine. Although the case of Christ Church was not adequately covered by the general principles of reform enunciated in the Act, it is doubtful whether the attempt in the early draft of the Bill to legislate specific solutions would have met it any better. In his early draft of the Bill Gladstone proposed that the Commissioners should by the terms of clause XLIX 'provide for the government of the said College by the Dean and Chapter, together with so many as the said Commissioners shall think fit of the Students thereof'. At first glance the clause seemed to bring the Students fully into the Governing Body, but when its ambiguities were exposed such was not found to be his intention.

Is it [Osborne Gordon asked him] the intention to include Students in the government and not in the corporation? I believe there is no collegiate precedent for such an arrangement and no good to be anticipated from it . . . The Dean and Chapter . . . object to the scheme because they do not wish anyone to be associated with them in their position at all. I object to it just as strongly because I do not wish to be associated with them on unequal terms.[1]

Or again,

Fellows in other colleges are really in authority, and have the entire control over the affairs of the corporation, whereas we should be, at best but stipendiaries called into Council.[2]

To this Gladstone replied with what seems remarkably like wilful disingenuousness 'the question about the corporation I should say is a very small one'.[3] When Longley inquired whether the association of the Students with the Governing Body extended to the control of capitular estates, Gladstone replied that the teaching body ought *de jure* to have an influence in the government, but that the provisions of the Act would 'leave open the question whether any portion of

[1] P.R.O., H.O. 73/44, undated letter to Gladstone written in 1854.

[2] *Letter to the Rt. Hon. W. E. Gladstone* (1854), p. 7.

[3] P.R.O., H.O. 73/44, letter to Gordon in 1854.

the Students should have anything to say to the management of college property. The studies, the discipline, the economy of the college are what they have in view'.[1]

Power is no less indivisible in Oxford than elsewhere, and an attempt to separate the educational from the other functions of the college was bound either to fail or to split Christ Church into its two components, the Dean and Chapter on the one side and the Students on the other.

[1] B.M. Add. MS. 44378, f. 260v.

III

The Christ Church Ordinance of 1858

(*a*) THE DEAN AND CHAPTER AND THE ORDINANCE, 1855–1857

HARDLY had the Commissioners been appointed when on 2 June 1855 Gaisford died. They can scarcely have regretted his passing, for he it was who had greeted the Oxford Bill with the uncompromising statement, 'I think it not merely inexpedient but unjust and tyrannical.'[1] The succession was thus a matter of unusual importance. Dr. Jelf informed Gladstone that what was needed was a 'Dean Jackson redivivus'. He added, 'The man we want must be not only a ripe scholar and apt to teach but a thorough gentleman, a man skilful and experienced in *governing* young men of the upper classes, a man of sound judgement, unflinching firmness, good temper, courteous manners, business habits, incorruptible integrity. Such men are doubtless rare.'[2] His brother William, he thought, was well suited. Pusey, who admired Gaisford, was filled with forebodings. 'Now', he wrote, 'nothing but what is evil is threatened as his successor. They imagine Liddell.'[3] Imagination speedily became fact and four days after Gaisford's death Liddell was named as Dean.

Liddell came to Christ Church with the reputation of a belligerent reformer. He had been an active member of the Royal Commission, and, much to Gladstone's annoyance, a troublesome champion of its ideas during the passage of the Oxford Act. Yet despite his reputation he seems to have had little interest in many of the ideas shared by the reformers

[1] B.M. Add. MS. 44378, f. 44.
[2] B.M. Add. MS. 44381, f. 31^{v}
[3] B.M. Add. MS. 44281, f. 181.

DEAN LIDDELL in 1858
(aged 47)

with whom he was associated. He was, for example, in favour only to a limited extent of opening Fellowships, and, as we have seen, he was a supporter of non-resident Studentships. On only two matters did he hold what might fairly be called reformist opinions. These were the relaxation of the obligation to take Orders, and, above all, the extension of the professoriate. Recalling his own share in the preparation of the Report of the Royal Commission, he stated in 1886 that 'my chief interest was in the restoration of the professors to life and action'.[1] So far as Christ Church was concerned the question of extending the professoriate hardly existed, for the college had proportionately many more Professors than any other college. Throughout the discussions on the Ordinance, Liddell, either through policy or conviction, displayed a great desire to retain as much as possible of the old Christ Church. The hostility of the Chapter to reform made his position difficult, but he remained throughout apparently unsympathetic to the demands of the Students (although himself a former Student and Censor) and approved almost without comment the first drafts of the Ordinance which were highly obnoxious to them. His enthusiasm for reform seems to have diminished further after his serious illness in 1857, and he took relatively little part in the negotiations leading to the Act of 1867. In his later years he devoted himself increasingly to what he perhaps erroneously conceived as the improvement of the college buildings.

Although the reforms which were about to be introduced into Christ Church concerned the Students more than any other section of the college, the Commissioners conducted negotiations not with them but with the Dean and Chapter, who composed the Governing Body, and Liddell's appointment was important not least because his presence ensured that reform, although inevitable, was not imposed without consultation. In the Chapter his only ally was the cautious and conciliatory Jacobson, but even he was not an enthusiast

[1] Lambeth Palace Library, MS. Tait 104, f. 73.

for reform and had told Gladstone in 1851 that he did not see the necessity for the Royal Commission.[1] The rest of the Chapter saw little need for change. The aged Barnes, who had matriculated in 1790, had indicated his hostility to any disruption of the existing order many years before when the young Charles Wordsworth had complained of a smoking chimney. 'Oh, Mr. Wordsworth', he had replied, 'the chimney has smoked for three hundred years, and I suppose it must continue to do so.'[2] Ogilvie, a reformer in his youth, was now 'quite without enthusiasm for reform, and inclined to resent all novelties'.[3] Pusey, although basically hostile to the main purposes of reform, was more selective in his opposition and welcomed an increase in the number of Tutors and believed that studious well-selected Fellows would be of great benefit to the University.[4] For the rest, Archdeacon Clerke, the Sub-Dean, and Heurtley held strong conservative convictions, Bull was a sick man 'away two terms out of three',[5] and Jelf lived in London 'and has never had anything to do with the place'.[5]

The University Commissioners held their first meeting to consider Christ Church in April 1856, almost two years after the passage of the Oxford Act. Since the Dean and Chapter had submitted no scheme of their own by the first day of Michaelmas Term 1855, as required by the Act, and showed no sign of doing so subsequently, the Commissioners were obliged to take the initiative and draw up an Ordinance for Christ Church. It soon became apparent that their powers were insufficient for the purpose. In other colleges it was possible to redeploy college finances by altering the statutes, but at Christ Church the Dean and Chapter, in whom the wealth of the foundation was vested, manifested little inclination to divest themselves willingly

[1] B.M. Add. MS. 44218, f. 18v.

[2] C. Wordsworth, *Annals of My Early Life* (1891), p. 76.

[3] Thompson, *H. G. Liddell*, p. 137.

[4] *Report and Evidence . . . Presented to the Board of Heads of Houses . . .* (1853), p. 79.

[5] B.M. Add. MS. 44386, f. 298.

of their emoluments for the benefit of the Students, and the Commissioners had no power to interfere with corporate revenues. The Commissioners had nevertheless to find additional finances if the stipends of the Students were to be increased to the level of Fellowships. The question was how much was wanted and where was it to be found. The sum required depended on three factors: on the amount of the improved emoluments, on the sum available under the existing foundation for emoluments, and on the number of Students. There was no difficulty about the first two of these. The basic stipends were settled by the general policy of the Commissioners of equating Fellowships and Scholarships throughout the University, and inquiry revealed that the sum devoted in 1856 to the payment of the Students was approximately £5,480 a year. With regard to the number of Students which the college was to have in the future, the Commissioners had at this time reached no firm conclusion, and although this was an important factor in estimating the income which would be required, the absence of definite statistics did not prevent them from taking measures to provide further funds.

The Royal Commission had proposed to obtain extra funds by suppressing the two Canonries which were not annexed to Professorships, and a clause to this effect was actually incorporated in the Oxford Bill. It was subsequently omitted through what Goldwin Smith tactfully called an 'oversight',[1] though in truth the Bill probably had enough difficulties to contend with without incurring the charge of overt spoliation of the Church. This was the scheme which was now revived. It was not, however, the only way in which funds could have been raised. Pusey was of the opinion that 'the Commissioners would have been equally satisfied in whatever way the money should have been raised'.[2] One method would have been by means of an annual grant by the Dean and Chapter and such a proposal

[1] B.M. Add. MS. 44303, f. 88.
[2] Ch. Ch. Archives, MS. Estates 117, f. 19.

was later made by that body. Although the Commissioners could not make use of corporate revenues, it was lawful for the Chapter to do so, since the disposal of their income depended on custom and the Chapter alone decided what was custom. The objection to such a method was simply that by 1856 the Chapter had displayed such implacable hostility to reform that there was no guarantee that what they granted by custom they would not subsequently revoke by the same token. As Jacob Ley, another Student and former Censor, observed, 'there seems to be no reason for suppressing the two canonries, except that the Commissioners have no other security for the employment of their revenues'.[1] Yet another method of raising income was advocated by Osborne Gordon. On 1 July 1856 he wrote to Liddell, who immediately forwarded his letter to the Commissioners, arguing that the abolition of Noblemen and Gentlemen Commoners, then much discussed, would inevitably lead to an increase in the cost of a university education for Commoners. He produced calculations demonstrating that a sum of £3,916. 8*s*. would become available from the Senior Masters' estate and from an increase in fees and room rents, and claimed that no sum from college funds 'properly so called' was therefore needed.[2] But this scheme too was unacceptable to the Commissioners. The mood of the time was so strongly directed towards reducing the cost of university education that they shied away from any proposal which involved an increase. They were determined that the basic emoluments of Studentships should be found entirely from the wealth of the foundation and not from the fees of undergraduates. It was in these circumstances that Lord Harrowby, supported by Lord Ellesmere, Liddell, and Goldwin Smith, introduced an Amending Act[3] to devote the proceeds of the two unappropriated Canonries to college purposes. 'The new Dean of Ch. Ch.', Goldwin Smith wrote to Gladstone,

[1] P.R.O., H.O. 73/44, 8 July 1857.
[2] Ibid., 1 July 1856.
[3] 19 & 20 Vict. cap. XXXI (Shadwell, iii. 191).

'has represented to Lord Ellesmere the necessity of such an amendment, and I am sure that no adequate improvement can take place at Ch. Ch. without it.'[1]

To Liddell the Amending Act was much more than a financial expedient. It would, he wrote to Gladstone, 'make Christ Church a College and not a Chapter for once and all'.[2] For Liddell's views on the reform of Christ Church at this time it was a revealing statement. The suppression of Canonries would make Christ Church a college and not a Chapter because it would place the government entirely in the hands of Professors, and the advancement of the professoriate was, as has been mentioned earlier, a cause dear to his heart.

On 24 April 1856, he developed his ideas in a remarkable letter to the Commissioners. 'To enable Christ Church to compete with other colleges,' he wrote, 'two things at least are necessary: 1 To improve the undergraduate Studentships so as to attract good men to the college as commoners or future competitors for Studentships. 2 To improve so many *at least* of the graduate Studentships as may induce good men to stay and become Tutors.'[3] He estimated that the undergraduate Studentships, as he called them, might be raised by between £30 and £40 a year by devoting to this end the Exhibitions previously reserved for Commoners. Turning to the graduate Students, he proposed that their stipends might be improved either by reducing the number of Students, or, coming to the business in hand, securing additional funds from the Chapter. After dismissing the possibility of a tax on the Dean and Canons as 'a question on which I forbear from making any remarks', he went on to propose that not two but *four* stalls should be suppressed. In addition to the two Canonries not appropriated to Professorships, he wished to suppress those attached to the Chair of Pastoral Theology and to the Lady Margaret

[1] B.M. Add. MS. 44303, f. 87.
[2] B.M. Add. MS. 44236, f. 286^{v}.
[3] P.R.O., H.O. 73/44, 24 Apr. 1856.

Professorship, both of which had recently been annexed. Of the former he wrote, 'the Professorship of Pastoral Theology can scarcely be made to work well *in Oxford*. Nor is it, considering its nature, a valuable piece of patronage . . . If such an office is required there are enough theological professors in Oxford to undertake its duties. They might be attached, for instance, to the Margaret Professor.' Of the latter he observed, 'Its annexation to a Canonry was done (in Mr. Gladstone's words) "in the dark, though with the best intentions". It might be endowed partly from Christ Church, partly from Magdalen (which is bound to maintain a Theological Professor) and left free from college connexion.'

The constitutional result of this very radical proposal would have been to reduce the already small Governing Body still further, so that it consisted of the Dean, the Archdeacon, and the Professors of Divinity, Hebrew, and Ecclesiastical History, all of whom, with the exception of the Professor of Divinity, Jacobson, were in 1856, as it happened, Christ Church men by origin. But it was not as a constitutional but as a financial measure that Liddell proposed it, and as such it was, to say the least, a remarkable proposal. Since the undergraduate Studentships were to be increased in value by the application of Exhibitions available to Commoners, and since Liddell apparently did not intend the income of all the remaining sixty graduate Students to be increased, and was probably aware that a big reduction in this number was intended by the Commissioners, the revenues of four Canonries were excessive for the purpose. It would, therefore, seem reasonable to conclude that Liddell had some other purpose in mind. What this was he did not say, but there comes to mind the complaint which Robert Hussey made to Gladstone in 1854 against a proposal to assign the revenues of two Canonries to maintain lay Professorships of Latin and Greek.[1] It was in this year that the Dean and Chapter themselves suggested

[1] B.M. Add. MS. 44377, f. 215^{v}.

the endowment of the chair of Greek with £300 a year.[1] What more natural than that Liddell, one of the best Greek scholars in the University, should have desired to improve the Professorship of Greek, which was still miserably endowed with the sum of £40 a year provided at the foundation, at a time when the equally ancient and inadequate stipends of the Students were about to be raised? The possibility that some such course was in his mind is increased by a correspondence, now unfortunately incomplete, which took place between him and Goldwin Smith in November of the same year, in the course of which Smith, commenting on a letter he had received from Liddell, remarked that although a chair of Pastoral Theology served no useful purpose, it would require an Act of Parliament to annex the Canonry to the chair of Greek.[2] Whatever Liddell's intentions may have been, Gladstone refused to consider the suppression of four Canonries, since he believed that such a proposal would not only reopen the Act of 1840 but probably defeat the intended suppression of the two unappropriated Canonries.[3] His opinion was shared by the Commissioners, and Edward Twisleton, who had taken the place of Sir George Cornewall Lewis, was fearful that such a measure would open the way for a general discussion in Parliament of the proceedings of the Commission, which could only be harmful at that juncture to further reform, and that it would be hotly contested by the Bishop of Oxford, Samuel Wilberforce, who would interpret it as an attack on the Chapter as a religious body.[4] The Amending Act was passed in June 1856, and by devoting the revenues of the two unappropriated Canonries to College purposes, paved the way for the practical reform of Christ Church. It did not augur well for the future of reform at Christ Church that the Canons

[1] *The Dean and Chapter of Christ Church, Oxford, to Viscount Palmerston* [1854].

[2] Ch. Ch. Archives, MS. Estates 117, f. 28. 'I think', he wrote, 'we must make an effort to relieve you of Pastoral Theology and give you the Regius Greek.'

[3] Ibid., f. 17.

[4] Ibid., f. 11v.

were not even consulted on a matter affecting them so intimately.[1]

In drawing up an Ordinance for Christ Church, the Commissioners had to take account of three separate elements of reform. They were, first, the principles enunciated in the Oxford Act; secondly, reforms on matters of less importance but of wide application to colleges in Oxford; thirdly, the particular needs of Christ Church. The test of their work was whether the first two of these could be combined harmoniously with the third. Of the few essential principles which the Act laid down for colleges, the most important without doubt were the award of Fellowships and Studentships for merit and the conversion of undergraduate Studentships into Scholarships, with safeguards for the rights of schools (in the case of Christ Church for Westminster). On these matters there could be no compromise. In the second category came matters which, while not specifically included in the Act though in many cases in the early stages of the Bill, had been generally enforced by the Commission, such as the proportion of clerical Fellowships to lay, provision for the study of mathematics and science, the qualification of residence. On some of these questions the Commissioners had been, and were still, divided. Some for example, wished to abolish the obligation to take Orders, but others feared that to do so would encourage sinecure Fellows and proposed to prevent this by limiting Fellowships to ten years in order to instil a measure of competition. There was division of opinion on the introduction of mathematical and scientific studies. Goldwin Smith, for example, wanted a college entirely devoted to science, with married Fellows and with laboratories within the college walls, but it seems to have been Edward Twisleton who successfully pressed for Fellowships in these subjects in every college, despite Goldwin Smith's contention that it would encourage mediocrity and disgust the colleges with science.[2]

[1] Ch. Ch. Archives, MS. Estates 117, f. 19.

[2] Ibid., f. 21.

It was, however, in the application of these reforms to Christ Church that the greatest difficulty was to be experienced. It had been far from Gladstone's intention in setting up the Commission to impose reform from without, but at Christ Church such a development was an imminent threat. By refusing to submit any proposals for reform, the Chapter had abdicated the right to take part in the preliminary discussions. The Commissioners had no communication with the Chapter until the outlines of the Ordinance had been framed, and none at all with the Students until it had been drafted. The Students, although in many instances favourable to some of the objects of reform as their support of the Tutors' Association illustrates, had no *locus standi* in the discussions because they formed no part of the Governing Body. Osborne Gordon sent to the Commissioners a copy of his correspondence with Gladstone in 1854, but it received scant attention. Almost the only channel of communication between Commission and College was Liddell.

The procedure adopted by the Commissioners was to draw up a memorandum of fourteen points enunciating the main principles of reform. On 1 July 1856 Goldwin Smith, who was one of the two secretaries to the Commission, described their intentions in an important letter to Gladstone.

It seems to me [he wrote], that the revenues which in other colleges maintain sinecure Fellows being here absorbed by the Chapter, we must devote what remains and all that we can get from suppressed Canonries to the Tutorships and Scholarships so as to make the college a first rate place of education, leaving its functions as a place of learning to be discharged mainly by the Professor Canons. We might make 60 undergraduate Studentships on the footing of Scholarships at £70 each, or near it; and 10 or 12 Senior Students, all educational officers, whose incomes, including tuition fees, would average £700 at least. This would be a great change no doubt but I think something of the kind is required by the necessities of the case. It seems to me also that the Dean and Senior Students should be the governing body of the College as a place of education, and elect to all the

Studentships senior and junior. I do not see how you can have an efficient government otherwise. Besides, the dignity, and therefore the value, of a Tutor's place at Ch. Ch. is lowered by their present position there as compared with the position of a Tutor in the Governing Body of another College. The Commission seems inclined to adopt some such scheme as I have mentioned but: I fear the Chapter will prove very tenacious, especially in regard to the right of election.[1]

Early in November, he wrote to inform Liddell of progress.

The 12 Seniors [he said, referring to the Students] are to be elected from the whole University. They are intended to be the educational staff of the college, and it was thought that with the aid of the Lee's Reader and the University Professors, 12 would be enough and something to spare . . . How many of them are to be in Orders is not settled: according to the analogy of what has been done in other colleges, 4 out of the 12 would be allowed to be permanently laymen. It is intended that the Undergraduate Studentships should be tenable for 5 years: the exception being proposed in the case of the Westminsters on account of the Carey benefaction which is too recent to be altered. The Commission will not touch the Fells [i.e. the Fell exhibitions]: at least their inclination is not to do so.[2]

On 10 December 1856 the memorandum reached Liddell. It proposed that there should be sixteen Senior and sixty-one Junior Studentships. The Senior Students, who were to furnish the educational staff of the college, were to be elected out of the whole University, and were to receive £200 a year. They were required to reside for ten years. Of the Junior Studentships, forty, including the Vernon, were to be awarded by open competition, and the remaining twenty-one appropriated to Westminster. The open Junior Studentships were to be raised to £80 a year and to be tenable for five years, as was usual in other colleges. The Westminsters were to receive £40 from the funds of the

[1] B.M. Add. MS. 44303, f. 107^{v}.

[2] Ch. Ch. Archives, MS. Estates 117, f. 30.

college, but it was calculated that the Lee Trust would permit their emoluments to be raised to £120 a year. They were to be tenable for seven years owing to the Carey Benefaction, which was available to graduates. Of the eight open Junior Studentships which it was believed would be vacant annually, three were to be set aside for the encouragement of mathematics and science, but the appropriation 'shall terminate at the end of twenty years'. The Students, both Senior and Junior, were to be elected by the Dean, Canons, and Senior Students, and the instruction and discipline of the House was vested in the Dean, Sub-Dean, and Senior Students. The power of deprivation remained with the Dean and Chapter. The two Canonries defined as college emoluments by the Amending Act were to be suppressed if necessary, and the income, except for half that of one of them which was to be assigned to the Domus Fund, together with the revenues of the existing Studentships and the Bostock Exhibitions, was to be applied to the objects of the scheme. A fund was also to be formed from the Fell, Boulter, Pauncefort, Gardiner, Frampton, Cotton, and Paul Exhibitions for Prizes and Exhibitions, partly for open competition and partly for the relief of poor students without competition. Finally, the number of Cathedral Chaplains was to be reduced in order to increase the stipends of the remainder.[1]

In essential matters these Fourteen Points followed the scheme described by Goldwin Smith in his letter to Gladstone of the previous July, and sought to make Christ Church a first-rate place of education by separating the educational from the other functions of the college. It created a second Governing Body, consisting of the Dean, Sub-Dean, who as Censor Theologiae performed certain educational duties, and the Senior Students, with powers independent of the Chapter in fact, though not in name, to control discipline and education. The scheme went beyond Gladstone's proposal in 1854 to associate some of the

[1] Ibid., f. 32. Printed (Appendix I) as the Fourteen Points.

Students with the Dean and Chapter in the government of Christ Church, for it gave the sixteen Senior Students an overwhelming majority vote, but it did not, any more than the earlier proposal, meet Osborne Gordon's objection that the Students were excluded from the corporation. The scheme went some way towards elevating the status and powers of the Students, both by making them independent of the Chapter in the educational work of the college, and also by constituting the electoral board, which appointed Students, in such a way that the sixteen Senior Students on it outnumbered the Dean and Canons. But independence was illusory so long as the fundamental question of the corporation remained unsolved. The scheme suffered from a further, and perhaps even graver disadvantage, for it severed the Students from the Dean and Chapter, who retained only the power of deprivation, and threatened to divide Christ Church into two parts, Chapter and College.

The Fourteen Points were open to amendment 'to almost any extent in detail'.[1] They reached Liddell as he was about to set out for Madeira to recover his health,[2] and were considered by the Chapter in his absence on 13 February 1857. A few days later the Sub-Dean, Archdeacon Clerke, wrote to inform him of their reception. 'It would be uncandid not to state [that] the majority of them dislike the scheme', he wrote.[3] In fact they had not a good word to say for it.

The only foundation for the proposed alteration [continued the Archdeacon] appears to lie in the poverty of the Studentships and the inadequate remuneration of the tutors. It is assumed that without making the ordinary stipend of the Students larger no sufficient number of good candidates will offer themselves for admission and election, and that without increasing

[1] Ch. Ch. Archives, MS. Estates 117, f. 31.

[2] Liddell was gravely ill with a chest complaint, diagnosed by Acland as acute bronchial pneumonia (*ex inf.* Dr. H. C. Harley).

[3] Ch. Ch. Archives, MS. Estates 117, f. 41.

the income of the tutors fit men will not be induced to take the office.

The Chapter argued that, on the contrary, provided the college was well taught and well governed there would be no lack of good candidates, and, ignoring the inconvenient provision of the Oxford Act abolishing undergraduate Studentships, they asserted that permanency of tenure was a full equivalent for smallness of income. The problem, they thought, was to ensure the continuance of enough Students on the foundation, 'of men attached to the place and disposed to act harmoniously in the maintenance of its usefulness and credit, provided their services are adequately rewarded'. They proposed, therefore, to charge the college revenues with the sum of £1,000 a year to augment the stipends of the Censors, the two Readers, and four other Tutors, and this sum, in addition to tuition money better levied and distributed, would provide ample remuneration for at least eight of the forty Senior Students. 'There does not appear to be the least occasion for augmenting the stipend of those who are not engaged in college tuition.' Those in Orders were rewarded by college preferment, which made up for limited stipends in previous years, and their residence in Christ Church was for the most part undesirable. In this way, the Chapter considered, the younger Students, elected by examination of Commoners of Christ Church according to the regulations made in 1854, would have a prospect of succeeding to the enriched Tutorships within a reasonable period of time and would therefore remain at the college. Thus the evils of suppressing Canonries, reducing the number of Students, and limiting their tenure would be avoided. Such a scheme could be implemented by the Commissioners more rapidly than their own scheme.

The Canons had other objections to the Fourteen Points. They deplored the failure of the Commissioners to recognize the clerical character of the college, for it was not stipulated that any of the Senior Students was to be in

Orders. Furthermore, they considered the opening of Studentships to general competition in the University highly detrimental.

> To associate such men with the Dean and Canons in the election of Students or to give them a voice in the discipline of the college equal to that of the Dean, Subdean and Canons would be to provoke contention and jealousy. The Head of an ordinary college with his fellows may contrive to manage their election and exercise their discipline without much collision of opinion or interruption of peace, but with two different bodies, the Canons and Students, it would be impossible to maintain harmony. The 8 Canons would feel it but a mockery if invited to join 16 other gentlemen in the election and would necessarily abdicate their function. It would be small consolation to them that they were left of [*sic*] the one most invidious prerogative, that of expelling a Student.

Having complained that none of the Students was in Orders, the Chapter also objected with some lack of consistency that the secular studies hitherto provided for by the lay Faculty Studentships were neglected.

> But above all [they concluded], the Canons would deprecate the loss of that Christ Church feeling which, if in former times it may have been thought to have fostered conceit, is yet when well directed and regulated capable of producing in a community the best effects. But [with] a division of the Students into Senior and Junior, temporary and permanent [*sic*], with a wide gap between the two classes, between the natives and the aliens, there can be little or no communion between them. They will be as it were members of two different societies—the Juniors at 23 or 25 cut off from the foundation will betake themselves elsewhere and to other employments . . . the college can hope for no recruits from among its own alumni, from among those who have been brought up in its bosom, and have been bound together by all the ties of undergraduate friendship and the still more beneficial relations of tutor and pupil.

It was the essence of the Chapter's position in this uncompromising statement that the old system at Christ Church required little alteration and that any difficulties from which the college may have been suffering could be rectified within that system. They rightly maintained that the opening of Studentships and the loss of permanency of undergraduate Studentships would weaken and perhaps destroy that solidarity of feeling which gave immense strength and cohesion to the society, though the force of the argument was somewhat diminished by the fact that so many of the Canons themselves came from other colleges; but they were mistaken in their belief that this feeling and the benefits it conferred on Christ Church could be preserved by maintaining the old system virtually unchanged. For Christ Church could not be considered in isolation from the rest of the University. The central fact, of which they failed to take account, was that Fellowships were being opened to competition throughout the University, and the inferior status of the Studentships compared with Fellowships would prevent the best men from other colleges seeking them and would cause the best undergraduate Students of Christ Church to migrate to Fellowships in other colleges. It followed that the Chapter's proposal to augment the stipends of college officers and Tutors was inadequate to ensure a sufficient supply of Tutors, for the fundamental question was not one of finance but of the powers of the Students. By their defence of the old system the Chapter not only countered the proposed suppression of Canonries but repudiated the scheme of the Commissioners to enlarge the powers of the Students by placing the educational work of the college largely in their hands. Their negative attitude to reform deprived them of any positive share in the work of drawing up the Ordinance, but it had one important consequence. The Commissioners were irrevocably committed to their proposals for the election and tenure of Studentships, but in the face of the Chapter's opposition they withdrew their scheme to separate the educational work of the college. When they came to draft the Ordinance, this proposal was greatly modified and the revised arrangements weighed heavily in the Chapter's favour, and the inferiority of the Students compared with Fellows was thereby further aggravated.

The immediate effect of the Chapter's letter to Liddell with its opposition to the essential principles of reform was to suggest a headlong collision with the Commissioners, and Liddell, still convalescing in Madeira, at once sought to prevent this happening. On 24 March 1857 he replied to the Chapter's letter with a mixture of threat and reassurance, seeking to persuade them that reform could not be resisted and that its consequences were less evil than the Canons supposed.[1] His letter is as important for what it left unsaid as for what it said. It contained no reference to the proposal to enlarge the powers of the Students in educational matters. Even if Liddell had been more favourable to the claims of the Students than there is reason to suppose that at this time he was, it is doubtful whether he would have supported a proposal which tended to split the college into two parts and his inclination would probably have been to favour some form of association of the Students with the Dean and Chapter. It was a different matter with the essential principles of reform concerning Scholarships and the opening of Studentships, and it was on these that he concentrated his attention.

The essential question was how to ensure a sufficient number of first-rate Senior Students, if possible recruited from men who had been undergraduates of the House. It was the same question to which the Chapter had addressed themselves. He agreed with the Chapter that it was necessary to encourage Junior Students to seek Senior Studentships rather than to apply for Fellowships in other colleges, but whereas the Chapter had argued that it was enough to improve the stipends of the Tutors only, Liddell insisted that the stipends of all Students should be increased. The Chapter's argument depended on the permanency of Studentships, which enabled the undergraduate Student to

[1] Ch. Ch. Archives, MS. Estates 117, f. 45.

progress to a Tutorship without examination. But, Liddell pointed out, the Commissioners intended to destroy permanency whether the Canons agreed or not, for, he wrote, 'I was assured by the Commissioners that they are resolved to insist upon the division [of Studentships] as a principle.' If Junior Students were to be discouraged from seeking Fellowships in other colleges, it was necessary to increase the stipends of all the sixteen Senior Studentships proposed in the Fourteen Points and not only the few which the Chapter had proposed to augment, and in order to attract the best men to compete for Junior Studentships it was necessary to increase them also. The poverty of Studentships was not, therefore, the only foundation for change, as the Canons had alleged: 'the necessity for change arises wholly from the poverty of the Studentships'. It followed from Liddell's argument that, if the stipends of all Studentships were to be raised, the sum of £1,000 offered by the Chapter was inadequate. The suppression of the two Canonries, or some equally drastic measure, was thus inescapable. He admitted that the suppression would cause difficulties in the offices of Treasurer and Sub-Dean, but

> I fear [he wrote] that if a Commission so friendly as that which is now sitting thinks that two of our stalls may be spared without serious loss, there is no doubt what will be the opinion of other persons who are even now enquiring into the duties of capitular bodies. If these stalls are suppressed now their proceeds will be secured to the uses of the corporate body for purposes not alien to the intention of the founder. If they are suppressed by other hands hereafter we shall lose them altogether.

The need to suppress Canonries thus depended on the need to increase all stipends, and this in turn depended on the intention of the Commissioners to divide Studentships. The increase in stipends would attract able Junior Students and encourage them to compete for Senior Studentships rather than move to Fellowships in other colleges. Having established this point, Liddell turned to the matter which the

Canons said caused them the greatest concern, namely the belief that the opening of Studentships would destroy the *genius loci* of Christ Church. He sought to allay their fears by using a curious, and some might think cynical, argument. He urged them to accept open competition, not because the Commissioners insisted on it or because it was good in itself, but because it could be ignored at Christ Church.

With regard to the question of electing foreigners to the Senior Studentships [he wrote], I am disposed to agree with the Chapter. The Commissioners and other persons whose opinions I greatly respect think that it is highly advantageous to a college to have infusions of new blood. In a small college or in an ill endowed college this is true. But in so large a body as Christ Church, if the Junior Studentships are properly increased in value by a bold use of the funds at the disposal of the Commissioners, we might elect such young men as should enable us to dispense with foreign aid. Even if we are required to admit the members of other colleges to competition, we should, in that case seldom elect them.

Competition within the college for Studentships could be stimulated by applying the existing Exhibitions for Commoners to the augmentation of Junior Studentships, reserving only a small sum to assist indigent scholars on the grounds that 'most poor scholars *who could benefit from academical education* will find places on Foundations in some college or other'. The Lee funds, he suggested, should be devoted to the further instruction of men entering the medical profession by augmenting the Anatomical Lecturership, perhaps providing a Lecturership in Chemistry and endowing those Junior Studentships which the Commissioners wished to set apart for Physical Science.

Allowing for the circumstances in which this letter was written, the views which it expressed were remarkably conservative. Liddell accepted those reforms on which the Commissioners were known to insist, but not for the reasons and even less in the enthusiastic spirit in which they had been adumbrated by the Royal Commission. He advocated no sweeping changes in the college, notably in the position of the Students, and he accepted in practice the existing system, as reformed by the Chapter in 1854, for their election. By the improvement of stipends and by sharpening competition within the college by the suppression of Exhibitions for Commoners, he believed that the size of Christ Church would enable it to find sufficient first-rate Senior Students, and that so far as Christ Church was concerned the opening of Studentships to competition in the University was an irrelevance. He wished to reduce change to a minimum and retain as much as possible of the old Christ Church. He failed to recognize that it was not enough to increase the stipends of Students unless their powers and status were made commensurate in other respects with those of Fellows elsewhere. With the social composition of the college and the academic quality of its intake from the schools, where so many of its educational problems lay, he showed little concern, and his proposals would have reduced even further the number of poor students.

Liddell's continued absence in Madeira effectually prevented any further discussion between him and the Chapter, and later in the year Jelf was to complain that 'we have never had an opportunity for a single conversation even for a few minutes with you'.[1] The Commissioners, who had been alarmed by the tone of the Chapter's letter to Liddell, a copy of which had been sent to them, required a formal answer from the Chapter before proceeding to draw up the Ordinance. If they had hoped for a last-minute conversion, they were disappointed. At the end of May 1857 the Chapter, with Jacobson abstaining, replied that they considered the proposed reduction in the number of Studentships, their division into two classes, the limitation of their tenure, and the suppression of the two Canonries prejudicial to Christ Church as a place of learning and education. By

[1] Ch. Ch. Archives, MS. Estates 117, f. 60.

implication they accepted the opening of Studentships, perhaps convinced by Liddell's argument that none but Christ Church men need be elected, but they rejected the proposal, on which he had placed particular emphasis and which depended for its implementation on the suppression of the Canonries, to augment the stipends of all Students.

Protesting to the end, the Canons thus surrendered their last opportunity of influencing the Ordinance. Although their hostility caused the Commissioners to frame an Ordinance more conservative than that outlined in the Fourteen Points, the specific objections raised by the Chapter were entirely disregarded: the number of Studentships was reduced, they were divided into two classes, their tenure was limited, and the two Canonries were suppressed. In the absence of any constructive contribution by the Chapter, Liddell's influence with the Commissioners became the greater, and was acknowledged to be so by Pusey, who wrote to him, 'unhappily, yourself, my dear Dean, and Jacobson, I suppose, have an entirely different view of what would benefit Christ Church from the rest of the Chapter. The Commissioners have adopted your plan and ignored every suggestion with regard to the college made by any one else.'[1]

(*b*) THE FIRST DRAFTS OF THE ORDINANCE, 1857

The Ordinance was drafted by early June 1857, and was immediately submitted to Liddell, who, with the assistance of Jacobson, made some emendations in points of detail. On 22 June a revised version was sent, and the Commissioners intimated that they were willing 'to receive any observations . . . which the Chapter or any of its members may consider themselves at liberty to make'.[2] In the months that followed the Ordinance underwent many alterations in its details before it was finally approved early in 1858, but

[1] Ch. Ch. Archives, MS. Estates 117, f. 17^{v}.
[2] Ibid., f. 57.

before turning to these and to the manner in which they were introduced it may be useful to consider the initial proposals. The Commissioners abandoned their original scheme in favour of one more conservative, which, while retaining the main principles of reform, sought to preserve where possible and to translate into written form where necessary the customary regulations and traditions of Christ Church. The Ordinance thus fell into two main sections. In the first were measures designed to raise the level of learning and education in the college, and in the second measures defining the machinery needed to implement them.

Among the measures designed to improve Christ Church as a place of learning and education were the reduction in the number of Students from 101 to 85, and their division into two groups, the first of which contained 24 Senior Students—a large increase on the figure of 16 suggested in the previous December—and the second 61 Junior Students. The Senior Students were to be appointed by open examination designed to encourage all branches of study in the University. Of the Junior Students, who were in reality Scholars, 21 were to be elected from Westminster by examination, and the remaining 40 were open. The Westminsters were tenable for seven years and the open Junior Studentships for five. By the application of the revenues of the two suppressed Canonries when they became vacant, except for a deduction from each of them of £150 to the Domus Fund, and of the Fell, Boulter, and Bostock Exhibitions and a proportion of the Lee Trust, the stipends of the Senior Students were raised to £200, of the Westminster Junior Students to between £115 and £125 from the Lee funds as some compensation for the loss of their rights to Senior Studentships, and of the open Junior Studentships to £75. Other measures were taken to encourage learning in addition to these designed to stimulate competition for Studentships. Of the twenty-four Senior Studentships, two at any time could be appointed without examination from men of eminence in literature, science, or art, and such Students were permitted to marry. They were full and not honorary Students: the latter formed a further category under the Ordinance and could be elected without limitation of number. Mathematics and science were encouraged by devoting the Vernon[1] and nine other Junior Studentships to these subjects.

To effect these changes administrative machinery had to be created, powers regulated, rights and duties defined. Whereas in other colleges such matters were an ordinary function of the Governing Body, at Christ Church the Ordinance proposed to discharge them by setting up various bodies which were empowered to act independently of the Governing Body, and on most of these bodies the Senior Students were represented. An Electoral Board consisting of the Dean, Canons, and Tutors was created for the election of all Students, and the same persons exercised control over the instruction and discipline of Junior Students. The Dean, Canons, and Senior Students were to constitute a further body to make by-laws binding on the Students and enforceable by pecuniary penalties. The Dean and Chapter, unaided by the Senior Students, retained the power of depriving Students for immorality, negligence, or misconduct, and the Dean and Chapter alone were required to draw up regulations for the residence of Students to be enforced by pecuniary penalties. The Senior Students were required to be members of the Church of England; eight were laymen and the remainder clergy; they were appointed for a probationary period of one year; they were not to possess income, in addition to their stipends, exceeding £500 a year. Finally, the Ordinance provided that a Treasurer and Sub-Dean should be elected by the Dean and Chapter from those who had been Senior Students, providing that funds permitted.

[1] Lord Vernon himself wished that the Vernon Studentship should be awarded for the study of biblical history, and especially cuneiform and hieroglyphics. P.R.O., H.O. 73/44, 26 June 1857.

In view of the defects of the Oxford Act, to which reference has been made, the first draft of the Ordinance could hardly be other than unsatisfactory, and many of its faults could not be removed by amendment. It gave Christ Church a constitution which did not mention the Governing Body. The Commissioners were appointed to introduce certain educational reforms, but since their limited powers prevented them from reconstituting the Governing Body, thereby giving the Students, who were closely affected by the reforms, a share in the powers of that body, they were obliged to separate the educational from the other functions of the college. In the Fourteen Points they had proposed to do this by giving the Senior Students a majority vote in matters relating to the election of Students and to education and discipline. Obliged to abandon this scheme, they proposed in the Ordinance to associate some of the Senior Students, and in one instance all of them, with the Dean and Chapter in implementing these reforms. Educational reform thus became involved with constitutional issues.

Far from settling a constitution for Christ Church, the proposals of the Ordinance created two serious constitutional problems. First, it set up several subordinate Governing Bodies. One, consisting of the Dean, Canons, and Tutors elected to Studentships, and the same persons in another capacity controlled the education and discipline of the undergraduates; another consisting of the Dean, Chapter, and all Senior Students was created to make by-laws, and yet another consisting of the Dean and Chapter alone exercised the power to deprive Students and was required to make regulations for their residence. It was a system which might have been designed to promote conflict and, in such a situation, the Dean was at the centre of power. Secondly, by its inability to reconstitute the Governing Body, the Ordinance failed to raise the Studentships to an equality with Fellowships, and by destroying the old system at Christ Church it demolished the position of the Students which had evolved over three centuries, and provoked constitutional difficulties between them and the Chapter which were not resolved until 1867. By giving the Students equal powers with the Chapter in some areas, the Ordinance exposed their inequality in others, and indeed accentuated it by removing the protection of unwritten custom and tradition. If in some respects the Students were the equal of Fellows, in others their position was worse than it had been under the old system. On the one hand they now legally possessed a voice in elections, but on the other they were subject to inquisitorial powers with regard to their private means, to regulations for residence which the Dean and Chapter were not merely permitted but positively required to draw up and enforce by pecuniary penalties, to deprivation by a body in which they were not represented, and which, with the suppression of the two Canonries, seemed likely to be composed increasingly of men educated at other colleges than Christ Church. The effects of these measures, accompanied by the suppression of undergraduate Studentships and the opening to competition of Senior Studentships, might place Christ Church at a considerable disadvantage in finding suitable candidates for Studentships when there existed Fellowships elsewhere undistinguished by similar marks of inferiority.

Compared with these defects, other shortcomings of the Ordinance, many of which again stemmed from the inadequate powers of the Commissioners, were of minor importance. Nothing was done to alleviate the dependence of the college on Westminster; the internal economy was left in confusion; no provision was made for the disposal of the ecclesiastical patronage in the gift of Christ Church; the arrangements for a Sub-Dean and Treasurer were so speculative that they were dropped almost at once by the Commissioners.

Liddell approved of the provisions of the draft Ordinance with only a few criticisms, mainly of a comparatively minor nature. Of the proposal to elect men of eminence in literature, science, and art to Studentships he wrote that the clause 'is to me quite novel and I do not apprehend its practical utility'.[1] On his own copy of the Ordinance he wrote that the Student body was too small for such a luxury. He also proposed that regulations for discipline should be taken out of the hands of the Dean, Chapter, and Tutors and placed in those of the Dean and Chapter alone, and that regulations for the instruction and attendance at divine service of Junior Students should remain as under the old system in the hands of the Dean. '*Any* change', he wrote, 'from existing rules which is not positively required will give offence here.'[2] Towards the end of June 1857 the draft Ordinance was before the Chapter, and early in the following month Pusey communicated the views of the Canons to Liddell. They did not, he reported, object to 'the matters of principle', on which the Commissioners insisted, namely the division of the Student body and the admission of Juniors to the ranks of the Seniors by examination.[3] On the other hand, they disapproved of the abolition of Canonries, of the early terminability of Junior Studentships, and the reduction in the number of Students. Pusey probably expressed the opinion of the majority when he wrote that 'Old Christ Church with its good and its defects is by this Ordinance among the things which have been. May God give those who have to form the new Christ Church vision to conduct it. I do not hope much either for new Christ Church or for new Oxford.'

(*c*) THE STUDENTS AND THE ORDINANCE, 1857

Up to this time the Students had taken no part in the discussions on the Ordinance. Although the terms of the Ordinance concerned them more directly than other members of Christ Church, they had no constitutional standing, and neither the Chapter nor the Commissioners displayed much desire to obtain their views. Although the Students

[1] P.R.O., H.O. 73/44, 11 June 1857. [2] Ibid., 16 June 1857.
[3] Ch. Ch. Archives, MS. Estates 117, f. 18.

thus had no right to be heard, it was a matter of practical sagacity that they should be. Yet the Ordinance was drafted and its main provisions decided before this step was taken. It is difficult at this period to speak of the collective opinion of the Students for there was no institution through which it could be expressed. In so far as the Students may be said to have held opinions on the Ordinance, they were the opinions of the Censors and Tutors, for the non-resident Students were unable and the undergraduate Students unqualified to contribute to the debate, and even the relatively few residents spoke as individuals and not, except on one occasion, as a group. It is possible that had the draft Ordinance reached the Students earlier during that Summer Term of 1857, they might have opposed it as a body, but, either by accident or design, it did not do so until the Long Vacation was at hand and with it the possibility of organized opposition receded. Yet the remarkable unanimity of opinion then expressed suggests that, as would be expected, considerable informal discussions had taken place. Whether the opposition would have been more effective if it had been more organized is doubtful. On some aspects of reform the opinions of the Students were known both to the Commissioners and to the Chapter some time before the Ordinance was drafted. On university reform in general their views were readily ascertainable through the papers of the Tutors' Association and the evidence given by Osborne Gordon to the Hebdomadal Board in 1853. On domestic matters this was not so. Only Gordon among the Students had been so much as invited to communicate his views to the Commission;[1] he had transmitted to it a copy of his correspondence with Gladstone in 1854 at the time of the passage of the Oxford Act. In it he expressed his conviction that unless there were to be 'an entire reconstruction of the college', by which he meant giving the Students the same degree of power in the Governing Body as Fellows exercised in colleges, it was better to leave things as they were.

[1] B.M. Add. MS. 44385, f. 357.

Most of the Students who now took part in amending the draft Ordinance have vanished into the shadows of history. Dodgson, to whom fame came later, was Mathematical Lecturer and a very junior don in 1857, and his criticisms of the Ordinance, which were expressed with clarity and brevity, were confined to matters of comparative detail and carried little weight.[1] The name, however, of one of these long-forgotten Students of Christ Church may profitably be rescued from oblivion—Osborne Gordon. Gordon, who has appeared many times in these pages, was, as Senior Censor from 1849 to 1861, the most respected and influential voice on behalf of the Students. He was a Shropshire man by origin and came up to Christ Church on a Careswell Exhibition from Bridgnorth School in 1832. His proficiency in Greek soon brought him to the attention of Gaisford who nominated him to a Studentship in 1834, and a firm friendship developed between the old Dean and the young scholar. In 1845 Gordon became Reader in Greek and a year later in Rhetoric. In 1846 he succeeded Liddell as Censor and, more briefly, as Proctor. Those of his contemporaries who knew him whether as Tutor or colleague clearly regarded him with esteem and much affection. Dean Kitchin described him as 'lean and haggard, with bright eyes, long reddish nose, untidy air, odd voice, and uncertain aspirates. Of quaint wit, exquisite scholarly tastes, extraordinary mathematical gifts, and of a very kind heart.'[2] Others remembered him vividly and succinctly as 'the sick crow'. The best and most perceptive portrait of Gordon was written by John Ruskin, who became his private pupil in 1839. Ruskin says of him,

He was a man of quite exceptional power, and there is no saying what he might have done, with any strong motive. Very early, a keen, though entirely benevolent, sense of the absurdity of the world took away his heart in working for it: perhaps I

[1] Dodgson's letters on the subject are in P.R.O. (H.O. 73/44).

[2] G. W. Kitchen, 'John Ruskin at Oxford', in *Ruskin in Oxford and other studies* (1903), p. 24.

should rather have said, the density and unmalleability of the world, than absurdity. He thought there was nothing to be done with it, and that after all it would get on by itself.

In another passage Ruskin speaks of him as

> a practical Englishman, of the shrewdest, yet gentlest type; keenly perceptive of folly, but disposed to pardon most human failings as little more. His ambition was restricted to the walls of Christ Church . . . His own scholarly power was of the highest order; his memory (the necessary instrument of great scholarship) errorless and effortless; his judgement and feeling in literature sound; his interpretation of political events always rational, and founded on wide detail of well-balanced knowledge.[1]

He was deeply attached to the old Christ Church which he had known for twenty-five years, and although ready to accept that some changes were necessary, he viewed the aspirations of the liberal reformers with scepticism and their practical measures with incredulity. He was soon required to defend his beliefs.

It was the Chapter who, perhaps hoping that the Students might also oppose the Ordinance, in February brought them openly into the discussion by seeking their views on the Fourteen Points. The Students held seven meetings and on 8 May 1857 returned the result of their deliberations to the Chapter.[2] On 19 June, when the draft of the Ordinance was already in circulation, a copy of their memorandum was sent to the Commissioners. It was an important document which proposed a constitution differing widely from the draft Ordinance and extending the principle implicit in the Fourteen Points of separating the educational from the other functions of the college. 'We advocate', wrote George Marshall, the Junior Censor, 'a distinct endowment for College Officers, [and] that the administration

[1] J. Ruskin, *Praeterita* (*Works of John Ruskin*, ed. Cook and Wedderburn, xxv. 250–2). Ruskin also wrote Gordon's epitaph. See also the references to Gordon in Joan Evans and J. H. Whitehouse, *The Diaries of John Ruskin* (1956–9).

[2] Ch. Ch. Library, MS. 354; Ch. Ch. Archives, MS. Estates 117, f. 53.

OSBORNE GORDON

of Christ Church "as a place of education" should be kept separate from its duties and functions as a Cathedral Body.'[1] It was proposed that (the number of Students remaining undivided and undiminished) there should be twelve college officers, Tutors, and Lecturers financially independent of the Chapter by the provision of distinct endowments, and that the sum of £1,500 should be made available for this purpose in addition to funds from the Lee Trust estate. In addition, two Lecturers were to be appointed to teach Physical Sciences, endowed if possible from Lee, and funds were to be found for increasing the stipends of a sufficient number of B.A.s to assist the educational staff. It was further proposed that 'the person next in authority to the Dean in the government of the House "as a place of education" be a Student or someone who has been a Student', and that such a person should be appointed by the Dean. Studentships, apart from those filled from Westminster, were to be elected by open competition from members of the House, a counter-proposal to open them to the whole University having been defeated, and elections were to be in the hands of the Dean, Sub-Dean, and six college officers. Education and discipline were to be entrusted to the Dean, Sub-Dean, officers, Tutors, and Lecturers, and the general economy of the House placed under the control of the Dean, Sub-Dean, and officers and a fund provided for contingent expenses. Exhibitions were to be thrown open to competition by members of the House and in some cases applied to the relief of indigent students. Finally, Lecturers were to be relieved of the obligation to take Orders unless they were Theologi.

There are unfortunately no records of the discussions from which this document emerged, but Osborne Gordon has left an account of the principal considerations which inspired it.[2]

> He felt [he wrote, referring to the memorandum] that all reforms in Christ Church must be based on one of two definite

[1] P.R.O., H.O. 73/44, 19 June 1857. [2] Ibid., 1 July 1857.

principles—viz., of retaining the present constitution, but strengthening and invigorating it, or of recasting the House in the mould of other societies in the University. He is not prepared to say that the latter might be the better course (if done completely) but, looking to facts, he could not see that the Commissioners had either the pecuniary means at their disposal, or the legal powers necessary to effect that purpose. For the present he will only observe that he considered it indispensable for Christ Church, if reorganised on the system of other colleges, to have, 1st, an equal number of fellowships, 2ndly of not less value, 3rdly invested with the same powers as those of any other college in the university.

On the other hand [he continued], he thought that there were ample means for strengthening the present system for the competition which it will have to undergo if the present foundation and constitution could be preserved. He considered number itself a great element of strength, and that perpetuity of tenure was to a certain extent a compensation for smallness of value. He wished the Studentships to be thrown open to the whole House, and through it to the whole kingdom. What was most wanted, was reasonable constitutional powers, and means of rewarding and retaining and so of attracting men who might be trained to the spirit of the House, and afterwards be of service in it. He believes that the propositions of the Senior Masters would have this effect. . . . Having no access to information on the present state of the revenues of the House, the Students did not indicate the source from which the funds necessary for carrying out their ideas might be derived. But if the returns published in 1835 may be depended upon, it appears that besides the sum of £12,547 divisible among the Dean and Chapter . . . there is a further sum of £2,153[1] divisible in respect of College Offices. Supposing the Sub-Dean and Treasurer to retain the two unappropriated canonries, the Senior Censor knows of no College Officers who can have any claim upon that sum based upon work

[1] This sum presented a mystery. Dr. Jelf informed the Commissioners that 'I have failed in the attempt to discover the meaning of the phraseology used in the Report of the Church Revenues Commissioners respecting the sum of £2,153. Dr. Bull cannot, at this distance of time and without referring to the original calculations, offer any explanation.' He does not seem ever to have done so (P.R.O., H.O. 73/44, 22 July 1857).

done, except those who are engaged in the House as a place of education, and the revenues of the House exclusive of that amount would still give the Dean and Canons a larger income than is received by the members of any other Chapter.

The Students' memorandum, in which for the first and only time in the history of the Ordinance they spoke as a body, was at once a conservative and a radical document. It was conservative in that many of the essential features of the old Christ Church were retained, such as the number and permanency of Studentships and their restriction to members of the House. In this it represented the opinion of those who believed that the condition of Christ Church was fundamentally sound and that its decline, if decline there was, was due to temporary and transitory causes. So far indeed their statement had much in common with the views expressed by the Chapter on the same subject. It was conservative too on those educational principles, such as the opening of Studentships to general competition and the abolition of undergraduate Studentships, by which the Commissioners set great store. But the constitutional changes it proposed were, on the other hand, of a very radical kind, despite the disarming phrases used by Osborne Gordon. The demand for 'reasonable constitutional powers' in effect took the form of establishing a second Governing Body, from which the Chapter was excluded, to elect Students, appoint college officers, control education and discipline, and administer the internal economy of the House. It rejected the idea of 'associating' the Students with the Chapter in favour of an autonomous and financially independent body, which, it was envisaged, would place the Students on a similar footing to Fellows of other colleges. There can be little doubt that, but for the limitation in the Commissioners' powers, the Students would have gone considerably further and recast the constitution of the House, setting up a Governing Body from which the Chapter would probably have been entirely excluded. Such a scheme appears to have been in Osborne Gordon's mind as early as 1854 when he corresponded with Gladstone, and he subsequently wrote of this correspondence,

> I did not like to say so when I troubled you with a correspondence during the passing of the [Oxford] Bill, that the college should be made complete in itself and separated absolutely from the Canons, they receiving such incomes out of its revenues as may be thought fit, and the college as such having the control of the property.[1]

Since such a drastic measure had no prospect of success, the Students were obliged to recognize that the Chapter would continue as the Governing Body, even if only in the non-educational sphere, and their financial proposals contained an important consequence of this conclusion. For it was a striking feature of them that they did not envisage the suppression of the two Canonries, and indeed there is reason to suppose that the Students were averse to such a measure. If the Chapter were to continue as the Governing Body, it was important for the Students that it should not be composed entirely of men from other colleges out of sympathy with the traditions and customs of Christ Church. Their fear was perhaps illusory but it was real. Liddell wrote scornfully of it that 'as long as I remember Christ Church it has been a complaint that the Governing Body necessarily stands much more aloof from the governed than is the case in other Colleges'.[2] The anxiety of the Students concerning the composition of the Governing Body was undoubtedly increased by the sudden death on 2 December 1856 of Robert Hussey, the first Regius Professor of Ecclesiastical History and a former Student, before the Canonry destined for his chair became vacant. He was succeeded by A. P. Stanley, a Balliol man in origin. It was not so much Stanley's theological opinions which worried the Students, though these caused something of a flutter in the canonical dovecot, but the fact that he had been the secretary

[1] B.M. Add. MS. 44386, f. 266.
[2] Ch. Ch. Archives, MS. Estates 117, f. 48v.

to the Royal Commission on the University in 1850 and the principal author of its report. His appointment meant also that in 1857 four of the five Professors whose chairs were already or were about to be annexed to Canonries were men from other colleges. Hussey's death caused concern on another account also, for he had been destined for the important office of Sub-Dean,[1] an office which had recently increased in significance with the uncertain state of Liddell's health and his prolonged absence in Madeira. It was an office which, like the Treasurership, had always been combined with one of the unappropriated Canonries, but were these now to be suppressed it must be held by one of the professorial Canons, and almost inevitably by a Canon who was a 'foreigner'. It was this possibility which perhaps accounted for the stipulation in the Students' memorandum that the person next in authority to the Dean should be a Student or one who had been a Student. It was thus perhaps less a high-minded disregard for pecuniary advantage than a fear of the effects of abolishing the two Canonries which caused the Students to limit an increase in stipend to the twelve seniors in their body.

The Students' memorandum reached the Commissioners too late to have any effect on the drafting of the Ordinance, but in any case it never had much chance of acceptance. It failed to accept the main educational reforms and went far beyond the constitutional changes which the Commissioners were prepared to contemplate. Considered as a solution of the constitutional problem at Christ Church it left much to be desired. If Chapter and College were to be separated, the basis of the division must embrace the control of college buildings and revenues. Yet it is perhaps a verdict of hindsight to brand the scheme as impracticable because it did not allow for the many purposes for which college revenues were used in later years. Until the passage of the University and Colleges Estates Act in 1858 and a spate of legislation in the following decades, there was very

[1] B.M. Add. MS. 44236, f. 70.

little flexibility in the use of college income, and fixed sums were applied to fixed purposes, whether these were salaries, the upkeep of the Cathedral, or the employment of gardeners. It was thus not unreasonable for the Students to believe that the educational work of the college could be financed on a completely separate basis from the rest of the college activities. Despite its defects the Students' scheme is of considerable interest because, although it was not the last occasion when it was proposed to separate College and Chapter, it was the only scheme to be advanced entirely by clerics and perhaps also the only one which has not been urged from a spirit of anti-clericalism or anti-secularism.

On constitutional issues the Students' memorandum was a radical extension of the scheme embodied in the Fourteen Points to separate the educational work of the college. But, as we have seen, in the face of opposition from the Chapter and probably from Liddell also, the first draft of the Ordinance abandoned this scheme in favour of one less favourable to the Students. It was on this scheme that the Students were asked to express an opinion in June 1857. The commencement of the Long Vacation obliged them to communicate their opinions individually. They could hardly be expected to welcome the Ordinance. The ink was barely dry on their own version of the constitution before they were confronted with a very different one on which they had not been consulted. As Vere Bayne, then a relatively Junior Student, put it, 'the invitation [to comment on the Ordinance] came somewhat late, and . . . if the Commissioners had asked the Educational Staff some months ago they would have received information on several points touching the requirements of the House which it is not too much to hope would materially have modified their views'.[1] Initial prejudice was nourished by a sense of injustice when, owing to an error in drafting, it appeared that the existing Students were excluded from the future benefits of the Ordinance, conjectural though these might seem to be, and

[1] P.R.O., H.O. 73/44, 21 July 1857.

that they were thereby collectively condemned as incompetent. The college officers and Tutors, while believing that the difficulties which Christ Church was experiencing in purely educational matters were due to temporary causes, were not opposed to many of the educational reforms introduced by the Commissioners, though critical of details, and in some matters, such as the special position of the Westminsters, prepared to have carried reform much further. They welcomed the increase in lay Studentships, and accepted, but without enthusiasm, the proposed opening of Junior Studentships to competition and the manner of electing Senior Students. The compulsory election of Junior Students in Science was less well received on the grounds that it tied the hands of the electors and that elections should be on as wide a basis scholastically as they were for Senior Studentships.

On the other hand, the measures proposed for the introduction of these reforms into Christ Church seemed so injurious to the Students that with almost complete unanimity they took the position that unless a radical alteration were made in the constitution of the college, the tinkering of the Commissioners would be productive of more harm than good. So injurious did the Ordinance seem in this respect, that some Students felt obliged to take an extreme position even beyond their own statement of the previous May. George Marshall, the Junior Censor, for example, wrote, 'Make the Students the college and the Canons the cathedral, and both bodies will have work for which they are suited', and again, 'no satisfactory scheme can be framed for the well-being of Christ Church which does not give to the Students charged with the education of the House some control over part of the funds of Christ Church beyond their own stipends and some share in its economical management'.[1] Jacob Ley proposed that the Canons be placed on fixed incomes, and that the remaining revenues of the College should go to Domus for the endowment of

[1] Ibid., 21 July 1857.

college officers, the Students being joined with the Canons in the management of the property as a common concern.[1]

Criticism of the draft Ordinance inevitably focused on its constitutional rather than on its educational provisions. The destruction of the old Christ Church dissolved the ancient relationship between Students and Chapter by removing its twin supports of confidence and custom. 'The position of the Students towards the Dean and Chapter', Marshall observed, 'was regulated formerly by custom and tradition and by the feeling subsisting between those who had been for the most part Students themselves, and those who were not unlikely some day to succeed to the stalls as they became vacant.'[2] With the suppression of the two Canonries the gap between governors and governed became an abyss. 'All prescriptive right is abolished,' wrote Vere Bayne, 'and indefinite authority given to the Dean and Canons, the majority of whom in all probability will never have been practically acquainted with the education or discipline of the House.'[3]

The substitution of a written for an unwritten constitution involved the definition and interpretation of rights and duties previously regulated by tradition, and as a function of power this had necessarily to be discharged by the Governing Body. Although the Ordinance sought to preserve continuity between old and new by retaining as much as possible of the old system, it kept the forms without the essence. It was not the intention of the Ordinance to increase the powers of the Chapter or to diminish those of the Students, but the effect of many of its measures was to shift the balance in favour of the Chapter and away from the Students. While the Fellows of other colleges were liberated by their new statutes, the constitution proposed for Christ Church increased the inferior status of the Students. The most important achievement of the Students

[1] P.R.O., H.O. 73/44, 8 July 1857.
[2] Ibid., 21 July 1857.
[3] Ibid., 21 July 1857.

at this time was to secure some revision of the clauses of the Ordinance which had this consequence.

Their criticisms were directed to three matters in particular—the provisions for residence, deprivation, and financial qualification. The Ordinance, it will be remembered, gave the Dean and Canons power to make regulations for residence, to deprive Students for immorality, conduct bringing disgrace upon the House, gross negligence or misconduct in any office, contumacious non-observance of statutes and by-laws, offensive conduct towards a member of the House, and non-conformity with the liturgy of the Church of England, and it empowered them to investigate the financial position of any Student with a view to ensuring that his income did not exceed the statutory figure. The fears of the Students were expressed by Osborne Gordon.

> It may indeed be said [he wrote], that no more power is given to the Dean and Canons than they at present possess, and that there is no reason to apprehend that it would be exercised in a more irksome manner, but no one can be more sensible than the writer that the Students are entirely under the authority of the Dean and Chapter, and have strictly speaking no constitutional rights.[1]

Deprived of the shield of custom, hedged with by-laws and regulations framed by an alien body on which they were not represented, and with no voice in the internal economy of the college or the management of its estates, the Students compared their position unfavourably with that of Fellows in other colleges, and considered the increase in their stipends, in the previous inadequacy of which Liddell had considered the sole necessity of change to lie, small compensation. 'He cannot think', wrote Osborne Gordon, 'that £200 a year will be much sought after by able men with these marks of inferiority attached when it can be had elsewhere without them.'[1] The same point of view was expressed by Charles Sandford, 'I believe', he wrote, 'that the power

[1] Ibid., 1 July 1857.

hereby vested in the Dean and Canons would destroy the independence of the Students, and deter many eligible persons from offering themselves as candidates for Senior Studentships.'[1] The question of residence was a particularly sore point. Under the old system residence had not been required, but with a considerably reduced number of Senior Students the Commissioners considered such a provision essential and that there would not be sufficient Tutors for the educational work of the college without it. The Students objected not only to the method by which residence was to be enforced but to the consequences of enforcement, and in particular to its effects on their claim to college patronage. Formerly, they had had a right to the patronage, but was it, they asked, now to be exercised by the Dean and Chapter as a favour to be granted or withheld by varying the rules of residence. Moreover, a residential qualification would prevent them holding many of those curacies which in the past had been tenable with Studentships, and would render nugatory the provision of the Ordinance that preferment could be held to the value of £300 a year.

The Students did not resent the inferiority of their position simply because they distrusted the Chapter but because they believed that it increased the difficulties in the way of obtaining suitable candidates for election to Senior Studentships. The Ordinance, it was held, insisted on competition in order to improve the quality of Students, but at the same time defeated its own object by weighing the odds heavily against Christ Church. Their concern was less that men from *other* colleges might be deterred by these disadvantages from competing for Senior Studentships than that the Junior Students of Christ Church might be so deterred and might therefore seek Fellowships in other colleges where the Fellows did not labour under similar marks of inferiority. They shared the belief which the Chapter had expressed to Liddell in the previous February

[1] P.R.O., H.O. 73/44, 13 July 1857.

that elections to Senior Studentships should be restricted to members of Christ Church. Sandford stated the case in these words, 'My chief reason for wishing that the Senior should be elected out of the Junior Students is that I am convinced that men educated at Christ Church are more likely to make good tutors for Christ Church undergraduates than those elected elsewhere.'[1] This not entirely self-evident proposition he defended on the grounds that 'the majority of those educated at Christ Church has consisted of men somewhat higher in social position than those educated at other colleges'. To a generation in which the majority of Students do in fact come from other colleges this may seem an argument that history has disproved, but circumstances alter cases. Sandford's statement derived from the belief that the college officers would be unable to maintain discipline among the undergraduates if the bond of common origin and unimpeded progression from Discipulus to Theologus which united the Students were broken, for their authority was based to a large extent on sentiment since it was not exercised through the Governing Body. The mere number of Students, undergraduate Students, Tutors, and Bachelor Students engaged in tuition, was sufficient to create a moral ascendancy over the mass of the undergraduates. In 1857 the sentiment was of even more immediate potency, for not only were the Students still excluded from the Governing Body and that body likely soon to be composed perhaps entirely of foreigners, but if the Senior Studentships were opened to general competition in the University those bodies, such as the Electoral Board, which the Ordinance proposed to establish, might also be dominated by foreigners. Such men, it was believed, would be placed in an untenable position in their dealings with undergraduates. It was this situation that Sandford had in mind when he lamented that the Ordinance would 'annihilate the genius loci'.[1] It followed from this argument that if the Senior Students were to be elected from the

[1] Ibid., 13 July 1857.

ranks of the Junior, it was desirable that the roll of 101 Students should not be diminished, since mere number was a powerful guarantee of an adequate supply of suitable candidates. The retention of the Student roll undiminished made it impossible in practice to raise the stipends of all the 101 Students to the levels recommended by the Ordinance, and the solution which was advocated by the Students was to endow the college officers. It was the solution they had advocated in their memorandum of May, and was not unlike that suggested by the Chapter in February. With regard to the Junior Students, it was held that the possibility of election to the ranks of the Seniors would afford them a greater incentive to remain at Christ Church than an increase in stipend and would compensate for the loss of permanency of tenure.

These were the principal objections levelled against the draft Ordinance by the Students, but they were not the only ones. Objections were levelled against the number of boards and committees created and the conflict of jurisdiction which might arise, against the failure to appoint a Steward, against the longer tenure of Westminster Junior Students compared with open Junior Students and the election of the former from the Queen's Scholars and not from the whole school. The general attitude of the Students was well summarized by Sandford. If the Commissioners had proposed, he wrote,

> to endow a sufficient number of college officers with distinct endowments, improving the condition of the Tutors by granting them larger powers in the general economy of the House, and a voice in elections; and to throw open the Studentships to general competition, dividing them into two classes, the Senior 30 to be elected out of the Junior 71, the recommendations would have been welcomed by some at least of the present working body. As it is, not one of the College Officers and Tutors, not one of the resident Student Masters is there who does not condemn it[1]

[1] P.R.O., H.O. 73/44, 13 July 1857.

Although the correspondence revealed a profound dissatisfaction with the fundamental arrangements of the Ordinance which augured ill for the future, the Commissioners were optimistic of its eventual acceptance. On 11 July Goldwin Smith wrote to Gladstone, 'Even with Christ Church, a rupture with which at one time appeared inevitable, the Commission has now got into friendly negotiation.'[1]

(*d*) THE ORDINANCE OF 1858

In the months that followed, the draft Ordinance was amended in some important respects and purged of many of its more objectionable features. The bodies charged with the election of Students and with the discipline and education of undergraduates were redefined to include the Censors, four senior Tutors, and the Dean and Chapter instead of simply the Tutors and Dean and Chapter. The power of regulating residence and of deprivation was placed in the hands of the Censors and four senior Tutors together with the Dean and Chapter, instead of exclusively in those of the latter. The Dean, Chapter, Censors, and four senior Tutors were to decide which college livings should be tenable with Studentships. The Ordinance was also amended to increase the number of Senior Students from 24 to 28, of whom 19 were to be clerical and 2 were the Lee's Readers in Anatomy and Chemistry, the latter being an entirely new appointment. The increase in the number of Senior Students involved a reduction in that of the Junior Students from 61 to 52, and of these 7 were to be known as Fell Students, 2 Bostock Students, and 1 each Vernon and Boulter Students. At the same time the Dean and Chapter were empowered to establish a further 12 Senior and 7 Junior Studentships if their funds permitted, but the clause allowing the appointment of men of distinction to Studentships without examination was dropped. The effect of this was

[1] B.M. Add. MS. 44303, f. 126.

in theory to restore the original roll of 101 Students, but in practice there was very little possibility that funds would be forthcoming for the purpose, and since the Commissioners offered no thoughts on how such a measure was to be financed it seems unlikely that it was seriously meant except as a gesture of their willingness to meet the Students' criticisms. The reduction in the number of Junior Studentships was made at the expense of the open Juniors, for the number of Westminster Studentships remained constant at twenty-one. This apparent prejudice in favour of Westminster was strongly resisted by the Students, who maintained with consistency that little good could be expected from the school in the future. The revised Ordinance was also made more precise with regard to the use of funds for the stipends of the three groups of Students, the Senior, the Westminster, and the open Junior. The proceeds of the suppressed Canonries were to be applied to the Clerical Senior Studentships only. The emoluments of the Fell, Boulter, and Bostock Trusts were to be applied to the open Junior Studentships, and, since the Lee Trust was no longer available for undergraduate purposes because it was to support the Lee's Readers, the Westminster Junior Students were to be maintained by an annual grant of £1,260 from the college estates and the proceeds of the South, Hill, and Frewin Trusts.

In its final form the Ordinance omitted the draft clause to provide a Treasurer and Sub-Dean from those who had been Senior Students. It is difficult to understand how the Commissioners could ever have supposed that the Sub-Dean need not be a Canon. As to the Treasurership, Jacobson, the Regius Professor of Divinity, had already succeeded the ailing Bull on 1 July 1857, and the Commissioners presumably intended that the Treasurership should henceforth be held by a Canon-Professor. The volume of estate business in the nineteenth century made it very undesirable that the duties of Treasurer and Canon should be combined, though it was a course approved by Liddell.

Such a practice had been abandoned for many years under the old system at Christ Church, and Pusey rightly deplored Jacobson's appointment. These were the main alterations incorporated into the final version of the Ordinance, apart from a reduction in the number of Cathedral chaplaincies to four and permission for the Dean and Chapter 'to alter in such manner as they shall think fit the designation of the Servitors'.

In its revised form the Ordinance went far to meet the criticisms of the Students. It relieved them of humiliating restrictions and brought them more actively than before into the educational work of the college. But the limited powers of the Commissioners prevented them from dealing with the principal difficulty, which was the exclusion of the Students from the Governing Body. They were thus unable to provide a satisfactory constitution for Christ Church, and their proposals were necessarily of a temporary nature. It is probable that the crisis of 1865–7 would have developed sooner if the Ordinance had taken effect more quickly, but through its respect for vested interests many years were to elapse before its main provisions came into force. In strictly educational matters the Commissioners were more successful, and their reforms on the whole beneficial. They did little to alter the choice of candidates for Studentships, but they prepared the way for an increase in the number of resident Senior Students and for some degree of specialization by Tutors, which eventually terminated the old system whereby a Tutor taught almost every subject in the curriculum. The indirect achievements of the Ordinance, on the other hand, were considerable. It averted, at least for a time, the threat that Christ Church would split into its two parts, Chapter and Students, Cathedral and College. It gave the college experience of a written constitution which gradually revealed those problems which needed to be settled in 1867. It also indicated the direction which the final settlement would take, both by exposing the untenability of its own compromise between the claims of

Chapter and Students and by demonstrating that it was possible to associate Chapter and Students together in the Electoral Board and elsewhere without the dire consequences which both parties had anticipated. This experience may well have restored the confidence of the Students in the Chapter which the Ordinance had done so much to destroy and so paved the way for the solution of 1867.

The final form of the Ordinance was drawn up by Mountague Bernard.[1] It was sealed by the Commissioners on 9 January and received the royal assent on 5 June 1858. At the Chapter meeting on 16 June Dr. Ogilvie entered a formal protest against the Ordinance,

First, Because I consider it wrong in principle as involving arbitrary changes, and such disregard for the Wills and intentions of Founders and Benefactors as no alleged necessity has justified. Secondly, because in its details it seems to me less suitable to the character and less conducive to the ends of a place of Religion, Learning, and Education than the previously existing constitution of the College.[2]

From the Students the document received a frigid welcome. Osborne Gordon, in that chill and formal third person which he favoured in his communications with the Commissioners, informed them that he

feels bound to say that they have now made every alteration in it that could be expected from them considering their inadequate powers and the principles they deliberately adopted. In all that they have done he is convinced that they have looked solely to the good of the House, and if his own views are different from theirs, he hopes still that the result will correspond to their expectations.[3]

Privately he confided to Gladstone, 'I fear the Commissioners have made a bad affair of Christ Church. If change was necessary they ought to have put the Students here on

[1] Bodleian Library, MS. Top. Oxon. c. 309, f. 2.
[2] Chapter Act Book, 16 June 1858.
[3] P.R.O., H.O. 73/44, 14 Nov. 1857.

the level of Fellows elsewhere.'[1] He had no taste for the new Christ Church which was being created, and in 1861 took the Berkshire living of Easthampstead. 'Our new Ordinance', he told Gladstone, 'has cut off any prospect of permanent settlement here.'[1] Marshall, Gordon's friend, fellow Censor and biographer, had departed for the living of Pyrton before the Ordinance was completed. Stokes, for some years a Tutor with Gordon and Marshall, left for the living of Staines in 1859.

Of the younger Students, Prout, who was to take the leading part in the agitation for the statutes, was even more hostile in his verdict on the Ordinance. Like Gordon, he complained that the Students had not been made the equal of Fellows. 'I regret therefore,' he wrote, 'that I cannot assent to the scheme as proposed by H.M. Commissioners nor can I think that it yet meets the requirements of the case.'[2]

[1] B.M. Add. MS. 44389, f. 166.
[2] P.R.O., H.O. 73/44, 29 Oct. 1857.

IV

New Christ Church Under the Ordinance, 1858–1865

SUCH changes as there were in the Chapter in the years immediately after the Ordinance were not calculated to assuage the Students' discontents. Archdeacon Clerke was to remain Sub-Dean until his death in 1877 and Pusey, Jelf, Jacobson, Ogilvie, and Heurtley remained in office; but, as has been seen, death had already cheated the Students of their hope of seeing one more former Student, Robert Hussey, become a Canon.

The fourth vacancy among the Canonries occurred with the death of Dr. Bull on 21 February 1858 at the age of sixty-eight. Bull is best known as a pluralist, in which capacity his achievements are celebrated in a well-known verse;[1] he had also enjoyed some notoriety as an unpopular Proctor. But there was much more to Bull than this: he was in fact a fine example of the old order of Canons of Christ Church. A King's Scholar at Westminster, Student and Censor of the House, and also (a fact little remembered) a

[1] W. Bright gave the following version ('which I heard many years ago from an old Christ Church man') in *Our Memories* (ed. C. H. O. Daniel, 1893), p. 139:

> On the Box with Will Whip, ere the use of the Rail,
> To London I travelled: and inside the mail
> Sat a Canon of Exeter: on the same perch
> Sat a Canon of Oxford's Episcopal Church:
> Next came one who held—I will own the thing's small—
> In the Minster of York a prebendal stall.
> And there sat a Parson, all pursy and fair,
> With a Vicarage fat and three hundred a year.
> Now, good reader, perhaps you will deem the coach full:
> No, there was but one traveller—Dr. John Bull!

Double First, he had left Christ Church in 1821 for a living and returned as a Canon in 1830. From 1832 until his resignation in 1857 he was Treasurer. Dr. Pusey, for one, thought he had a 'fine mind, which was wasted on Treasurer's business'.[1] On 1 July 1857 the Dean and Chapter elected Jacobson to succeed Bull as Treasurer; suddenly the Treasurer was no longer a Canon who had formerly been Student and Censor, but instead a 'foreigner'.

When Bull died Hussey's successor as Professor had already been in office for a year, living in his lodgings in the High Street, and he could hardly have presented a greater contrast to Bull or Hussey. A. P. Stanley, who was installed in 1858, had been a Scholar of Balliol with his lifelong friend Benjamin Jowett in that great decade, the 1830s, and had gone on to be a Fellow of University College. His friend Dean Liddell had welcomed his appointment, but the University in general did not, and to the Students of Christ Church it was another gloomy landmark in the disappearance of the Christ Church they knew.

In 1859 the process continued, with the death on 19 August of the eighty-eight-year-old Dr. Barnes, like Bull a King's Scholar of Westminster and Student and Censor of Christ Church, and even more than Bull a member of a family loyal to Westminster and the House. Soon after an engaging interlude as an officer of the Oxford Volunteer Corps,[2] Barnes had spent a mere five years away from Christ Church before returning as a Canon as far back as 1810. Barnes's Canonry (the Seventh Stall) now lapsed in accordance with the Amending Act of 1856 and the Ordinances of 1858, and accordingly the number of Canons was

[1] Pusey wrote to Bull's brother Henry on 17 Mar. 1861 (the occasion was Bull's epitaph): 'It vexed me so that his fine and polished talent should be wasted on Treasurer's business. . . . My only comfort was that his good management of the Chapter property, enabled them to augment the small livings to a large amount. I think they were augmented by £5000 a year in his time. But I used to groan inwardly, over his fine mind being wasted on what an acute professional man would do as well' (Pusey Papers).

[2] A lampoon on 'Major Barnes' was issued as late as 1831.

reduced to seven,[1] at which it remained until it became six by the lapse of the Eighth Stall on the death of Dr. Jelf in 1871.

At the beginning of 1864 Stanley became Dean of Westminster. Some in Oxford (Pusey, naturally, among them) saw H. P. Liddon, who had been a Student of Christ Church since 1846, as a possible successor;[2] but Palmerston did not take the opportunity to renew the succession of Students to Canonries of Christ Church, nor did he meet the wishes of Dean Liddell by appointing G. G. Bradley. In the event Palmerston nominated Walter Waddington Shirley to the vacant Professorship and Canonry.[3] Shirley's tenure was in some ways successful[4] but in one respect it was disastrous, though to some extent this was the result of a system for which he was not himself to blame: he was made Treasurer in 1865, and was belaboured by critics of the internal economy of Christ Church in the 'Bread and Butter row' which broke out in November of that year. Shirley's pedigree

[1] Barnes's canonical residence became the present Peckwater IX staircase in 1868.

[2] J. O. Johnston, *Life and Letters of H. P. Liddon* (1904), p. 71.

[3] Liddell heard from W. W. Shirley that he (Shirley) or A. S. Farrar, a Tutor of Wadham, was certain to be nominated, and wrote a pained letter to Gladstone: 'I shall never cease to deplore Mr. Bradley [Dean Stanley's Liberal friend G. G. Bradley of University College, then Headmaster of Marlborough] being put after either of those gentlemen. It would be the greatest loss to the University and to Christ Church. I should, as now, be left singlehanded in the Chapter. . . . To me at Christ Church he [Bradley] would be indeed a valuable ally.' Farrar's appointment would be a joke, and Shirley was certainly better than Farrar; but the Dean 'conscientiously' believed Bradley the best man (B.M. Add. MS. 44236, ff. 313–14). Gladstone was mortified that R. W. Church did not succeed Stanley (J. Morley, *Life of W. E. Gladstone*, bk. vi, chap. X).

[4] Stubbs wrote to Freeman, 28 Nov. 1866: 'Shirley... was accidentally a good appointment, but it was very like an accident altogether' (ed. W. H. Hutton, *Letters of William Stubbs* (1904), p. 112). There is a panegyric in J. W. Burgon, *Twelve Good Men* (1891), p. vii. Stubbs, Freeman, and Shirley (and also Church and Froude) had all been unsuccessful candidates for the Chichele Professorship of Modern History when Montagu Burrows was appointed in 1862 (Dorothy M. Owen, 'The Chichele Professorship of Modern History', *Bulletin of the Institute of Historical Research*, xxxiv (1961), 218).

could hardly have been better: his ancestor Saswalo appears in Domesday Book, his father was a bishop, and he himself (being the great-grandnephew of the 4th Earl Ferrers, the only Christ Church peer ever hanged for murder) had a remote chance of succeeding to the earldom of Ferrers, as in fact his son did do in 1912.[1] But he had been a Scholar and Fellow of Wadham; and perhaps worst of all, as far as the Students were concerned, he was relatively young, a mere thirty-six. (He had overlapped with Sandford and Dodgson at Rugby.) Students who were of much the same age as Shirley, or even (like Prout) somewhat older, could not be expected to tolerate exclusion from power when appointments like Shirley's were seen to be inevitable.

Thus, after Stanley's departure, the Chapter contained six Canons of some standing in Clerke, Pusey, Jelf, Jacobson, Ogilvie, and Heurtley, and one very junior member indeed in Shirley. A majority of the Canons during the first years of government under the Ordinance come from other colleges; and the three gremial members of Christ Church (Clerke, Pusey, and Jelf) were in a minority after the death of Barnes in 1859. Since 1846, when Archdeacon Clerke had obtained his Canonry, no Student of the House had been made a Canon of Christ Church; in these conditions no special 'Christ Church sentiment' could be expected to flourish. Moreover, of the six senior Canons early in 1865 four were born in the eighteenth century, and the other two, Jacobson and Heurtley, were both older than the Dean. Only Clerke had been a Student; Canons who had themselves been Fellows of other colleges, even (as Pusey, Jelf, and Ogilvie had been) Fellows of Oriel and Balliol, were unlikely to abdicate their supreme power as Canons without a struggle; and the advent of younger ones, of whom Shirley was the first, was bound to stimulate the Students' desire for change.

Within a few weeks of his installation Stanley wrote that 'certainly the Chapter here contains very explosive

[1] Shirley was also related to the French diplomat Waddington.

elements';[1] it does not seem to have occurred to him that his own past as Secretary to the Commission set up in 1850 was likely to add to them. There is also evidence of tension between Dean and Canons as a result of what the latter regarded as the former's highhandedness.[2] Nevertheless, in these years after the Ordinance the Chapter was far from idle. Apart from the usual round of leases and presentations to be sealed, railway plans to be contested, college offices to be filled and Students' places to be voided, the Chapter carried through one measure crucial to the future of Christ Church: Meadow Buildings were erected in place of Fell's Buildings and the Chaplains' Quadrangle. This project was essential if the undergraduate numbers were to expand; as early as 1791 the Dean and Chapter had been exercised by 'the heavy expence which must be incurred at no great distance of time by taking down and rebuilding' the Chaplains' Quadrangle, and a special fund for the purpose was set up as far back as 1809.[3] For good or ill it was Dean Liddell who had the new building erected, at a cost of some £21,000.[4] Staircases 1 and 2 were occupied at Michaelmas 1864, and the remaining four twelve months later.[5] But above all there were Studentships, Senior and Junior, to be

[1] R. E. Prothero and G. G. Bradley, *Life and Correspondence of Dean Stanley* (1894), ii. 2.

[2] Chapter Act Book, 17 Dec. 1862.

[3] Ch. Ch. Archives, xxxiii. b. 4 ('A Fund for Extraordinary Reparations'), pp. 13, 59–60. A fund was indeed set up in 1791 and reached £4,051 by 1805, but was apparently diverted to other college purposes.

[4] Accounts in Ch. Ch. Archives, xxxiii. b. 7 ('Funds for New Buildings 1810–65'); in 1862 the fund set up in 1809 had an annual income of nearly £700. In 1862–5 £21,213 was paid out from it—£18,000 to the builder, J. R. Symm, and £850 to the architect, T. N. Deane. It was prophetically observed in *The Builder* for 29 Nov. 1862 that 'The style of the building . . . will doubtless produce conflicting criticisms.'

[5] The Dean and Chapter undertook another building venture during these years in the 'Model Dwellings for Working Classes in Oxford' built in St. Thomas's Parish in 1866–7—an important pioneer housing venture on a site 'where recently stood some of the worst tenements which could be found in Oxford'. The 'Model Dwellings' contained 12 first-class, 12 second-class, and 12 third-class dwellings let at 4*s*., 3*s*., and 2*s*. per week respectively; they cost £4,700.

created in compliance with the terms of the Ordinance; and new bodies on the educational side of the House to be operated in conjunction with the Senior Students.

By 1865 gremial members of Christ Church were in a minority not only among the Canons but also among the Senior Students. Under clause 20 of the Ordinance 'the present Censors, Readers, Tutors, and Lecturers of the House' became Senior Students 'without election or admission'. By this provision eight Students under the Old Foundation became Senior Students: Osborne Gordon, Charles Lloyd, T. J. Prout, C. W. Sandford, F. H. Joyce, T. Vere Bayne, H. A. Pickard, and C. L. Dodgson.[1] The first three of these were Theologi; Sandford, Joyce, Bayne, Pickard, and Dodgson were 46th, 52nd, 57th, 63rd, and 69th on the list of 101 at the end of 1858. As Senior Students they naturally retained among themselves their previous order of seniority as Students. All were in Orders (though Dodgson, of course, only in Deacon's Orders); the most senior of them, Gordon, had matriculated in 1832, and the most junior, Pickard and Dodgson, in 1851 and 1850 respectively. Between them they had considerable experience of the educational side of Christ Church. Gordon and Prout were the two Censors and Librarians; Gordon was also Catechist, and had served two terms as a member of the new Hebdomadal Council. Sandford was the Greek Reader and Joyce became the Rhetoric Reader in October 1858; Bayne and Pickard were Tutors; and Dodgson was the Mathematical Lecturer.

Changes in this small body were rapid. Liddell's forecast in 1857 that members of other colleges would 'seldom' be elected to Senior Studentships proved inaccurate, to say the least.[2] It was the Chapter which (because it controlled the

[1] H. L. Thompson, *Christ Church* (1900), pp. 214–15, omits Lloyd from his list of the 'educational staff' when he came up in Michaelmas Term 1858. For Gordon, see above, pp. 65–6; for Prout, Sandford, Bayne, and Dodgson see below, pp. 112–13. *Francis Hayward Joyce . . . A Short Memoir of His Life, Work and Character*, By a few of his Friends, was published in 1907.

[2] See above, p. 56.

finances of the House) determined the rate at and the subjects in which new Senior and Junior Studentships were created; but elections of individuals to fill them were made (after examination) by the new Electoral Board of Dean, Canons, Censors, and four senior Tutors set up by the Ordinance.[1] In December 1859 this new body elected the first two new Senior Students, one an archbishop's grandson, the other a baker's son, A. G. Vernon Harcourt (who became Lee's Reader in Chemistry) and G. R. Luke. There were two other candidates for Harcourt's Studentship. Both new Students were 'foreigners'; and in view of the dominance of their college in the Honour Schools, it was natural that both should be Balliol men. Harcourt (1834–1919) matriculated in 1854; one of the first pupils of B. C. Brodie, Aldrichian and later Waynflete Professor, he had taken a First in Natural Science in 1858; between 1861 and 1885 inclusive he was to examine in Natural Science no fewer than ten times. He was made F.R.S. in 1863.[2] Harcourt is surely a good example of an able man who by family tradition would in former times automatically have gone to Westminster and Christ Church but may have gone elsewhere because of the decline apparent in those institutions in the 1840s and early 1850s. He was a descendant and kinsman of those Barons Vernon who nominated to one Studentship of the House. His grandfather, Edward Vernon (later Harcourt) (1757–1847), had been first a Student and later a Canon of Christ Church before becoming Archbishop of York. The Archbishop's first, second, third, seventh, ninth, and eleventh sons had all proceeded from

[1] Details of elections are taken from the minutes of this body (Ch. Ch. Archives, xxxix. a. 1).

[2] Brodie himself and F. T. Conington (Fellow of Corpus) were the assessors in the examination taken by Harcourt; the papers set are in the Bodleian Library (2626 d. 31). Dr. P. W. Kent kindly drew my attention to the obituary of Harcourt in *Proc. of the Royal Society*, 1920. Harcourt had attended demonstrations and lectures by the Lee's Reader in Anatomy in the Lee Gallery at Christ Church; in 1859 the anatomical books and specimens were removed to the new University Museum, and in 1866 Harcourt took over the Gallery for the study and teaching of Chemistry.

Westminster to Christ Church (where the second died); the eleventh and youngest son, Egerton, had obtained a Double First in 1824 and with Robert Hussey was a great favourite of Dr. Bull, then Censor. But only one of the Archbishop's grandsons went to Westminster and the House.[1] Luke (one year Harcourt's junior) had taken a Double First in Classical Moderations and Greats, and he won both Gaisford Prizes and the Ireland. Luke's devotion to the House and his pupils altogether won the heart of H. L. Thompson, who says of him:

He was a man of singular beauty of character, of intense earnestness, and of contagious enthusiasm. He took us in hand, spent infinite trouble upon us, made us do our very best; and four first classes at the next examination were his reward. His good work met the warmest encouragement from the Dean, and its stimulating effect was felt throughout the college.[2]

In November 1860 W. S. Church, who like Harcourt was required by the terms of Dr. Lee's will to be a layman, was elected and became Lee's Reader in Anatomy, i.e. Tutor in Medicine; one year junior to Luke, he had taken a First in Natural Science at University College, and was thus another 'foreigner'. In the examination he defeated the only other candidate, Dodgson's friend Reginald Southey, Student of Christ Church.[3] Church's Readership dated

[1] i.e. G. E. Harcourt-Vernon, the eldest son of the Archbishop's seventh son, in 1835; his next brother, E. H. Harcourt-Vernon, went from Westminster to University College in 1839.

[2] Thompson, *Christ Church*, pp. 218–19; the First Classes (in 1860) were T. A. Gaisford, W. H. Gladstone, A. F. Pope, and Thompson himself; the first three were Junior Students, and Thompson one of the last Students on the Old Foundation. Alas! Pope did not read for Honours in the Second Public Examination; in Easter Term 1862 Gaisford got a Third in Classics, Gladstone and Thompson got Seconds (Gladstone got a Third in Modern History in Michaelmas Term). Thompson's comment may no doubt be used to condemn the whole examination system at the time: Luke had had precisely one term's work with his pupils.

[3] George Rolleston (the outgoing Reader, elected only a few weeks before the Ordinance) and H. W. Acland (Rolleston's predecessor, now Regius Professor of Medicine) were the assessors in the examination. Church's brilliant career ended only in 1928.

from 1767; Harcourt's was a new appointment. Next year Gordon's Studentship lapsed as he was now incumbent of Easthampstead, but two new Senior Students were elected. In March 1861, at the last meeting of the Electoral Board attended by Osborne Gordon, his former pupil G. J. Blore became the first gremial member of the House to be elected by examination to a Senior Studentship under the Ordinance. Blore (later a mild Headmaster of King's School, Canterbury) was the only Student on the Old Foundation to be advanced in this way between 1858 and 1867; in 1856 and 1858 he had taken Firsts in Classical Moderations and Greats. In January 1862 Blore's exact contemporary C. H. Hoole of Magdalen Hall was elected; his First in Classical Moderations, and Fourth in Greats may to some have presaged the difficulties which his presence certainly caused in later years. (He appealed to the Visitor as early as 1868.)

The year 1862 saw a most grievous loss, for on 3 March, at the age of twenty-five, Luke met a tragic death by drowning when his dinghy capsized on the Isis near Kennington, apparently as a result of giddiness induced by years of overwork.[1] The Dean was grief-stricken;[2] he later had a window placed in the Cathedral as a memorial to one from whom he had hoped so much. On 27 April Charles Lloyd died, and Prout became the Senior Student under the Ordinance. Two new elections were made in December

[1] Jowett wrote that day the obituary notice on Luke printed in *The Times*, 4 Mar. 1867, and quoted in part by E. Abbott and L. Campbell, *Life and Letters of Benjamin Jowett* (1897), i. 331–2. Abbott and Campbell relate that 'When told that Luke was killing himself with work, Jowett said, with a kind of fatherly pride, "Young men don't die so easily."' He was wrong: Luke became subject to fits of giddiness, one of which caused his death. That Luke did seriously overwork is clear from the account of his career in *The Museum*, ii (1862–3), 73–81, by his friend John Nichol, Regius Professor of English Language and Literature at Glasgow University 1862–89, who later published verses on 'G. R. L.' in *The Death of Themistocles, and other Poems* (1881), p. 151.

[2] Thompson, *H. G. Liddell*, pp. 180–1 (account by G. W. Kitchin, who as Censor presumably reported the event to the Dean).

1862: Charles Bigg and H. A. Giffard (a Guernseyman) both came from Corpus Christi College, the former with a Double First in Moderations and Greats and a Hertford Scholarship behind him, the latter with Firsts in both Classical and Mathematical Moderations and in both Lit. Hum. and Mathematics, not to mention a Junior Mathematical Scholarship, a Taylorian Scholarship, and an Eldon Law Scholarship. Giffard's sharp brain soon found defects in the Ordinances.

At the end of 1862 there were thus six Senior Students who had been Students on the Old Foundation, and six who had not, though of these one (Blore) was a Christ Church man. But in 1863 Joyce ceased to be a Senior Student and the Senior Students named in 1858 were henceforth in a minority. In March 1864 the Wykehamist Charles Martin was elected from New College and Robert Brodie (a younger cousin of the Professor of Chemistry) from Trinity; there were ten candidates. Martin (later Warden of Radley) had a Second in Classical Moderations and a First in Greats, and had won the Stanhope Essay Prize; Brodie had taken a Double First in Moderations and Greats. E. S. Talbot felt he owed much to Martin, 'who assisted me to see that to hold convictions or beliefs and to recognize difficulties in them which we could not solve was normal and right';[1] but A. B. Simeon thought that Brodie (like many tutors before and since) 'used to talk too much of subjects that interested him instead of teaching me Latin Prose'.[2] At the beginning of 1865, therefore, there were thirteen Students under the Ordinance, of whom the five senior had been Students on the Old Foundation (Prout, Sandford, Bayne, Pickard, and Dodgson, of whom Pickard was an Inspector of Schools and non-resident); the remaining

[1] E. S. Talbot, *Memories of Early Life* (1924), p. 47. Martin took his own difficulties to H. P. Liddon (MS. Diary of H. P. Liddon, 26 Nov. 1864 (Article XXIX), 24 Feb. 1865, 20 Feb., and 1 Nov. 1866). For Martin see *Over the Hills* . . . (1968), the autobiography of his son, W. Keble Martin.

[2] A. B. Simeon's MS. Autobiography, in Archives of St. Edward's School, Oxford, 1/1.11 (extract kindly supplied by the Warden).

eight had all been elected after examination. Six of the thirteen (i.e. the five senior and Blore) were gremial members of Christ Church; the other seven were 'foreigners'. Of the thirteen eight were in Anglican Orders: these were the five senior, Blore, Hoole, and Bigg, while Brodie was about to become ordained.

A number of Students on the Old Foundation still retained the Studentships to which they had been elected before the Ordinance of 1858, which naturally saved their rights, came into force. At the end of 1859 there were still as many as eighty-five of these (including the eight who had become Senior Students), but by the end of 1864 the number had declined to forty-three as death and marriage took their toll; no more were of course elected, and the last survivor died in 1915. In 1865 the Students on the Old Foundation ranged from C. W. Page[1] and T. Chamberlain, who were in their fifties and had been Students for over thirty years, down through resident members of Convocation like R. G. Faussett and H. P. Liddon to three very junior Students (H. L. Thompson, Thomas Waters, and E. W. Whitaker) who had been elected Students from Westminster School on Christmas Eve 1858, some months after the Ordinance had come into force. During these years the Dean was in no way debarred from designating Students on the Old Foundation as Tutors by his own fiat (as he had always done), and he had in fact so designated H. L. Thompson. As Students on the Old Foundation had vested rights under the Ordinance of 1858, they were bound at some stage to be consulted before that Ordinance was set aside; and a few resident Students on the Old Foundation took a prominent part in the agitation from the outset.

Throughout this period the college officers were Students who had been appointed before 1858.[2] In April 1861, on

[1] See p. 148.

[2] Details from Bayne's list of 'Censors for fifty Years', in first Scrapbook in Ch. Ch. Library, and from Chapter Act Book.

Gordon's departure for Easthampstead, Prout (his junior since October 1857) was appointed Senior Censor and Catechist in his place, and Sandford Junior Censor in place of Prout; Bayne succeeded Sandford as Greek Reader. Two months later, after only one term in office, for some reason unknown,[1] Prout resigned; like Gordon he found the new system unacceptable, but unlike Gordon he remained in Oxford. In October 1861 Sandford succeeded him, after a very short Censorial apprenticeship; Joyce became Junior Censor, Bayne succeeded to Joyce's place as Rhetoric Reader, and Pickard to Bayne's as Greek Reader. But Joyce never resided during his term of office and next February began his thirty-six years' incumbency of Harrow; in January 1862 G. W. Kitchin became Junior Censor. Kitchin had for some years been the successful Headmaster of a Preparatory School at Twyford,[2] and had kept his Studentship (on the Old Foundation);[3] he was not a Senior Student but there was nothing in the Ordinance to prevent his appointment as Censor. Kitchin's Double First in Classics and Mathematics in 1850 made him perhaps the most distinguished Student remaining from the days before 1858. But his term of office was short, and ended in June 1863. In September 1863 he married, and so forfeited his Studentship. In October Bayne succeeded him as Junior Censor; Pickard took Bayne's place as Rhetoric Reader, and Blore Pickard's place as Greek Reader.

These bewildering and rapid changes are not significant in detail; but they show how Students originally appointed under the old regime retained a monopoly of the college offices in the first years after the Ordinances: this was

[1] He appears to have been successful as Junior Censor. Thompson (*H. G. Liddell*, p. 168) records Archdeacon Clerke's favourable comment in a letter to the absent Dean in 1858: 'I am bound to speak well of Prout as Censor. He shows firmness, and knows how to manage men, and they seem to respect him.' Prout resigned as Proctor at the same time.

[2] See *The Story of Twyford School* (Winchester, [1909]), pp. 13–15, 20–1.

[3] He had been at Ipswich Grammar School, Wolsey's other foundation.

reasonable enough, as they were the most senior. Far the most important of the college officers were the Censors: Sandford and Bayne were to hold office together until January 1870; in the coming agitation Sandford was to preside over meetings of which Bayne took the minutes. Sandford had matriculated in 1847 and by early 1865 had nearly four years' experience of the Censorship; Bayne had matriculated a year later and had held office for fifteen months. The Censors occupied a curious position; nominated by the Dean,[1] they were his representatives in the maintenance of discipline among the undergraduates; but they were also the natural and inevitable representatives of the full body of Senior Students in all dealings with the Dean and Chapter.

These were the men with some of whom under the Ordinance the Dean and Canons shared a little of their former power. The 'Electoral Board' was empowered to elect Senior and Junior Students after examination, to admit Senior Students to full status after their twelve months' probation, to make regulations as to their residence, and to deprive them of their Studentships for specified offences (including 'grossly offensive behaviour towards any member' of the House—a curiously wide description). The Board could also elect Honorary Students, and at the end of 1858 elected ten members of the House to this honourable dignity;[2] and it could make regulations as to

[1] Formally, the Censors were 'elected' by the Dean and Chapter; but according to T. B. Strong (*Henry Parry Liddon 1829–1929: A Centenary Memoir* (1929), p. 12), were nominated by the Dean, as one would expect.

[2] Gladstone, Sir George Cornewall Lewis, Sir Frederick Ouseley (the first Professor of Music to make that profession respectable), Dr. Acland, John Ruskin, Henry Hallam, Lords Stanhope, Elgin, Dalhousie, and Canning. Ruskin's name was put forward by Osborne Gordon, once Ruskin's private tutor, seconded by the Dean. Lord Wrottesley (late P.R.S.) was added in 1860, and Chichester Parkinson-Fortescue in 1866. The most striking omission from the list was that of Lord Derby (already twice Prime Minister): it can hardly have been thought that the distinction was an improper one for a former Gentleman Commoner, for Ruskin had held this rank, and Stanhope had been a Nobleman of the House. Honorary Students of the House were not limited in Number until 1882.

the conduct of all undergraduates and Bachelors of the House. The Board had, of course, no financial powers whatever. The Ordinance gave the Dean and seven Canons a clear majority over the Students; had a case of possible deprivation of a Senior Student arisen, the unwisdom of this provision might have become apparent. When the number of Canons was reduced to six, the Dean would have a casting vote.

At first the Censors and Senior Students who attended meetings of this body were Senior Students named by the Ordinance itself, until Luke, Blore, Hoole, Bigg, H. L. Thompson (a Tutor but a Student on the Old Foundation),[1] and Martin became members in turn. The list alone reveals a curious anomaly: because the Lee's Readers, Harcourt and Church, who were both senior to Blore and Hoole, were not *eo nomine* Tutors, they were not eligible for membership of the Electoral Board; again, although Kitchin was not a Tutor, because he was Censor he sat on the Board to the exclusion of a Tutor. On the other hand, because he was not a Tutor Prout ceased to be a member of the Board when he ceased to be Censor. At the end of 1864 the Board consisted of Sandford, Bayne, Pickard, Blore, Hoole, and Bigg; but Harcourt and Church, both senior to Blore, were excluded, and as the number of Tutors eligible for membership in addition to the Censors was fixed at four, more and more Senior Students would have to wait longer and longer before becoming eligible to partake even in the limited business which was within the powers of the Board. Ultimately, some twenty of the twenty-eight Senior Students (including two of the nine laymen) envisaged in the Ordinance would have been excluded in this way. The Board did undoubtedly provide a means whereby Dean, Canons, and Students could collaborate together in the educational work of the House; but as far as the Canons (other than the Sub-Dean) were concerned this was in fact a novelty. The setting

[1] Thompson was made eligible for membership of the Board by a change in the Ordinance.

of examination papers by Canons as well as Dean and Students may have seemed to some framers of the Ordinance a proper recognition of the Canons' academic status;[1] but to the Students, especially those who remembered the old system, this was Canonical encroachment on matters which had previously been the preserve of Dean, Sub-Dean, and Students alone. Worst of all, the Canons did not have to teach the men whom they helped to select. The Electoral Board met seventy-two times during its life of nine years, an average of eight meetings each year. There were of course long intervals between meetings (there was no meeting between March 1864 and February 1865), and the business to be done was of a restricted kind; but the Board gave frequent opportunities for collaboration between Canons and Students, and on the whole it appears to have functioned harmoniously and with success. As might have been expected,[2] there were arguments over residence; there are hints of disagreements over the election of Senior Students,[3] but in the records this can only be detected in the case of Giffard, on whose classical attainments the electors were divided. Despite earlier fears, there is no sign that electors of Christ Church origin combined against the rest.

One defect of the Electoral Board must be mentioned: it did not in fact control all tutorial appointments. In February 1861 the Dean and Chapter, as trustees under Dr. Lee's will, were able to appoint a third Lee's Reader, this time in Law and Modern History. In so doing they acted without any reference to the Electoral Board.

The Ordinance envisaged one other type of meeting involving the Students: under clause 23, by-laws binding on the Senior Students could be made 'by the Dean, Canons and Senior Students'. At such meetings the Senior Students

[1] To Gordon it may have recalled the fact that years before he had beaten Stanley for the Ireland.

[2] Cf. above, p. 76.

[3] Thompson, *H. G. Liddell*, p. 184.

would almost at once have been in a majority; but no minutes survive of such meetings.[1]

At the end of 1864 it was probably still too soon to assess the results of the Ordinance in academic matters. In December 1859, following the publication of the Michaelmas Term Class Lists in Classical Mods., in which Christ Church had one name only, and that in the Second Class, the House, and the Dean in particular, had been taken to task by *The Times* in a severe leader, replete with that inaccuracy which has characterized so much Press abuse of Christ Church before and since. 'There is something so very remarkable in this falling off that people [*sic*] at a distance are seeking reasons for it.' Whether 'people' were or not (and *The Times* had no more means of knowing this then than we have now), *The Times*'s own facts were wrong: as shown earlier in this account, the decline in the Schools had begun (as letters to the newspapers during the following days showed) under Gaisford and by his encouragement. But to *The Times* 'the most remarkable phase of the decline and fall of this illustrious seminary of learning' was coincidental with Liddell's appointment in 1855 and even consequent upon his 'non-residence' since; there was an urgent need for the appointment of an efficient deputy—whether Canon or Student *The Times* did not venture to say. Liddell was vigorously defended by 'Ex Aede Christi' (in fact A. P. Stanley), who maintained—without damning Gaisford by name—that 'the blank years from 1855 to 1858 are the results of the state in which the College was found at his [i.e. Liddell's] appointment'; the years to come would show. Another defence came over the signature 'V.' from another Liberal, Francis Jeune, then Vice-Chancellor, who like Liddell had been a Royal Commissioner in 1850; Jeune happened to write on the day of Harcourt's and Luke's elections, and thought they augured 'the dawn of a brilliant

[1] Meetings of Tutors alone (held, as they still are, with the Senior Censor in the chair) must have been held from an early date; for examples just before the Ordinance, cf. ed. R. L. Green, *Carroll Diaries* (1953), i. 74, 248–9.

day for that great institution, even though the absorption of a large portion of its revenues for its purposes as a cathedral and its government, not by fellows but by canons, must *ever*[1] injure it as a College'.[2]

To some extent these prophecies were borne out by events. The inferior status assigned to Senior Students by the Ordinance did not prevent the recruitment of able men from outside Christ Church; on the other hand, before 1865 only one, Blore, had been recruited from within the House. In the Final Schools, to which as usual exaggerated significance was attached, the results improved. Between Easter 1856 and Michaelmas 1859 there were only eight Christ Church First Classes in all Moderations, and nine in all Final Schools (as against 29 and 18 respectively from Balliol), Blore of course figuring in both lists; between Easter 1860 and Michaelmas 1864 there were 18 Christ Church First Classes in Moderations (including the 4 immediately after G. R. Luke's arrival signalized by Thompson) and 16 in the Final Schools; 5 of these last were won at Michaelmas 1864 itself. The Balliol figures for the same period were 45 and 34 respectively.

But for Prout comparisons with Balliol were not the main point in determining the moment for agitation. The question was a constitutional one. If the constitution remained as it was, would the First Class men clearly still to be found within Christ Church seek Studentships at Christ Church rather than Fellowships elsewhere? If there was change, and change there must be, there must be agitation now, while some Students on the Old Foundation remained, to preserve what could be preserved of the old Christ Church. Jeune, with the self-satisfaction of the reformer content with existing achievement, had thought in 1859 that Christ Church must 'ever' suffer from the Cathedral connection;

[1] My italics.

[2] *The Times*, 17, 20, 21, 22 Dec. 1859; Vere Bayne's press-cuttings in his first scrapbook in Ch. Ch. Library identify Stanley and Jeune. Cf. Thompson, *H. G. Liddell*, pp. 181–2.

Prout, with a pragmatic readiness to change in order to preserve, had no intention of accepting the *status quo* under the ill-considered provisions of the Ordinance.

The contemporary sources confirm the gossip of later years: undoubtedly 'the man who slew the Canons' was T. J. Prout. No doubt he would have moved earlier had new Senior Studentships been created at a faster rate; at all events, in November 1864 he thought the time had come.

V

The Christ Church, Oxford, Act of 1867

(*a*) THE REGIUS PROFESSORSHIP OF GREEK, 1865

TOWARDS the end of 1864 Christ Church came once more under public attack: as a result the six-year-old controversy over the refusal of a majority of the Dean and Chapter to pay an adequate stipend to Benjamin Jowett as Regius Professor of Greek[1] was now made to serve the interests of the Students of Christ Church. On 29 November a letter appeared in *The Times* from that familiar character, 'Oxoniensis', who discussed in no friendly spirit the income of the Dean and Chapter. He understood (rightly) that Canonries of Christ Church were now worth about £1,500 yearly, whereas even those of Durham were now reduced to £1,000, 'and the same sum is surely enough for Oxford'; the next best endowed Oxford Professorship (of Sanskrit) was only worth £900 yearly, and many were not worth more than £400. 'Oxoniensis' then unkindly pointed to the Canons' other emoluments: Jacobson had the living of Ewelme, Ogilvie £1,100 yearly from the living of Ross-on-Wye (in the gift of a bishop), Heurtley £500 from that of Fenny Compton (in the gift of his college), Clerke had the living of Milton (in the gift of the Dean and Chapter itself), and Jelf was Principal of King's College, London. (It is fair to add that Canons of other cathedrals were similarly pluralist, and that Ewelme was attached to Jacobson's chair by Act of Parliament.) The writer then proposed a massive reapportionment of income: Canonries of Christ Church should be reduced to £1,000 and the Deanery to

[1] See Abbott and Campbell, i. 236 ff., 302 ff.

£2,000 (with perhaps a yearly allowance of £200 or £300), and the £3,000 thus freed should be used to increase to £1,000 the salaries of four lay Professors, those of Greek, Civil Law, Medicine, and Modern History (who, it was noted, would, unlike the Canons, be provided neither with free residences nor with additional incomes from pluralities). The writer chose to omit, even if he knew, the fact that for generations Deans and Canons had been among the most generous benefactors of the House.[1]

Prout's plans were now ready and (as one ex-Censor to another) he confided them to Osborne Gordon, with whom he was still in touch. On 29 November Gordon replied:

> I am very glad to think you are going to get up an agitation about Christ Church but I think the Greek Chair should still be endowed from its funds . . . Then as to the positions of Students the Ordinance is as I always told Longley a snare and a delusion. If the Commissioners intended the Students of Ch. Ch. to be as good as other Fellows and thought they would be so, why did they not put them in the same position? I always thought it unwise to go to the High Table—because it has an appearance of a proper position without the reality and I hate shams. It is better to accept facts and confess them. I think a letter to *The Times* would be a very good thing—and if I saw the subject attracted attention I might carry it on . . .[2]

(Before 1858 the Students had sat not at High Table, which was reserved for Noblemen, but in the body of Christ Church Hall.)[3] It does not seem from Gordon's opening remark that the letter in *The Times* that very day was part of

[1] Such attacks were particularly unfair to Pusey, whose frugal living and private generosity were notorious. In 1877 he advocated the reduction of Canonical stipends (including his own) to £1,000 (*Minutes of Evidence* (1881), p. 296); this was to enable the creation of a further theological chair by reviving one of the Canonries suppressed under the Ordinance of 1858. Liddon (p. 292) realized that a clerical Studentship would have to be suppressed to allow this.

[2] Ch. Ch. Archives, MS. Estates 117, ff. 95–6.

[3] In 1862 Dodgson thought a return to the old arrangement was preferable to some changes then in the Dean's mind (*Carroll Diaries*, i. 190).

Prout's plan, though if it was he was indeed ingenious. But the next letter was part of that plan: written from Oxford on 29 November, it appeared on 1 December, from 'A Student of Christ Church'. To the writer the rearrangement of the incomes of the Chapter among yet other Professors was of course anathema; if there were a redistribution, the College, not other Professors, had first claim. With £2,500 from savings on the incomes of the Canonries of the Professors and the Archdeacon money 'could be devoted to the work for which Christ Church was endowed—teaching Christ Church men'. 'The time indeed seems to have come when the imperfect reform of Christ Church sanctioned by the second University Commissioners [*sic*] may fairly demand revision.' The writer concluded with the observation, which perhaps stood in need of reiteration at the time, that Christ Church was 'a far more important object' than Benjamin Jowett.

Having organized a sighting shot by some unknown colleague, Prout then delivered a broadside himself: the letter dated 7 December which appeared in *The Times* next day over the signature of 'Ex-Censor' was his work. His lengthy 'few remarks' made up a cogent case. The Students, even the Censors and Tutors, had never been consulted on the Ordinance; Christ Church had never been 'thoroughly investigated'. 'She seems to have escaped the Ecclesiastical Commissioners because she was a College and the University Commissioners because she was a Cathedral'; partial reform had tended to aggravate rather than amend 'the original anomaly of her Constitution'. It might be proper for Canonries to be annexed to Professorships; but

that University Professors should by virtue of their Canonries become supreme governors of the largest College in Oxford with the internal organization of which they probably have no acquaintance, in the education of whose members they take no share and in which therefore they cannot be expected to feel any very lively interest is a practical evil which is making itself felt more and more every day.

The Students had 'little or no real power', no voice in the administration of the revenues, and in 'ordinary domestic and economical arrangements' were unable for the most part to do more than petition, and that in vain. In Prout's view difficulties were put in the way of the most obvious improvement, sometimes because of mere suspicion of the Students as such, but more often because of the financial situation within Christ Church: 'the Deans and Chapters have yielded to a not uncommon human infirmity' and 'allowed their own incomes to grow enormously, while all other interests have been starved; for instance, payments to College Officers and others (and I may add now the Regius Professor of Greek) had remained at their 16th century level. The result was that the proportion of revenue reserved for educational or other College purposes is very scanty indeed.'

Prout then turned to the position of the Students: in stipend and status they were inferior to Fellows of colleges. 'When it is considered that Studentships at Christ Church as well as Fellowships at Colleges are thrown open to public competition the immense disadvantages against which Christ Church has to contend will be readily understood': recently elected Senior Students from other colleges 'are not a little aggrieved when they realize their own inferiority, and "the elite of the University" would not much longer seek Studentships'.

Prout concluded that the Ordinance 'imperatively demands amendment'. Amendment should achieve three ends at least: '1. such an improvement of the condition of Students as shall raise them in all respects to the level of Fellows of Colleges; 2. either fixed stipends to the Dean and Chapter or a due allotment of estates; 3. a proper inspection of all accounts.'

But how was this to be achieved? Prout's expressed hope was that a Christ Church M.P. might have his attention dircted to the subject and be induced to bring in the necessary Bill. He ended: 'I cannot but fear that longer continuance of the present anomalous condition of things will mar the usefulness of Christ Church as a place of learning and education to an incalculable extent.'[1]

Gordon thought this a 'very excellent letter';[2] but—for the present—it was the last to discuss the state of Christ Church. At least one more letter was sent to *The Times*, by R. St. John Tyrwhitt, a Student on the Old Foundation; but to Prout's and Gordon's relief this was not printed, and from our next piece of evidence (a letter from H. A. Giffard to Prout, written from London on 20 December) it is clear that Tyrwhitt's solution was not Prout's. This is not the only sign of a divergence of views between Senior Students and Students on the Old Foundation.

Giffard himself, according to this letter of 20 December, was busy setting forth his own criticisms of the Ordinance to the Dean, but he clearly regarded Prout as the leader of the whole movement, for he wrote:

> You have very nobly led the van, and if you will allow me to enrol myself under your banner, I shall feel very proud of my leader . . . My chief fear is that if we agitate singly, we shall be crushed in detail . . . I do not think the Chapter can ignore us if we act in concert . . . We shall meet with an organised opposition: it is as well that we should make an organised attack.

Giffard suggested one of two methods: either a general meeting of Senior Students to put forward resolutions, or (preferably) for three or four or more Senior Students who were 'perfectly unanimous' to present a petition to the Dean and Chapter which all Senior Students could sign if they wished. This petition Giffard thought would be rejected, particularly if it was as radical as he himself wanted. Whether his views were fully in accordance with Prout's is not clear: 'I think you are prepared,' he wrote, '—as certainly I am—to petition for the severance of the Ecclesiastical from the Collegiate establishment';[3] Prout's phrase

[1] Draft in Ch. Ch. Archives MS. Estates 117, ff. 97–8.

[2] Ibid., f. 99 (10 Dec. 1864) (incomplete).

[3] Ibid., ff. 100–6.

'a due allotment of estates' did not necessarily mean such a severance as Giffard's phrase might imply. At all events, next month Giffard was at one with Prout and the other Senior Students; he had sent a draft of a possible petition to Prout on 8 January.[1]

During the first weeks of Hilary Term Prout continued his preparations; it was no doubt at this time that, as H. L. Thompson says, 'private meetings were held, and a plan of operations devised'.[2] The Canons were not unaware of developments: on 7 February H. P. Liddon, the most famous of the remaining Students on the Old Foundation, 'walked round [Ch. Ch.] Meadow with Dr. Pusey: who talked about the proposal of the Students to petition Parliament for a Reform of the Constitution of Ch. Ch. Thought Prout very "vain and inferior".'[3] Bayne lobbied Liddon.[4] A letter from the latter to Prout on 9 February reveals a serious difficulty which Prout had to face. The changes proposed at Christ Church involved application to Parliament for a Bill, and also what some would regard as expropriation of the Church. Liddon felt he could not render assistance because, while approving the objects of Prout's agitation, he objected to a 'direct application to Parliament' 'for further interference'. Such an application, in his view, condoned the 'original wrong' done by the recent forcible interference of Parliament with the University, and gave sanction to a theory as to the right of the State over the property of the Church which Liddon thought sinful. In any case, Liddon felt that internal divisions within Christ Church should not be exposed to the world unnecessarily.[5] Prout had written to Liddon to give notice of a meeting of Senior Students and of resident Students on the Old Foundation to be held on Saturday, 11 February.

[1] Ibid., ff. 107–8.
[2] Thompson, *Christ Church*, p. 205.
[3] MS. Diary of H. P. Liddon, 7 Feb. 1865. As Dodgson so inimitably put it, 'The locus of HPL will be found almost invariably to coincide' with 'the locus of EBP' (*The New Method of Evaluation, as applied to* π).
[4] Liddon Diary, 9 Feb. 1865.
[5] Ch. Ch. Archives, MS. Estates 117, ff. 109–12.

Liddon himself could not attend,[1] but Dodgson did, and recorded the event in his diary: 'A meeting of Students was invited by Prout in his rooms, on the subject of our position. We agreed on the necessity of Students being raised to the position of Fellows.'[2] No minutes were kept of this meeting; but Arthur Hassall gave a full account of it in 1911:

On Saturday, February 11, 1865, a memorable meeting took place in Mr. Prout's rooms, at which eighteen senior masters were present. Among them are the names of Benson, A. Vernon Harcourt, Faussett, Sandford, Bayne, Pickard, Dodgson, Thompson, Bigg, Church, Martin, Blore, and Chamberlain. Mr. (afterwards Dr.) Bigg proposed that the position of the students should be raised, and that proposal was carried by thirteen to four. Mr. Prout, supported by Mr. Dodgson, then carried *nem. con.* a proposal 'that the carrying out of the above proposition involves the admission of the Students into the Corporation of The House, with a due share of the administration of the revenues and in the government of the same, and also the possession of such other rights and privileges as commonly attach to the Fellows of other Colleges.[3]

Before another meeting of Students could be held a move was made by the Dean and Chapter. At their meeting on Tuesday, 14 February, when the Dean and all seven Canons were present, two important matters were discussed.[4] The first was the salary of the Regius Professor of Greek, as to which the legal opinions of Sir Roundell Palmer and Sir Hugh Cairns were laid on the table. The minute is exquisitely worded:

After a long discussion of the subjects of the liability of the Dean and Chapter to make adequate provision for the Regius Professor of Greek, it was resolved, on an unanimously expressed opinion, that the Chapter is not held by any legal obliga-

[1] He dined at All Souls to meet the Russian archpriest Vasiliev, whom he had met the day before at Pusey's (Liddon Diary, 10 and 11 Feb. 1865).

[2] *Carroll Diaries*, i. 227. (Original in B.M. Add. MS. 54344.)

[3] A. Hassall, *Christ Church, Oxford* (1911), p. 42. Hassall omits four names; perhaps Giffard, Hoole, and Brodie were among them.

[4] Chapter Act Book, 14 Feb. 1865.

tion to alter the original endowment of £40 a year. The Chapter was not so perfectly agreed as to the existence of moral obligation in the matter. The Chapter then took into consideration the question of expediency and it was resolved (1) that it was expedient to consider whether there be any mode of adequately endowing the Greek Chair which it might be advisable for the Chapter to adopt, and (2) that it would be a gracious act, and one relieving the University from a painful difficulty, if the Chapter were to augment the Professor's Stipend from funds at their command and (3) . . . that the Dean ber equested to communicate to the Vice-Chancellor the result of this deliberation.[1]

For the carrying out these resolutions it was further resolved, that the sum of £460 be charged on the incomes of the Dean and Canons yearly to be levied in due proportions until or unless some other means be found to defray this charge.

The actual terms of the Dean's letter to the Vice-Chancellor were approved in a Chapter meeting on 17 February, and then printed.

(*b*) THE STUDENTS' PROPOSALS AND THEIR REJECTION, 1865

The question of the endowment of the Regius Chair of Greek has some relevance to what the Senior Students doubtless thought the more pressing, if less well publicized, question of their own status and emoluments; it had already enabled Prout to write to *The Times*; moreover, as had already been noted in that journal, the amounts paid to the Censors and other college officers were fixed by the same ancient prescription and at the same now ludicrous levels as was the salary of the Regius Professor of Greek. If his salary could be increased at the expense of the Dean and Canons, could not theirs be increased by the same means?

[1] Thirty years later the Dean could still recall the difficulty which even at the last moment he had in bringing the Chapter to this decision (Abbott and Campbell, i. 320, n. 1).

Pusey too realized this, for he had told Gordon that an increase in Jowett's salary 'involved the general principle of increasing fixed payments, which would be inconvenient'.[1]

At all events, the Dean and Canons seem to have felt that some further move was called for, and at the end of the meeting of the Chapter on 14 February,

A statement having been made to the effect that considerable dissatisfaction exists among the resident students as to the present relative position of the canons and students, it was resolved that a committee be appointed to confer with the students on this matter; that the committee consist of the dean, the sub-dean, the treasurer, and Dr. Pusey, and that instructions be given them to ascertain what the grievances are of which the students complain, and what remedies thereof they desire to suggest to the chapter.

Next day Dodgson noted the proposal in his diary; the printed edition of this text omits the diarist's uninformative references to five subsequent meetings of the Students. On 15 February, however, he added: 'The idea occurred to me in the evening of writing some mock American news embodying some of our proceedings, and I wrote it at night.' On the 17th Dodgson wrote: 'Sent *American Telegrams*, with some additions, to be printed.'[2]

American Telegrams was followed next month by *The New Method of Evaluation, as applied to* π, a skit on the Jowett controversy. The latter is relatively easy to follow, but *American Telegrams* has long puzzled commentators; Carroll's bibliographers say it refers to 'proposed regulations at Christ Church, Oxford, about the Treasury, the Butler &c';[3] in fact at least half of it concerns the Students' agitation against the Dean and Chapter. The 'Confederate "platform"' of four points is Dodgson's version of the Students' proposals for the amendment of the constitution

[1] Ch. Ch. Archives, MS. Estates 117, f. 95^{v}. Cf. above, p. 45.

[2] *Carroll Diaries*, i. 227.

[3] Eds. S. H. Williams, F. Madan, and R. L. Green, *The Lewis Carroll Handbook* (1962), p. 25 (no. 39).

and domestic economy of Christ Church. The 'General Grant' whose 'almost dictatorial power' was to be 'largely curtailed, if not altogether abolished', was the conveniently named Butler of Christ Church, Henry Grant, who was also the 'General Butler' whose 'enormities' were to meet with their 'due reward'. The demand 'that the Treasury shall be placed under the control of Confederates [i.e. Students] and Federals [i.e. Canons] alike' speaks for itself. The Secretary of the Treasury who 'would be a blot in any conceivable system of government' was the Under-Treasurer, Blott.[1] The fourth demand, 'that the forces at present in occupation of Confederate territory be withdrawn' appears to be a demand for the exclusion of the Canons from their newly awarded share in the educational work of the House at examinations.[2]

The 'statement' at the Chapter on 14 February probably came from the Dean; the Committee itself was to consist of three Christ Church men (Liddell, Clerke, and Pusey) and one 'outsider' in the Treasurer, Jacobson, who could hardly be left out if, as was certain, financial questions were to be raised. But in the event Liddell acted as chairman at the meeting of Students and Canons, and the Chapter Committee consisted of three members only. By their move the Chapter may conceivably have forced the Students' hand: if there was to be a conference of delegates of the Students and of the Chapter, Giffard's idea of a small self-appointed committee of Students was hardly feasible: there must be a meeting of Students to make resolutions for the conference to discuss. This, at least, is what happened, and if the Chapter hoped, as it may have done, to divide the Students and weaken their leaders the hope was disappointed.

The Students held over two dozen meetings in all between February 1865 and March 1867; these were concentrated in three periods, February to March 1865, November 1865 to

[1] Blott died in 1868.

[2] The copy in Christ Church Library (first Bayne scrapbook, pp. 80–1) with annotations by T. V. Bayne, is reproduced as Plate iv.

June 1866, and November 1866 to March 1867.[1] In February and March 1865 four meetings were held: the Students saw these as an essential preliminary to further action, for they had first to discover whether the Dean and Chapter would co-operate with the Students in securing the desired changes.

The first meeting, on 18 February, was attended by eleven of the thirteen Senior Students (Prout, Sandford, Bayne, Dodgson, Harcourt, Church, Blore, Hoole, Bigg, Martin, and Brodie); Pickard and Giffard were absent, but concurred in the moves made. Four resident Students on the Old Foundation were also present; these (in order of seniority) were T. Chamberlain, R. M. Benson, H. P. Liddon, and H. L. Thompson.

Before the agitation launched at this meeting is traced, the agitators themselves deserve a brief survey. Prout himself came to Christ Church from Westminster in 1842; as a young athlete in the 1840s (he was in the House boat at the Head of the River in 1846), as an aged valetudinarian two whole generations later, he lived in Christ Church for nearly seventy years, until his death there in 1909. Apart from the conversation between Pusey and Liddon (neither, in the context, the most reliable of guides), no hostile comment on this man has been found. From 1856 he was Perpetual Curate of Binsey, a parish just west of Oxford for which he cared with intense devotion. He was too modest to leave any works behind him,[2] but he was a man of wide interests, among them geology and the related sport of mountaineering, for which he had a great love. Prout had won no more than a Third Class in Literae Humaniores; but there is ample evidence that he could express himself on paper with great clarity and force, and he was clearly a tireless and discreet organizer.

[1] All are amply recorded in the splendidly clear hand of T. V. Bayne in Ch. Ch. Library MS. 449 ('Minutes of Meetings of the Students'); except where otherwise indicated, the following account of meetings is based on this manuscript.

[2] Tuckwell (*Reminiscences*, p. 155) attributes to Prout a one-word contribution in pseudo-Greek to a well-known Dodgson parody.

C. L. DODGSON in 1863
(aged 31)

PLATE IV

AMERICAN TELEGRAMS.—(SUMMARY.)

The interview which has just taken place, between President L*iddell* and the Confederate Commissioners, has resulted in a proposal from the President that three representatives from each of the contending parties shall meet to arrange conditions of peace. The following is said to be the Confederate "platform":—

(1.) That the almost dictatorial power, held by General Grant, shall be largely curtailed, if not altogether abolished. It is understood that the President himself is so entirely under his influence as to be a free agent in name only: a state of things which, it is urged, cannot but be highly prejudicial to the Union. *Butler of Ch. Ch.*

(2.) That the enormities perpetrated by General Butler shall meet with their due reward. The document from which we quote urges that "he has cost his country more in battels *(sic)* than any other known in our time," and that "the interests of the few magnates, whose wealth he has augmented, cannot be suffered to outweigh those of the Commons he has so wantonly sacrificed." *v. supra*

(3.) That the Treasury shall be placed under the control of Confederates and Federals alike: the Confederates urge that their party is "inadequately represented under the present administration," and that the Secretary in particular "would be a blot in any conceivable system of government." *Mr Blott. under Treasurer*

(4.) That the forces at present in occupation of Confederate territory be withdrawn. "We can discuss no terms of peace," say the Confederates, "with an armed foe. It is unworthy the dignity of a nation to be thus dictated to by the roar of canons *(sic)*."

* In the summer Term Chapel used to be at 7 a.m. This year the Dean altered the hour to 8 a.m.

Other minor propositions may, it is understood, be presented to the Federals for consideration. One is, "that the services which General Early has rendered to his country be rewarded by advancement in the course of the ensuing summer." * This proposal, however, is said to be distasteful to the Federals, and the President himself is so opposed to the very idea of Early rising, that there is little hope of its being agreed on. Various charges are brought against this unpopular general, of which his abandonment of "Pillow," (the Federals' strongest fort) is one of the gravest.

Value of a Senr Studentship

Gold 200, at which price it occasionally excites a brisk competition.

The difficulties of transit from place to place are enhanced by the insufficiency of public conveyances, and most of the travelling is done by means of private coaches. So much of the country, however, is still under martial law, that passes are not easy to obtain: in some instances they have been refused altogether.

G. Marshall Examiner

The officers continue to send in long lists of sick and missing: much of this illness is supposed to be feigned for the sake of avoiding active service.

With a view to improving the condition of the lower classes, it is understood that collections will shortly be set on foot, under the authority of the President: this will probably have the effect of drawing attention to their number and wretchedness, but, beyond this, it is not anticipated that any great results will be derived from this measure.

C/

Feb. 17, 1865.

C. L. Dodgson
Ch. Ch.

by C. L. Dodgson (1865)

PLATE V

a. C. W. SANDFORD

b. T. VERE BAYNE

c. G. R. LUKE

d. A. G. VERNON HARCOURT

SENIOR STUDENTS OF CHRIST CHURCH

The Senior Censor, Sandford, now seems a remote figure, but he took the chair at the meetings of Students with great energy and competence. In later life he did not progress beyond the Bishopric of Gibraltar. However, no one who has ever concerned himself with the history of Christ Church can deny a grateful tribute to Thomas Vere Bayne. Bayne never wrote in anything but the clearest of hands, and seldom failed to record with precision significant events. When in 1870 he became Senior Censor, he 'ruled the College with great outward rigidity, but with a subterranean bonhomie which made him popular with many generations of Christ Church men'.[1] At the end, when to the general amazement he left £138,000, his benefactions were exemplary.[2] Dodgson in later years was clearly a difficult colleague; not so now. He emerges, in the year of *Alice in Wonderland*, as a man of much practical sense in college affairs; though unfortunately he chose to record almost nothing of what happened in his diary. Pickard, the other surviving original Senior Student, took little part, and attended only one meeting. Of the Senior Students elected after 1858, the most active were Harcourt, Giffard, and (until his departure) Bigg—a scientist, a lawyer, and a theologian respectively.

Five Students on the Old Foundation also played some part in the moves for a new constitution: Chamberlain, R. G. Faussett, Benson, Liddon, and Thompson. Chamberlain, the second senior Student on the Old Foundation, was from 1842 Vicar of St. Thomas the Martyr (a Christ Church living) in west Oxford; he kept his rooms in the House until 1869. His stormy career as a Ritualist and his reputation for inflexibility do not altogether prepare one for his emollient role in Christ Church.[3] Benson, a Student

[1] Strong, *H. P. Liddon*, p. 14.

[2] Dean Paget was much struck by Bayne's management and generosity (S. Paget and J. M. C. Crum, *Francis Paget* (1912), pp. 240–1, 274–5, 289). Bayne was a schoolmaster's son, and his wealth was acquired, not inherited. Sandford, by contrast, came from a Shropshire gentry family.

[3] For Chamberlain's strenuous career in the Oxford Movement and St. Thomas's, cf. T. W. Squires, *In West Oxford* (1928), pp. 18–26.

since 1846 on Dr. Pusey's nomination, and Vicar of Cowley, attended the first two meetings, but only one thereafter; for him this was the period of preparation for the foundation of the Society of St. John the Evangelist. Liddon had returned to his rooms in Christ Church in December 1862, and retained them, and his Studentship, until his death in 1890. At first, indeed, he simply could not afford to give up his Studentship; and no one would ever have wanted him to, for (though an opponent of the changes mooted in 1865) he was by all accounts a great ornament of the Christ Church Senior Common Room.[1] Faussett, the son of Dr. Faussett, once Lady Margaret Professor of Divinity, won a First Class in Mathematics in 1849 and had been Dodgson's predecessor as Mathematical Lecturer from 1850 to 1855; he had some capacity as a man of business. Thompson, one of the last three Students on the Old Foundation, later Bayne's junior as Censor, was the admirable biographer of Dean Liddell and historian of Christ Church itself. Prout, Sandford, and Thompson attended every single meeting of Students held during the next two years; Bayne missed only one.

It is easy to forget how well all these men and those who followed their lead knew one another. Nearly all had rooms on the south and west sides of Tom Quad, on staircases I to VII; the Deanery and the houses of four of the Canons were on the opposite north and east sides, with Dr. Pusey's house as a canonical enclave between staircases II and III—though (owing to the lack of suitably placed windows) not well situated for purposes of observation. The chief link between the Students was in all probability Vere Bayne, who was a great friend of Dodgson, and friendly too with Liddon, as were Dodgson, Martin, and E. S. Talbot. Perhaps Prout himself was rather an aloof man: he was clearly no great favourite with Dodgson or Liddon. One social occasion fell conveniently for the Students: the annual

[1] Cf. the accounts by later colleagues, E. F. Sampson (in Johnston, *Liddon*, pp. 255–64), and T. B. Strong (*H. P. Liddon*, pp. 13–14).

Censors' supper, one of the more searching tests of after-dinner oratory in Oxford, was always held in December, and in that month of 1864, 1865, and 1866 was surely a convenient occasion for the report of progress.

Sandford as Senior Censor had summoned the meeting of 18 February and presided over it; 'he had convened the meeting in order to lay before the Students a proposal of the Chapter communicated to the college officers [himself and Bayne[1]] by the Dean, viz. that the Students should appoint a certain number of their body to confer with the three members of the Chapter on matters affecting the general interests of the House'. The proceedings went with that smoothness which implies previous organization. Bayne and Harcourt proposed 'that instructions be framed first, and the Delegates appointed subsequently'; this was agreed *nem. con.* The Delegates were instructed to press for two changes; first, 'That the Students be admitted into the Corporation of the House, with a due share in the government thereof and in the administration of the revenues, and also that they should enjoy such other rights and privileges as commonly attach to the Fellows of Colleges.' This, appropriately, was moved by Prout himself, and seconded by Dodgson; it was carried by fourteen to one; Liddon voted against the proposal, and is the only Student who is known to have objected in principle to the whole plan. His attitude emerges clearly from the entry in his diary:

> At 9 a Common Room to decide on the Resolutions to be submitted to the Chapter with respect to the Constitution of Ch. Ch. These of the most radical nature. Although Chamberlain and Benson were present, I voted in the minority of one. Harcourt and Bigg were for going to Parliament and obliging the Chapter to admit Students to the position of Fellows.[2]

The second instruction, moved by Blore and seconded by Bigg, was 'that one of such right or privileges shall be the

[1] i.e. The 'Confederate Commissioners' mentioned in Dodgson's *American Telegrams.*

[2] Liddon Diary, 18 Feb. 1865. Cf. Johnston, *Liddon*, pp. 259–60.

right to vote in the election of Students'. As this was carried by ten to five, it follows that at least one of the Senior Students voted against it; although such a power might well be thought inherent in the position of a Fellow of a college, anyone could vote against it who thought that not all Senior Students should be members of the proposed enlarged Governing Body. Sandford 'then named certain minor practical changes, which the Delegates might be authorized to discuss and try to carry out, without prejudice to the great constitutional changes sought above. But the meeting declined to empower the Delegates to suggest them, lest the force of the more sweeping propositions should be weakened'; this rebuff to Sandford brings out once more the single-mindedness of Prout.

With the instructions safely framed, three Delegates were chosen by ballot: these were Prout, Sandford, and Harcourt. The meeting then agreed *nem. con.* to three propositions to be put by the Censors to the Dean; Harcourt and Blore proposed that college offices and lecturerships be endowed, in order to free part of the Tutorial Fund for the creation of additional Tutorships; Dodgson and Bigg broached the question of the domestic economy of the House, and proposed that college servants 'should receive fixed salaries, and not be paid by monopolies', and that a joint Committee of Canons and Students should examine the whole system of salaries paid to college servants; Thompson and Bigg proposed that Cathedral services attended by junior members of the House should be regulated by the Dean, Canons, and college officers who were in Orders. The first of these was essential to achieve a proper ratio of teachers to pupils; the second concerned the domestic economy over which a storm was already brewing; without agreement by the Students on the third proposition the Canons could never have been brought to a negotiation at all. It is clear that while the Students were prepared to submit these more detailed questions to the Dean through the Censors, they were not prepared to weaken their case for major constitutional reform by making them part of that case itself.

A letter from Gordon to Prout written on 20 February shows how opinion on a future constitution was still forming:

I feel convinced that you ought to stand upon some thing of this sort. The present Chapter to continue as it is with fixed incomes for its members, for all purposes for which Cathedral chapters generally exist but the College to be administered by the Dean, a Subdean, Treasurer, and 6 senior Students. I do not see how any combination is possible—and the Professors ought to be left to their professorial duties.

As the Treasurer was a Canon, this scheme envisaged a Governing Body of nine, the Dean, two Canons, and six Senior Students, and the exclusion of five Canons and (at that particular moment) eight Senior Students; it was in fact a scheme for a College Council with a clear Student majority. Gordon went on, 'The Dean will try to frighten you from Parliament by the prospect of the Bishop of Oxford getting his finger into the pie, appointing Honorary Canons etc., but I dont see what harm that will do you, if the two bodies are distinct. . . .'[1] (The question of Honorary Canons was settled between the Chapter and the Ecclesiastical Commissioners in 1865–6.)[2]

The delegates of the Chapter and of the Students met in the Chapter House on Saturday, 25 February, under the chairmanship of the Dean. Prout's rough notes of the meeting show that the phrase 'due share' in the Students' first instruction to their delegates involved two possible alternatives 'whether all the Students are to share in the government or whether supposing a Seniority was

[1] Ch. Ch. Archives, MS. Estates 117, ff. 114–15.

[2] Thompson, *Christ Church*, pp. 212–13; the Chapter was represented by Dr. Jelf alone at the installation of the first Honorary Canon on 23 July 1866 (Chapter Act Book). Relations between the Chapter and Bishop Wilberforce were by no means uniformly harmonious (Chapter Act Book, *passim*).

appointed that Seniority should have equal power in all respects to the Chapter'. Harcourt stressed forcibly that three propositions on 'minor or practical questions' had been given to the Dean to bring before the Chapter separately, but these were to be kept quite separate from the major constitutional issue. In answer to Pusey, Sandford bleakly refused to state to the Chapter the 'practical evils' complained of: 'They have been stated in the Paper handed to the Dean.' Archdeacon Clerke asked whether the difficulties of carrying out the larger proposition (i.e. the need for recourse to Parliament) had been considered; to this the answer was 'Not at any common meeting. The fact that the Dean and Chapter could not carry out the measure without recourse to higher authority was known.' From this exchange it emerges that Prout had as yet only put the difficult question of parliamentary intervention to individual Students.[1]

On 4 March the Dean and Chapter gave their answer which lacked nothing in clarity:

> In reference to the proposition submitted to the Dean and Chapter by the Students, the Dean and Chapter are sorry to find themselves in opposition to the wishes of the Students. They are not prepared to take steps towards promoting constitutional changes of the kind desired. At the same time the Dean and Chapter are most anxious to make provision for the Educational requirements of the House; and they are ready to assist in providing a Student Bursar for managing the portion of revenues set apart for domestic administration.

This flat rejection was accompanied by an overture of sorts, a letter from the Sub-Dean (Archdeacon Clerke) suggesting a Commission to inquire into the revenues of the House, the income of the Canons, and relations between the Canons and Students. Prout wrote at once to Gordon, who replied: 'I thought you were too sanguine about the Chapter and you must fight for it.' Gordon was prepared to sound two of the Commissioners (Jeune, now Bishop of Peterborough,

[1] Ch. Ch. Archives, MS. Estates 117, f. 116.

and Longley, now Archbishop of Canterbury) as to the plan for a Commission: Jeune, he thought, might speak to his great friend Lord Westbury, the Lord Chancellor. Gordon was even ready to name the members of a Commission: Jeune, his own former Christ Church pupils Ward Hunt and C. S. Fortescue, 'some good lawyer and some one well versed in the management of Chapter property'.[1]

On 7 March the Students met for the second time; once more fifteen were present, eleven Senior Students (Giffard came but Church was away) and four Students under the Old Foundation (Chamberlain, Benson, Thompson, and R. G. Faussett). Prout gave a summary of the Conference of 25 February, Sandford read a letter from Jeune to Gordon of 8 June 1855, and then the reply of the Dean and Chapter. Again it was Prout who moved the key motion, which Harcourt seconded: 'That whereas the Dean and Chapter have declined to take steps towards promoting constitutional changes of the kind desired by the Students, the Students proceed to consider whether, in order to promote such changes, they will appeal to higher authority, and if so, in what way it will be most expedient to do this.' This was agreed *nem. con.*; by thirteen to one it was agreed to seek advice 'from competent authorities as to the proper course to be adopted towards the attainment of those changes, which the Students think necessary, and which the Chapter decline to promote'. Prout, Giffard, and Harcourt were to do this, and the same three, with the Censors, were to draw up 'a statement of the principal defects of the present constitution'. A temperate reply to the Dean and Chapter was agreed:

The Students beg leave to acknowledge the communication made to them by the Dean and Chapter in answer to their propositions, and they regret to find that the Dean and Chapter are not prepared to take steps towards promoting those constitutional

[1] Ibid., ff. 121–2, where the Sub-Dean's letter is summarized. Longley was to be approached through his son Henry, a former Student (1853–61).

changes, which the Students think the interests of the House require. While they thank the Dean and Chapter for their offer to make provision for the educational requirements of the House, and to assist in providing a Student Bursar, they feel obliged to add that the offer made does not affect the main question at issue.

This reply was reported to the Chapter on 8 March. On the same day Prout was in London to begin the next stage. He had already written to the one man among the many Christ Church M.P.s on whom his hopes rested, G. Ward Hunt. Hunt has a safe reputation among the fattest, though not among the ablest, of Victorian politicians; he clearly possessed an abiding love of Christ Church. He was well known to the older Senior Students, and had been a pupil of Osborne Gordon;[1] he was admitted a Student on 24 December 1846 together with Benson, Kitchin, and Liddon, read for Honours, and took a Second Class in Literae Humaniores in 1848; Prout was a few years Hunt's senior, and doubtless had Hunt in mind in his first letter to *The Times*.[2] Hunt put the difficulties clearly in his reply on 6 March:

I will take the matter you write about into consideration . . . The difficulty that you will have to contend with will be re-opening a question that has been considered settled so recently as 1858. I will try and see some one of the University Commissioners before Wednesday on the subject. If you want Parliament to interfere you ought to petition—but this will require great consideration.[3]

Prout summarized the exchanges between himself and Hunt at the House of Commons on 8 March thus:[4]

[Hunt] Difficulty of opening the question supposed to have been duly examined and settled. Must show reasons for its necessity.

[1] Gordon (a very notable after-dinner speaker) spoke at the dinner given to Hunt by his friends on his appointment as Chancellor of the Exchequer (G. Marshall, *Osborne Gordon: A Memoir* (1883), p. 66).

[2] Cf. above, p. 105.

[3] Ch. Ch. Archives, MS. Estates 117, ff. 118–19.

[4] Ibid., f. 123. The names in brackets have been supplied in accordance with the sense and spacing of Prout's notes.

Students ought to have asked to be heard by Commissioners at the time. [Prout] Students had no status, were not consulted. Commissioners had not power to inquire into capitular revenue and incomes. [Hunt] Consult late Commissioners, endeavour to gain their support in House in event of petition being presented. Interview with Archbishop. Point out grievances and defects. Suggest new Constitution.

It was apparently on the same day that Prout met Archbishop Longley—perhaps at their club, the Athenaeum, on the notepaper of which establishment Prout's notes of both conversations were written. Hunt summarized Longley's reply thus: 'The object of late Commissioners was to raise the level of S. Students to that of Fellows as nearly as possible, and to make S. Studentships as attractive as Fellowships. If it can be shown that that object has not been fulfilled that is sufficient ground for re-opening the question.' Prout added succinctly: 'ArchBp would not oppose'[1] (i.e. the reopening); Prout had much more work to do, but he had surely won the essential point.

Prout's next conversation was with Lord Harrowby, another Commissioner, whom he saw in Grosvenor Square on 10 March after another talk with Hunt; Harrowby too was responsive, and echoed Hunt's advice: the Students should submit a statement of the changes required to all members of the late Commission. If they considered the Students' claims just 'a bill could be got through Parliament without much difficulty'. If Sir John Awdry, who represented the more conservative element of the Commission, supported the Students all would be well. In reporting all this to Hunt Prout found himself in a common difficulty:

I feel that our cause is really conservative. It is to conserve Christ Church by enabling her to put forth her resources and compete on equal terms with other Colleges in the University. I am sure she only wants fair play to enable her not only to hold her own but to become a greater place than she ever was before.

[1] Ibid., f. 123v.

The old spirit will rise again more vigorous perhaps than it ever was, inasmuch as it will be founded on a broader basis.

Prout's letter touched on another difficulty, for it is the earliest evidence of a point of importance: what was Dean Liddell's attitude? Prout found he had been too optimistic:

> I may possibly have spoken to you of the favourable views of the Dean of Christ Church in a way which might be taken to mean more than I was authorized to state concerning him. To prevent mistakes therefore it is as well to add that the Dean does not wish to be understood to have pronounced any opinion favourable or unfavourable in the matter. He wishes as far as possible to be considered neutral in as much as he is the Head of both bodies (Chapter and Students).[1]

Prout also reported his various conversations to Osborne Gordon, who replied on 12 March. Gordon was now uncertain as to both procedure and solutions: he thought that if the Commissioners of 1858 were reassembled 'the result might be satisfactory—but it is clear that they could not act without being reconstituted—and I do not quite see what is the next step. I think there must be a petition to the Visitor and that you will have to approach the Lord Chancellor some how.' (The Visitor of Christ Church was the Sovereign, for whom the Lord Chancellor would act.) Gordon went on:

> I send you a letter from the Sub-dean in which he suggests Sir J. Awdrey [*sic*] as a referee—and it might be well to consult him. But I think some improvement might be made in the Commission and I feel sure it would be a good thing if the Bishop of Peterborough—and some younger Ch. Ch. man—(say Ward Hunt) could be got upon it.
>
> As to the claims to be advanced the Sub-Dean's letter expresses what *was* my mind 5 years since—but it may not go far enough to satisfy *present* Students—and it is quite possible that the time for compromise may have passed away.

[1] Ch. Ch. Archives, MS. Estates 117, ff. 127–8; f. 124 contains what seems to be a longer version of Harrowby's advice.

The new Senior Students, as he rightly said, 'certainly have nothing to do with the former history of the college—but with the facts of their actual condition'. He added advice on the content of the case to be submitted by the Students; and, with his usual practical sense, was clear that a solution could only be achieved by Act of Parliament.[1]

The letter from the Sub-Dean to Gordon has not been traced: that it should have been written at all shows that Gordon was viewed as a man who might exercise a powerful influence on the discussions, and that Archdeacon Clerke himself saw that some change was inevitable and was quite ready to give private advice to the Senior Students, indirectly, not only as to procedure but also as to their claims. (In 1865 he was, after all, the only Canon who had ever been a Student himself.)

The next meeting of Students was held on 13 March: all those present on 7 March came again, except Giffard. Prout duly reported the views of Longley, Harrowby, and Hunt; Harrowby's and Hunt's advice was taken, and Prout moved and Bayne seconded 'That the Committee previously appointed be requested to consider what amendments and additions to the late ordinance are essential, and to sketch out such a Constitution as may appear to them to satisfy the requirements of the House.' A week was spent on this, and after further discussion at a meeting held on the 21st the statement was ordered to be printed. This meeting began, however, with trouble of a kind which Prout had hitherto avoided: the attendance rose to sixteen with the appearance for the first time of a non-resident Student on the Old Foundation. This was J. M. Collyns,[2] who inquired why non-residents had not hitherto been summoned; but Bayne and Prout virtually promised that Students on the Old Foundation would ultimately be consulted whether or not they were resident, and the trouble was smoothed over.

[1] Ibid., ff. 125–6.

[2] A friend of Dodgson and once Kitchin's second master at Twyford School (*Carroll Diaries*, i. 132).

This was the last formal meeting of Students for seven months. Four days later the Dean and Chapter agreed 'That the sum of £500 yearly be placed at the disposal of the Dean for educational purposes in the College, and that the Treasurer be empowered to charge the Dean and Canons' general account with this sum.'[1] But half-measures would no longer suffice, and Prout now began the circulation of the Students' printed case to the surviving Commissioners (Lord Harrowby, Archbishop Longley, Sir J. T. Coleridge, Sir John Awdry, and Edward Twisleton) in accordance with Lord Harrowby's suggestion.

(*c*) THE STUDENTS' CASE, 1865

The Students' case[2] was a concise, temperate, and cogent statement, which sought first of all to explain why Christ Church had not been 'finally settled' by the Commissioners in 1858: their powers had been limited, and the Students had not had access to them. The document then outlined 'the principal defects of the present constitution' under the Ordinance: the government of the House by Professors (who in other colleges were seldom even Fellows),[3] the anomalous position of the Censors, the objectionable system of 'monopolies' operated by the chief college servants, in spite of the Students' unavailing protests, and above all the patent inferiority in status of Senior Students to Fellows

[1] Chapter Act Book. Pusey told Sir William Heathcote on 13 July 1867 that before the 1867 Act the Dean and Chapter had intended to devote another £500 to tutorial purposes 'as soon as we are secure in the funds' (Pusey Papers).

[2] See Appendix III.

[3] At the end of 1864 there were thirty-eight Professors in the University, some of them supported by college revenues assigned to that purpose by the executive Commissioners in 1854. Some Professors (like Jowett) retained their Fellowships on becoming Professors, some Professors were made Honorary Fellows, and an Honorary Fellowship (of Corpus) was actually attached to the Corpus Chair of Latin; but only to the Canon-Professors of Christ Church did a professorship give a place on the governing body of a college.

of other colleges, and the consequential likelihood of the decline of the House 'as a place of religion, education, and learning'. The Chapter had refused to promote constitutional change; the Students were therefore forced 'to make an independent appeal to higher authority': Senior Studentships must offer the same reward as Fellowships, and the financial system must be 'entirely remodelled'. The Students' more detailed proposals were well and succinctly put: they themselves must be included in the Corporation, and be admitted to the Governing Body, of the House. Two alternative schemes were sketched out: a Governing Body of Dean, Canons, and Students to administer the revenues and elect to all Studentships; or a Governing Body of the Dean and an equal number of Canons and Students, with, in the latter case, a separate electoral body. The former scheme was for one body with a majority of Students, the latter for two bodies in one of which the Dean would have a casting vote while the Students would have a clear majority in the other. The Dean's deputy in the House as a place of education was to be a Student holding the office of Censor Theologiae; there was to be a Student Bursar to control the 'general economy of the House'; college officers were to be appointed by the Governing Body; the incomes of all members of the Governing Body were to be fixed within certain limits. The Dean and Chapter's authority in purely Cathedral matters was not to be affected.

Late in March this document was sent to all members of the late Commission, and also to Hunt. The Archbishop with a prudent economy of words promised 'attentive consideration'. Prout drafted his letter to his most difficult quarry, Sir John Awdry, with some care. Their exchanges were not ultimately of great importance—but they illustrate well the opposition to be overcome. Prout's immediate object, he wrote, was

> to ascertain whether in the opinion of the late Commissioners our claim for further alterations in the constitution of Christ Church

is fairly made out, and whether therefore we should be justified in seeking the interference of Parliament on our behalf. I need hardly say that those acting with me as well as myself feel no little delicacy in asking the countenance of the Commissioners to the reconsideration of an Ordinance framed by themselves and we admit that we are rightly called upon to show that we have good cause for putting forward the present request. We venture to hope that when all the facts of the case are considered that request will be found to be not unreasonable. The questions on which the issue is raised as we have endeavoured to point out were necessarily left untouched by the late Commission and the present movement has been commenced from the conviction that if Christ Church is to hold her own in the University and country a satisfactory adjustment of these questions by some such changes as are indicated in the accompanying pages is imperatively needed . . .[1]

Awdry's reply was not in all respects comforting. He explained the attitude of the Commissioners: 'to depose the Chapter from its position as Governing Body would probably have been beyond our powers—certainly beyond the spirit of our Commission'; to that extent, therefore, the Ordinance was not final, and further changes, 'if otherwise desirable', could be made, as they had in the case of Winchester College. Awdry thought it incorrect to say, as the Students did in their memorandum, that they had had no chance to make their views known to the Commission; in his recollection, 'Papers' from Osborne Gordon and other Students had been received and considered. But above all Awdry saw

no middle course practicable between retaining the Governing Body substantially as at present, and either placing it in the hands of the Students (which will hardly be advocated) or an entire severance of interests. For the latter much might be said, though it is painful to think of such a disruption. But I fear the arrangement of buildings would be impracticable. If that difficulty could be surmounted, a division of property, and a merely

[1] Ch. Ch. Archives, MS. Estates 117, ff. 130–1.

personal union through the Dean (the Dean and Students constituting a distinct Corporation) might be possible. But I do not desire to see it . . . In regard to the application of the 'vast resources' of the House, I do not believe that a joint Government could be so constructed as to work. Perhaps part of the Estates of the House might be handed over to the Students for the educational department. I will not say that it is impossible. But I cannot imagine a working scheme of this kind, short of total severance.

Awdry saw no great problems in the questions of ecclesiastical patronage and control of the college servants; but he felt his main objection, the difficulty of producing a workable scheme for a 'joint government' to be 'inherent and insuperable'.[1]

This was a clear expression of the conservative case against change. Prout disagreed fundamentally, and wrote back to say so. His twenty years at the House, he delicately observed, had given him 'opportunities of gaining an insight into the inner working of the College, which are hardly granted to those who by their position necessarily stand somewhat aloof'. Prout believed that a 'joint government' would work: 'There are absolutely no points on which the interests of the Canons and Students should clash'; new Canons would have no difficulty in accepting a new system already in being. If a joint government did not work, a change could then be made; what was certain was that the existing government could not work. In the changed conditions after 1858 Studentships were no longer as attractive as in the former days when Awdry himself had been at the House: 'Already I am sorry to add Christ Church is spoken of as a place to be avoided among those who think they can command a Fellowship at a College.' On one point Prout was on weak ground: the Students had made no representations to the Commissioners between December 1856 (when the first scheme of the Commissioners was sent to the Dean) and July 1857 (when the Commissioners

[1] Ibid., ff. 136–41.

sent copies of a draft to Students who were Tutors). They had 'waited anxiously for an opportunity of speaking: it was felt that having no status they could not address the Commissioners except through the Chapter as the Governing Body. The Chapter however gave no sign.' In July 1857 Gordon and others had sent in papers to the Commission; but had felt, rightly as it turned out, that they were too late.[1] In retrospect, the Students' conduct during those eight months seems both pusillanimous and shortsighted. Awdry wrote back to make two concessions. He accepted that the position of Students had deteriorated; matters must change now that 'both [Canons and Students] are to a great extent imported from other Colleges'. (He added truly: 'The decline of Westminster also must have an unfavourable influence', but gave no explanation of the fact that he himself had already sent two sons to Balliol and was about to send a third to New College.) Awdry could still not see how a joint government would work, but he went on: 'If however the Archbishop, who from his character and experience must be the best living judge of the question in all its aspects, thinks the remedy practicable, I have no doubt that I shall concur with him.'[2] Once again, Longley's views appear crucial.

Prout then approached a much more important personage who had not been a Commissioner, Lord Derby, Chancellor of the University and the only living Christ Church man who had been Prime Minister. His letter must be quoted in full, for it is an admirable expression of the feelings which actuated Prout and others:

> I take the liberty of forwarding herewith a copy of a statement regarding Christ Church. I need hardly say that the reopening of a question supposed to have been settled by the late University Commission is felt to be a matter of no little delicacy. At the same time those acting with me as well as myself dare to think that when all the facts of the case are fairly considered the claims of the Students of Ch: Ch: will be found to be not unreasonable.

[1] Ch. Ch. Archives, MS. Estates 117, ff. 142–7. [2] Ibid., ff. 148–9.

Indeed if Ch: Ch: is to continue to hold her own, some such changes as those pointed to in our suggestions seem to be imperatively needed. In former days under the ancient system there was, as your Lordship is well aware, a Ch: Ch: patriotism which led Students to feel proud of the House to which they belonged and of the position they occupied as Students therein. It hardly occurred to them to compare themselves with the Fellows of a College. They were a distinct order, and they were content so to remain. Moreover when the Canons were for the most part, not as now University Professors, but men who had been educated at Ch: Ch: themselves there was a bond of union between governours and governed which does not and cannot exist under present circumstances. Now that Studentships as well as Fellowships are thrown open to public competition it is not difficult to see how immense the disadvantage is under which Ch: Ch: labours from the very inferior position of a Student in Ch: Ch: as compared with that of a Fellow in a College. There is too much reason to fear that the mere title of 'Student of Ch: Ch:' will not stand in the place of more substantial dignity when Fellowships & Studentships are put forward together as objects of ambition. The growing feeling of dissatisfaction & disappointment among those who have won Senior Studentships & the probability, as the facts of the case become more generally known that the most desirable men will decline to compete for Studentships when they can obtain Fellowships elsewhere are evils partly present partly future which no well-wisher to Ch: Ch: can contemplate without the deepest concern. That the new order of Senior Students will never rest satisfied with the existing state of things is certain; & I for one have taken part in the present movement from the hope that, while some members of the Old Foundation remain, a system may be inaugurated which shall as far as possible be conservative of Ch: Ch: as Ch: Ch:; i.e. that Ch: Ch: shall not be broken up into a College & a Cathedral distinct from each other, as has been suggested, but that there shall be a joint government of Canons & Senior Students under the presidency of the Dean. If the incomes of Dean & Canons for the future were fixed by law there would seem to be really no points on which the interests of the Chapter & the Students need clash; & there would be good reason to hope that, when the members of the two bodies met together on common ground to consult together for the common good of the House to which they belonged, a sympathy & community of feeling would grow up between them which would be productive of the best results . . .[1]

There could hardly be a clearer expression of the motives of Prout and others: to them the attachment of Canonries to Professorships by the Act of 1840 and the destruction of non-Professorial Canonries had destroyed the old order in Christ Church; as a consequence of this, and of the throwing open of Studentships to general competition, Students of Christ Church could no longer regard themselves as an order of men distinct from but equal to Fellows of other colleges; changes were essential now, before Students on the Old Foundation were altogether swamped, if anything of the old Christ Church were to be retained, a split between College and Cathedral averted, and Christ Church raised again to its proper position in the University without losing its old characteristics. Derby's reply shows that he too saw all this clearly; but his position was still that which he had taken up in 1854, and he had to confess to Prout that he would 'strongly deprecate a renewed application for the interference of Parliament, as I cannot but feel that any such interference seriously interferes with the independence of the University, and should not be recurred to except in cases of great emergency'.[2] Prout replied that the Students were unanimous in seeking that 'interference'.[3]

However, 'interference' was not yet possible; Prout had been over-sanguine in hoping for a successful conclusion during the session then in being: for Parliament was dissolved in July 1865, and a new one elected. Energies were briefly diverted to the question of Mr. Gladstone's future as Member for the University (and, in Dodgson's

[1] Ch. Ch. Archives, MS. Estates 117, ff. 152–5.

[2] Ibid., ff. 156–7.

[3] Ibid., f. 158. Prout also wrote to another University Commissioner, Lord Harrowby, to Harrowby's son, Lord Sandon, who had come up as a Nobleman in 1849, and to Sir John Mowbray, a former Westminster Student (ibid., ff. 159–64).

case, to the first edition of *Alice in Wonderland*); the Dean departed to Switzerland with Dr. Acland; and the Students held no formal meetings until Michaelmas Term.

In June 1865 there was one addition to the body of Senior Students. Herbert Salwey came, like Osborne Gordon, from Shropshire; he had been a Westminster Junior Student of the House and had won Firsts in Classical Moderations and Literae Humaniores (the former as a pupil of G. R. Luke); Salwey was the first Westminster Junior Student and the second gremial member of Christ Church to be advanced to a Senior Studentship, and his election was a good omen both for Westminster and the House. There had also been one change in the Chapter. In July Jacobson had been made Bishop of Chester and within eighteen months Liddell had thus lost both Canons, Stanley and Jacobson, who had been nearest to him in views; *The Guardian* mentioned Liddon for the vacancy, and Dr. Pusey wrote to the Archbishop of Canterbury to press his claims; but even before this kiss of death Liddon thought his own appointment 'not very likely',[1] and in October another 'outsider', Robert Payne Smith, a former Scholar of Pembroke College, was installed as Regius Professor of Divinity in Jacobson's place. Payne Smith was born in 1820, and so was four years older than Prout; he seems to have played a conciliatory role. More important to the Senior Students was the fact that the Treasurership of Christ Church was vacant by Jacobson's departure; into this office on 1 August 1865 the Dean and Chapter thrust W. W. Shirley, the Regius Professor of Ecclesiastical History, who had been a member of Christ Church for a mere eighteen months. The promotion to this all-important administrative position of one who was not only a newly appointed Professor but also a very recent member of the House was a direct result of the system prescribed by the Act of 1840 and the Ordinance of 1858; but Shirley was the only relatively young Canon available for a thankless office.

[1] Liddon Diary, 6 and 28 July 1865.

The new Treasurer was soon in trouble; for on 11 November, the very day on which the Students resumed their meetings, the internal affairs of Christ Church came before the public in the pages of *The Times*, which on that day published the first letter and leader in the great Bread and Butter Row.

(*d*) 'THE BREAD AND BUTTER ROW', 1865

In the early months of 1865 the Dean and Chapter had suffered even more trials than those already outlined. Not only had they been forced to solve the problem of the salary of the Regius Professor of Greek, and been charged with diverting to other purposes endowments which should have been devoted to education; they had also been attacked by the undergraduates of the House for their management of the internal economy of the college. The trouble began on the very day on which the Dean and Chapter rejected the proposals of the Students: on 4 March 1865 108 commoners of the House presented a petition to the Dean and Canons, complaining of the price charged by the college butler for certain articles. At the head of these were bread and butter—hence the title given to the dispute. The butler bought these wholesale; but whereas the retail market price for two daily commons of bread and butter (i.e. 1 lb. 3 oz. of bread and 2⅔ oz. of butter) was 5*d*., the butler charged 8*d*., a profit of 60 per cent on his purchase price. There was also a general complaint with regard to the dinners and the quality of the beer. The petitioners therefore suggested that the butler and all other college servants be put on wages, that they be no longer allowed to realize a profit on any articles sold, and that 'the entire management of dinners and attendance in Hall be entrusted to one college servant, on fixed wages'. Dean Liddell is said to have disbelieved the facts as stated, but promised to call in an accountant.

The Chapter did in fact take action: on 8 March it agreed

'That the resolution passed December 21st 1860 be acted upon and that steps be taken for appointing a professional auditor or auditors for the purpose of examining all the College accounts and reporting to the Chapter thereupon.' (In fact, in 1860 the Dean and Chapter had merely resolved 'That it is very desirable to appoint an Auditor to audit the accounts of the House each year at the usual time of audit.') A firm of accountants (Messrs. Begbie, Robinson, & Hockley) was appointed on 18 May 'to examine and report upon the present state of the finances of the College, and on the present mode of keeping the accounts'.[1] By great good fortune Messrs. Begbie, Robinson & Co., still possess the day-books recording the execution of their commission. The entries run as follows:

Dean and Chapter of Christ Church, Oxford

30th May 1865	Travelling to Oxford and there conferring with the Treasurer, Dr. Jacobson, and afterwards engaged with Mr. Blott, the Sub-Treasurer, inspecting the College Books and obtaining information therefrom.
3rd June	Engaged on long inspection of Mr. Grant's (the College Butler's) Books. Travelling to London.
15th June	Engaged on form of the proposed new system of Accounts.
16th June	—ditto—and arranging with Mr. Lawrence, the Chapter Clerk, for an appointment to confer on proposed alterations.
27th June	Engaged with Mr. Lawrence on the proposed alterations in the Accounts.
13th July	Commencing drawing patterns for new Books and writing Mr. Blott.
17th July	Engaged on new proposed system of Accounts and commencing draft report.

[1] Chapter Act Book, 18 May 1865.

21st July Completing Report, engaged on fair copy Accounts and writing the Bishop of Chester therewith.[1]

A report[2] was made to the Dean at the end of the Long Vacation—but, not surprisingly, only on the form of the accounts, not on the system which they enshrined. The Censors never saw the accountant, let alone the report. At the beginning of Michaelmas Term the Dean tried to find an accountant who would report on the system itself; but before this search could succeed the whole issue suddenly became public.

On 11 November a fortnight's acrimonious correspondence began in the columns of *The Times* and leaders there and in the *Pall Mall Gazette*, *London Review*, the *Morning Post*, the *Saturday Review*, and *Punch*, called for 'a thorough constitutional change in the government of Christ Church'.[3] *The Times* said, on 11 November, 'It is quite evident that the system itself is vicious. It is like that of the "Clothing Colonels" and a good many other obsolete usages. The butler it would appear is a contractor of a schedule of prices fixed unaccountably high.' '*Miserans Inopem*', 'A London Incumbent', 'An Undergraduate of Christ Church', '*Paterfamilias*', '*Querulus*', '*Inops*', 'A Tutor of Christ Church', 'An M.A. of Christ Church', '*Oxoniensis*', 'A Barrister', '*Quondam Inops*', 'An Undergraduate of the House', and 'An Old Student', all fulminated in turn. The system complained of was, of course, of medieval origin, and had once been universal in Oxford; but under similar pressure other colleges had remedied or were remedying it. Osborne Gordon had effected a few improvements in 1850 and 1853; but at Christ Church the butler (who supplied the bread, butter, and beer), the manciple (who supplied the meat at dinner), and the cook (who supplied the meat at breakfast and lunch) were all appointed by the Dean and Canons, and

[1] These extracts were provided by the great kindness of Mr. R. F. Cox, of Messrs. Begbie, Robinson & Co., Grays Inn.

[2] Not traced.

[3] Also printed in pamphlet form.

received only nominal salaries: their remuneration came almost wholly from profits on articles which undergraduates were compelled to buy at excessive prices in order to prove their residence or eat meals for which they would in any case be charged, and thus indirectly to subsidize their seniors. The whole question of the government of the House was involved: for the revenues from which the butler and other college servants might be paid adequate salaries were controlled by the Dean and Canons.

At this point a letter written over forty years later by W. T. Thiselton-Dyer, a doctor's son who matriculated in December 1863 as a Junior Student, deserves quotation.[1] Time may have distorted his recollections in one respect, but the whole picture rings true:

'. . . Christ Church was in a curious state in my day. The old hands . . . resented the changes made by the Commission. Junior Students had been in the gift of the Chapter . . . The new Natural Science Students were regarded as an invention of the devil. They were assumed to be incompetent of taking a pass degree. The Dean summarily rejected eleven candidates at the Election preceding mine. The consequence was that the first two Science Students were classical men and both took honours in Greats. I was the third, and when I tried it seemed a forlorn hope. However I could write Latin prose of a sort with fluency, and that passed...

There was a dull apathy amongst the men and a good deal of sullen discontent which broke out occasionally in coarse rowdyism. They did little in the Schools, the Westminsters who should have led the House were chiefly remarkable for getting into debt and getting ploughed. Our appearance on the river was ignominious. The Etonians would not play cricket.[2] 'Peck' was a

[1] W. T. Thisleton-Dyer to J. G. C. Anderson, 8 Dec. 1909 (bound in a volume of pamphlets given by Dyer to Christ Church Library); quoted in part by W. G. Hiscock, *A Christ Church Miscellany* (1946), p. 96. Dyer was later Director of the Royal Gardens at Kew and was elected an Honorary Student of Christ Church in 1899; he died in 1928.

[2] Edward Stanhope, a notable Christ Church cricketer just before Dyer's time, was a Harrovian.

barbarous community dominated by the Duke of Hamilton[1] and mainly occupied with hunting.

But there was a strong and quiet set who held their own:—the Duke of Northumberland, the Bishop of Southwark, Sir Walter Phillimore, Salwey . . ., Stephen Gladstone and others who alas are dead.[2] John Walter, to whom we put up a window in the Cathedral, was a leading spirit amongst us. He was a prime mover in the 'Bread and Butter Row'. This was supported by the best men of those senior to ourselves. The whole thing was engineered with consummate skill, for which John Walter was largely responsible. I can see now, and this is the reason why I trouble you with this long letter, that it was momentous in the History of the House. It was the first serious blow to the capitular citadel. I believe it was dear old Prout who delivered the next blow on behalf of the Senior Students. Everything else followed. But history must I think credit the undergraduates with having set the ball rolling . . .

The evidence set out earlier suggests that Dyer's view of the prior importance of the 'Bread and Butter Row' as a means to the destruction of the 'capitular citadel' can hardly be sustained; for Dodgson and Bigg had raised the question of college servants' salaries on 18 February, and the Students had seen the importance of the issue back in 1857.[3] Dyer's very exaggeration of the importance of the 'Bread and Butter Row' may be evidence not so much of undergraduate self-importance as of the admirable discretion of the Students of 1865 in their proceedings. However, on the decay of Westminster School, the tribulations

[1] i.e. the 12th Duke of Hamilton (1845–93) (matriculated Oct. 1863); *The Complete Peerage* (ed. G. E. C.), vi. 276, note (*a*) amply confirms Dyer's remark; but the statement by Vicary Gibbs (ibid., note (*d*)) that the Duke was involved in the Christ Church Library riot (of 1870) cannot be right.

[2] i.e. the 9th Duke of Northumberland (matriculated Apr. 1865), Edward Stuart Talbot (matriculated Oct. 1862; for his impressions of the House, 'not then in a very stimulating condition', cf. his *Memories of Early Life*, pp. 31 ff.), (Sir) W. G. F. Phillimore (matriculated May 1863; a Junior Student, later Fellow of All Souls), Herbert Salwey (see above, p. 131), S. E. Gladstone (W. E. Gladstone's second son; matriculated Oct. 1862).

[3] Cf. above, p. 67.

of would-be scientists, the different 'sets' within the House, and above all on the organization of the 'Bread and Butter Row', Dyer seems admirably sound. Some of his recollections are confirmed by those of his contemporary A. B. Simeon, who came into residence in October 1865. Simeon too wrote in old age:

At that time Christ Church was not a leading College, and there was a great deal too much cardplaying, drinking, and rowdiness. There were a lot of young noblemen, and rich men. In fact my allowance was not sufficient for a Commoner of Christ Church, and I found it very difficult to keep out of debt. But it was some help to be living in the Old Library instead of in Peckwater where all the rowdy men lived. There were wine parties almost every night, and we had to give at least two a term. Then followed cards, and often the play was very high, but I generally managed to evade gambling, and played whist for small points . . . Ch. Ch. in those days was cut up into sets, and you were bound to join one unless you lived an unsociable life . . . There was a Musical and Literary set . . . There was no boat on the river till the following year . . . But no one took much interest in it . . . I think I was too lazy to row, though often pressed to do so, and spent my time in mere amusement on the river, or sometimes on the cricket ground. The only thing I did in the Athletic line was to win the pole-jump. I should have done much better at a smaller College I believe. . . .[1]

John Balston Walter, whom Dyer singled out as the moving undergraduate spirit in 1865, had matriculated in March 1864, and as the eldest son of John Walter III, chief proprietor of *The Times* from 1847 to 1894, may fairly be held responsible for the prominence given to the 'Bread and Butter Row' in the family newspaper, perhaps even for

[1] Simeon's account (in MS. Autobiography, St. Edward's School Archives, 1/1. 11) goes on to describe how, fired by the example of M. G. Davidson, and encouraged by Liddon, Simeon was 'converted' in Jan. 1867 and from then on resolved to lead 'a high Christian life'; he survived persecution, regularly attended Evening Chapel in the Cathedral and sang in the choir at St. Thomas's, where Thomas Chamberlain (to Simeon's 'great astonishment') arrayed his choristers in surplice and cassock.

some of the pseudonymous letters;[1] his promising career came to a tragically early and sudden end in 1870.[2] (However, H. L. Thompson, whose rooms were on the same staircase as Walter's in Tom Quad, gives the main credit to Dr. Acland's nephew C. T. D. Acland, who was one of the seven main signatories of the undergraduate petition presented in March 1865.)[3] There was an additional reason why *The Times* should have given publicity to affairs at Christ Church (of which John Walter III himself had, after all, been a member): the editor under Walter was J. T. Delane, who was brought up at Easthampstead and retained an intimate connection with that place all his life. The Rector of Easthampstead from 1861 was Osborne Gordon himself, and his parish lay conveniently almost half-way between John Walter's house at Bear Wood and Delane's at Ascot Heath.[4]

It was 'A Tutor of Christ Church' who took the opportunity to point out the connection between the 'Bread and Butter Row' and the agitation set on foot in February 1865:

It is hoped that in the course of next year the government of Christ Church may be placed in the hands of those interested in it as a place of education—the Students, as distinguished from the Chapter. Were this done such abuses as those complained of would not last for a single day, and the noble revenues of Christ Church would be applied to their proper object—the cheapening of education.

[1] The late Mr. John Walter IV (b. 1873, d. 1968) kindly told me that he could not recall any reference to his uncle's activities in 1865 by either Dean Liddell or Dean Paget.

[2] He was drowned during a skating party at Bear Wood on Christmas Eve 1870: for the full circumstances see *The History of The Times, 1841–84* (1939), p. 499.

[3] Thompson, *Christ Church*, p. 217. J. B. Walter lived in Tom. III.1, opposite J. E. L. Shadwell, then an undergraduate (III.2), and underneath Harcourt (III.3); Thompson lived in Tom. III.4.

[4] A belief that Gordon was 'connected with the Times' was held by Sir William Gregory, who matriculated at the House in 1835 (ed. Lady Gregory, *Sir William Gregory . . . An Autobiography* (1894), p. 46); Gordon had been Gregory's 'coach' (ibid., p. 45).

The Times leader on the whole question was sadly unhistorical and deplorably inaccurate; for instance, it was quite untrue that the canons 'have in reality nothing to do with the colleges as a portion of the university', and it was going too far to say that 'the Dean usually cares little, and the Canons rarely care anything, for the undergraduates, unless they have a gilt tuft to their caps, or wear the Gentleman Commoner's silk gown'. The error, according to *The Times*, was that 'the government of Christ Church' was left in the hands of the Dean and Chapter, 'instead of being vested in the Dean and a select number of the Students of the college'.

Only three letters appeared in *The Times* over the real names of their signatories. As was perhaps intended, Shirley, the Treasurer, was goaded into a reply—and a singularly ill-advised one. He maintained that 'The commissariat of Christ Church was in the hands, not of the Dean and Chapter, but of the Dean and Censors, both of them tutors; the present tariff was the work of a late Senior Censor, and that only once in recent years had the commissariat as such been considered by the Dean and Chapter.' These points were effectively refuted by a letter from the two Censors (had not the Dean and Canons appointed the accountant, they asked?), and by a more vehement letter from Osborne Gordon who had drawn up the current tariff. Gordon's acid comment must be given in full to show the depth of feeling aroused by the ignorance of a canon from another college whose experience of Christ Church was limited to a few months, 'Had Dr. Shirley been Censor for 10 or 12 years, and not a novice in the House, of which he is one of the supreme governors, he would not have ventured on this assertion.' Gordon also made Shirley regret the statement that the Dean and Chapter had only once in late years considered the commissariat: 'That is to say, that the governing body of the House exclude habitually from their consideration matters which intimately concern the interests and comforts of every resident member of the House except themselves.' And he returned with vigour to the basic question at issue. The day before a letter had appeared from the Senior Censor, who was partly concerned to defend the Dean against 'the monstrous charge of indifference'; but Sandford brought into the open the whole question of the agitation which had begun in the previous February and stressed again the root of the matter; the Dean and Chapter, not the Dean and Censors, controlled the finances, and therefore the obvious remedial measure, a salaried bursar, required the concurrence of the Dean and Chapter. 'The system is to blame and not the man'; and as a result of recent publicity, the system he hoped could not long endure. *The Times* itself eventually waxed extremely sarcastic (22 November): 'at this very hour, for aught that appears to the contrary, Dr. Liddell may be searching the counting houses of London for a man who was at once acute and anxious enough to unravel the accounts of Christ Church.' It could only hope

> that the radical defects in the constitution of the House will at the same time come in for a share of attention, and that the government of the educational side of Christ Church will be, in some measure, withdrawn from a body which, separated from all intercourse with the Undergraduate world, and wholly removed from the work of tuition, is about as much fitted for the functions it professes to discharge as the Dean and Chapter of Ely would be to undertake the management of a College at Cambridge.

The 'Bread and Butter Row' resulted in victory for the agitators. On 8 December, a fortnight after the last letter on the subject in *The Times*, the Treasurer, as the Dean's representative, and the two Censors met to draw up recommendations on 'the general economy of the House':[1] they recommended the establishment of the office of Steward, the

[1] The four words, 'as the Dean's representative', were inserted by Bayne in the printed copy of these recommendations and modifications in Ch. Ch. Library MS. 449, f. 89; this is another expression of the Students' preference for the rule of the Dean rather than of the Dean and Chapter. The meeting of Dean and Canons on 9 Dec. was not regarded as a regular Chapter meeting, and is not recorded in the Chapter Act Book.

election of the Steward by the Senior Students and Resident Students, the abolition of the office of manciple, the remuneration of both cook and butler by fixed salaries plus half the net profits of their respective departments, the provision of dinner at a fixed price, and so on.[1] Next day Dean and Canons accepted these proposals, with minor modifications; and on 11 December R. G. Faussett was unanimously elected Steward at a meeting of Students presided over by the Dean. This was held in 'the old Common Room', i.e. the present S.C.R.; it was a departure from precedent that the Dean should meet the Senior Students on their own ground.

(*e*) COMMISSIONERS, ARBITRATORS, OR REFEREES? 1865–1866

At the meeting of Students on 11 November Prout and Sandford reported progress. (There were fourteen present: eleven Senior Students, Chamberlain, Faussett, and Thompson.) Prout summarized the correspondence already surveyed here. Sandford had been in touch with two other University Commissioners; the Dean of Wells thought some improvement might be made in the Ordinance, Twisleton 'would be glad to see the disadvantages of Senior Students, as compared with Fellows of Colleges, removed'. Sandford had also seen Sir George Grey, who as Home Secretary was concerned with the appointment of Royal Commissions; Grey had been in touch with Gladstone, who had placed his services at the disposal of the House, 'noting that the Government could hardly take the initiative, and that there was no precedent for instituting a Royal Commission to complete a scheme for a single College'. (This offer was never taken up.) With one dissentient vote a

[1] The new rates appear in the (?first) 1866 issue of the College Regulations (Bodleian Library G.A. Oxon. 8°. 1110 (4)), already enclosed in the blue cover familiar to members of the House ever since.

Committee consisting of Prout, Sandford, and Harcourt (Bayne was added later) was appointed to decide the form of representations of which the Government could officially take cognizance, and submit the proposed communication for the Students' approval. The man whom Prout approached for advice was an old acquaintance, Chichester Parkinson-Fortescue (1823–98), a Westminster contemporary who had matriculated at the House in 1841 and taken a First in Classics in 1844; like Hunt he was a pupil of Osborne Gordon. Fortescue had been a Liberal M.P. for many years, and an Under-Secretary; he was now Chief Secretary for Ireland in Russell's last Government.[1] Back in 1855 Fortescue had been among those 'violently' in favour of Liddell as the new Dean,[2] and his answer to Prout naturally returned to an awkward point: was the Dean himself favourable, neutral, or hostile? As to procedure, it seemed to Fortescue that

> the best way would be to get up a Memorial from Ch. Ch. men, praying either for specific reforms, or for a Commission of inquiry with a view to reforms, to have this Memorial as largely and influentially signed as possible, and to present it to the Prime Minister, who, as it happens, was the author, as head of the Government at the time, of the former Commission. If such a Memorial were unfavourably received, it wd. form a foundation for action in the House of Commons.[3]

Prout accepted Fortescue's advice, and was sanguine enough to think that the Government would not decline to help; he added a description of the Dean's neutrality: 'At first he seemed to express himself favourably to the movement, but on my asking him directly what might be said of him, his reply was that he wished to be understood not to have

[1] Fortescue's wife (1863) was the much-married Countess Waldegrave, recently (1861) the widow of an uncle of Prout's colleague Harcourt (cf. . . . *and Mr Fortescue* (ed. O. W. Hewett, 1958), pp. 189–90, 198).

[2] Ibid., p. 82: Fortescue lobbied Palmerston on 3 June 1855 in favour of Liddell as soon as he heard of Gaisford's death, and next day lobbied Russell.

[3] Ch. Ch. Archives, MS. Estates 117, ff. 165–6.

pronounced any opinion favourable or unfavourable in the matter.'[1]

The Students held two meetings (1 and 9 December) to consider the form of their Memorial, which was printed, ready for signature, and about to be submitted; but on the 9th Sandford announced a countermove by the Canons, who on the same day had accepted the recommendations on the internal economy of the House. The Students' Memorial would produce a Commission selected by the Government to inquire into matters defined by the Government; there were other methods by which the selection of the equivalent of a Commission and of the points to be discussed by it would be left to the actual disputants. A Commission would sit in public, a body not sponsored by the Government would sit in private. Accordingly, the Canons proposed the submission of the differences between the Students and themselves to arbitration.

Eight meetings of Students spread over six weeks were necessary to deal with the Canons' proposal. At the outset the resident Students were, for the first time, divided on the two basic issues of whether to accept the Canons' proposal at all, and (if so) on what conditions. On 13 December Martin and Bayne, supported by Sandford, moved the conditional acceptance of the offer of arbitration; Hoole and Harcourt, supported by Giffard and Blore, proposed an amendment: 'That the Students are of opinion that the offer of the Canons has come too late, and that the preferable course is to proceed with their Memorial.' Sandford put forward two arguments for arbitration: 'we should come before the world better if we listened to so temperate a proposal, whereas we should damage our cause by a definite refusal'; and arbitration might involve less delay, for there would probably be a change of Government, which might involve the failure of any move to proceed by way of a Commission. In thinking a change of Government likely

[1] Ibid., ff. 167–8. In Jan. 1866 Fortescue was made an Honorary Student, apparently without objections from the Canons.

Sandford was of course proved right: it was during Derby's last Government, not Russell's, that the Christ Church, Oxford, Act eventually passed. (On the other hand, as the new Parliament had only just been elected, the likelihood of an actual dissolution could for the moment be disregarded.)

The amendment was lost by eight votes to six, and the motion for conditional acceptance of arbitration carried by seven votes to none. Another meeting was held at ten o'clock the same evening to draft the Students' answer to the Canons, and two more on the 15th (the second at 9.30 p.m.) to answer the Canons' successive rejoinders. The rapidity of these proceedings was due to the fact that the Christmas Vacation had now begun.

Throughout these exchanges the object of the Students was to widen and that of the Canons was to limit the terms of reference of the proposed body of arbitrators. The Canons' formal proposal (12 December) was to submit to arbitration the question whether the Canons should entirely keep or totally lose their share in the election of Senior and Junior Students and 'in the government of the House as a Collegiate Body' as assigned to them by the Ordinance, and also the desirability of change in the '(1) management, and (2) application of the revenues of the College'. At first glance this proposal might be viewed as one for the separation of Cathedral and College; but the Canons later explained that by 'revenues of the College' they meant in fact 'the whole estates and income of the House'. But the Canons' proposal as it stood said nothing of the status of the Senior Students themselves, and it was this point which most exercised Prout in his efforts to state the conditions on which arbitration could proceed: he wished the arbitrators to consider not those questions selected for decision by the Canons but the whole system of government of the House. As a result, there was at the second meeting on 13 December a divergence between Prout and the Censors which is concealed by Bayne's minutes and also by the printed summary of the exchanges later circulated by the Students among themselves.[1] Prout was highly suspicious of the Canons' eleventh-hour offer as being 'too good to be true',[2] and he and Thompson carried by seven votes to none a resolution to insert in the Students' answer to the Canons a clear demand that the Canons should consent in advance of arbitration to the principle 'that the position of Senior Students be assimilated to that of Fellows in other Societies with reference to the Finance, the Government of the College, and the Elections'. Prout thought this motion essential to secure the consent of some of the new Senior Students; the latter favoured a Government Commission because they thought it would be more thorough, Prout wanted a private arbitration (presumably as less wounding to the Canons) and hoped that new Senior Students would accept this if its scope were so widened that it might be looked upon as a 'private Commission'.[3] As twelve men attended the meeting, it follows that five did not vote on this key resolution; the five abstainers included both Censors, and Prout's correspondence with Sandford and Bayne shows that he much deplored their attitude, which seemed to him 'almost to give up our case'.[4] 'It is most important', he wrote to Bayne, 'that both parties should make themselves clearly understood to each other at the commencement, and at present I do not think that either party has done so.'[5]

The Students' answer was sent to the Canons next day (14 December), and the words by which Prout set so much store proved more than the Canons could accept; their rejoinder of the same day thought the arbitrators must be left absolutely free, but did agree to two other stipulations of a procedural kind made by the Students, that the arbitrators should have every facility to inquire into the

[1] Reference to the division was omitted in the printed statement (Appendix IV) when Prout insisted that if the document noted on this issue that the Censors were 'in the minority' (*sic*), it should also state that the senior Senior Student (i.e. Prout himself) was in the majority.

[2] Ch. Ch. Archives, MS. Estates 117, f. 175.

[3] Ibid., f. 176v.

[4] Ibid., f. 173.

[5] Ibid., f. 176v.

government and revenues of the House and to recommend any alterations to the Ordinance, and that the Dean, Canons, and Students should all combine to seek legal authority for carrying out the arbitrators' recommendations. Next morning (15 December) the Dean expressed his willingness to accept arbitration on the Canons' terms, and after a morning meeting the Students sent their answer to the Canons' rejoinder: this repeated the insistence on the admission of the Students to the government of the House in matters of discipline, elections, and revenues. (However, by using the phrase 'either as a body, or by representatives' this reply implied a readiness to accept a Governing Body in which Canons and Students should be equal in number.) The Canons sent a reply during the course of the day, repeating their view that such a condition would deprive the arbitrators of complete freedom; at the same time the Dean wrote to say that he found the Canons' views 'fair and temperate'. The Students had accepted the Canons' proposal that there be three arbitrators, and had adroitly gone on to suggest that the Dean and Chapter name one, the Students a second, and the two arbitrators thus named a third. The Canons thought that 'the position of the Dean, in some important points, is so different from their own', that he ought to have a personal voice in the nomination; they understood that he would name Sir Roundell Palmer. The Canons stated their readiness to name the Archbishop of Canterbury, affirming 'They believe that neither of these eminent persons has expressed any opinion on the points at issue.' The exchanges in March 1865 between Prout and the Archbishop show that Longley was at least not ignorant of the issues themselves.

The Canons, supported by the Dean, had therefore refused to meet the Students' basic pre-condition for arbitration; and accordingly at an evening meeting of Students on 15 December, a meeting of Students on both foundations, resident and non-resident, was summoned for 18 January.

In the second week of January Prout discussed the position at the Athenaeum with Arthur Milman. Milman, son of the Dean of St. Paul's, had been a Student from 1846 to 1860 and was a barrister. His letter to Prout of 15 January is the only evidence found of the views of lay members of the House outside the Governing Body apart from Hunt and Fortescue. Milman had discussed the position with two other barrister members of the House, Alfred Bailey and A. P. Whately; Whately had been a Student from 1847 to 1863. All three thought the Students should not consent to arbitration unless the Canons accepted the precondition insisted upon by Prout: otherwise the Students might find themselves bound in honour to accept not only for themselves but also for their successors an unsatisfactory award, whereas if the desired principle were once admitted, any scheme designed to effect it might be amended from time to time. Milman thought the number of arbitrators should be extended to five, and added that 'Bailey and Whately both agree with me in looking with some distrust upon the person whom you suggested as likely to be chosen by the Students to act on their behalf.' Presumably this was a reference to G. W. Hunt. On a future constitution Milman wrote: 'it has always seemed to myself that the only perfectly satisfactory result, if it could be achieved, would be, a complete partition and severance into two distinct societies, certain portions of the estates being assigned to the Dean and Chapter qua capitular body, others to the Dean and Students as representing the College.'[1]

Milman's advice on arbitration was perhaps over legalistic; when the time came Prout ignored it.

The lengthy meeting on 18 January 1866 was attended by twenty-six Students. Eleven of these were Senior Students, but fifteen were Students on the Old Foundation; these were Page, Chamberlain, Jeffreys, Harvey, Johnson, R. Faussett, Ingram, Collyns, Benson, Mason, Floyd, Andrews,

[1] Ch. Ch. Archives, MS. Estates 117, ff. 179–82.

Williamson, Thompson, and Whitaker.[1] Four of these (Chamberlain, R. Faussett, Benson, and Thompson) were resident in Oxford; others held college livings and came up from their parsonages to attend—Jeffreys from Hawkhurst in Kent, Harvey from Tring, Johnson from Flore (Northants), Collyns from Benson, Mason from Wigginton, and Andrews from Market Harborough. Page, who held a London living, was the senior Student and represented the quintessence of the Westminster–Christ Church connection;[2] but he did not play a notably large part in the meeting. The number of Students on the Old Foundation was still nearly forty, and this was the first time that non-resident Students of this status were actually summoned, though some had been present, apparently by accident, at a few earlier meetings. In the discussion on 18 January the Students on the Old Foundation naturally tended on the whole to take a more moderate view than the Senior Students; they were, of course, a majority of the meeting.

Much of the argument centred on the differences between a 'Government Commission', a 'Private Commission', and 'Arbitration'; the important point was, of course, the terms of reference of the inquiry itself. Prout and Harcourt eventually got through (by fifteen votes to four, with seven abstentions) a motion that in view of the Chapter's refusal 'to accept as a basis of arbitration the principle,[3] which the Students consider essential, no arbitration in the ordinary sense of the word is possible'; amendments by Jeffreys and

[1] Jeffreys, Johnson, Mason, Floyd, Andrews, and Williamson never attended another meeting. Apologies were received from Edward Rogers, G. D. Bowles, Liddon, R. T. West, W. A. Strong, W. W. Follett, and G. C. Robinson.

[2] Cyril William Page (1805–73), King's Scholar of Westminster 1819–23, Student of Christ Church 1823–73, and Perpetual Curate of Christ Church, Westminster, 1843–73, was the son of William Page, the last Headmaster of Westminster before the decline; his grandfather, father, and two brothers were all King's Scholars who came to Christ Church. According to E. S. Talbot (*Memories of Early Life*, p. 12) he was 'a very faithful and slightly pedantic Prayer Book Churchman'.

[3] i.e. the admission of the Senior Students to the status enjoyed by Fellows of other societies.

Williamson and then by Page and Collyns to accept arbitration by three persons as then envisaged without insisting on the pre-condition advocated by the Senior Students were narrowly defeated (by nine votes to thirteen and nine votes to eleven). A great diversity of view was expressed: Hoole refused to be bound personally by any arbitration, Thompson wanted to present the Memorial at once, Dodgson expressed what proved to be the unanimous feeling of the meeting: he thought it better to agree with the Chapter upon men who would draw up a scheme, than to have each party submit a Memorial to the Crown.

Prout, seconded by Hoole, then put forward a compromise which had been in his mind for some days.[1] His motion was ingenious. He abandoned the attempt to get the Canons' consent to the admission of Senior Students to full power in advance of an inquiry and instead made the terms of reference of the inquiry itself as wide as possible; and he produced the phrase 'Private Commissioners' to keep the support of those new Senior Students who wanted a Government Commission. The new motion dropped the pre-condition hitherto insisted upon, and the attempt to deny the Dean his own nominee on the adjudicating body, and proposed, in the interests of co-operation with the Dean and Canons, 'to refer the whole question of the Elections to Studentships, the Finance, and the Government of the College, to Private Commissioners, who shall be nominated by the Dean, the Canons, and the Students', and who after 'full enquiry' should 'frame such a scheme for the future Government of the House, and the management and application of its revenues, as they may deem most likely to conduce to the welfare and usefulness of Christ Church'. This was passed unanimously. It was also agreed to co-operate with the Dean and Canons in obtaining legal authority for the resultant scheme.

The minutes read as though Prout caught the exact moment when a compromise would be accepted; and the

[1] Ch. Ch. Archives, MS. Estates 117, f. 176 (5 Jan.).

rest of this important meeting was harmonious: Prout and Bayne proposed that there be five Commissioners, two named by the Dean and Chapter, two by the Students, and one by the Dean; and ten names (those of Sir W. P. Wood, G. W. Hunt, Dean Hook, E. Twisleton, Sir John Coleridge, Chichester Fortescue, Sir Stafford Northcote, Lord Lyttelton, Lord Stanhope, and Lord Cranborne) were agreed as proper persons to be named by the Students, with a preference for Page Wood, Hunt, Twisleton, and Lord Lyttelton in that order. Finally Page Wood and Hunt were selected. A motion by two more non-residents (Jeffreys and Johnson) to give the resident Students full power to receive and act upon the Dean and Chapter's answer was unopposed; and it was agreed that in the event of an 'absolute refusal' from the Dean and Chapter the Students should proceed with their Memorial.

There was no such 'absolute refusal'; the Dean expressed concurrence in the Resolutions of the Students; the Canons accepted them 'as substantially accepting the proposal contained in their letter of December 12', i.e. their original offer of arbitration. The Students could not let this pass, and the residents met again on the 20th to reiterate the scope of the inquiry as defined on the 18th; Sandford, in writing to the Sub-Dean, made clear that the object of an inquiry could not be 'limited to giving a simple affirmative or negative answer to the questions specified in the letter of the Canons dated Dec. 12, 1865'. (This was a fear expressed by several Students in discussion.) The Canons produced an explanation: their object in referring to their proposals of 12 December was to lead the inquiry to recommend one of two solutions to the question of election of Students. This the Students accepted on the 24th, and after thirteen meetings of Students the long exchange on the terms of reference was over.

It was the Canons who produced the answer to the question of terminology, by proposing the term 'Referees'[1]

[1] This helpful word had first been used by Archdeacon Clerke in a letter to Osborne Gordon nine months before (above, p. 122).

instead of 'Commissioners' or 'Arbitrators'; the Dean and Canons also won their point on another matter, for, reasonably enough, they objected to Ward Hunt as a Referee, and the Students accordingly substituted Twisleton.[1] The Students also agreed that the Dean should write to the Referees on behalf of all parties.

Only from this moment did Dean Liddell play that dominant part in the affair from which his neutral position had hitherto precluded him. At two further meetings of the residents, the admirably concise letter which he proposed to send to the Referees was accepted with one unimportant amendment (2 February); and at another (15 March) the Students agreed that he should submit to the Referees the 'Historical Sketch' of the House which he had prepared.

This last is an admirably concise, accurate, and perceptive paper which can still be read with profit.[2] It set out in turn with unfailing clarity the collegiate character of Wolsey's original foundation, the ecclesiastical character of Henry VIII's foundation, and the 'double character of a College and a Chapter' established by that King's second foundation in 1546, the annexation of Canonries from 1604 onwards, and the system under the Ordinance. A statement by the Dean and Canons was added describing their recent policy, notably their offers to augment their poorer livings.

During these arguments, another Senior Student, J. E. L. Shadwell, formerly Open Junior Student of the House, had been elected at the end of January; the field could hardly have been smaller, for only two candidates had presented themselves, of whom the other withdrew after the second paper. The poor field may have been due to the anomalous status of Senior Students—or to Shadwell's ability; he had won the Ireland and Craven, and two Firsts.

[1] Hunt showed some resentment: he told Prout that his advice 'had not been as to the merits, but only as to the mode of procedure' and that he would have acted as a Referee 'out of affection for the old House and with a wish to have acted without fear or favour' (Ch. Ch. Archives, MS. Estates 117, f. 184).

[2] See Appendix VI.

(*f*) THE REFEREES AND THE AWARD, 1866

The Dean named as a Referee Sir Roundell Palmer; the Canons named Archbishop Longley and Sir John Taylor Coleridge, of whom the latter had been on the Students' list of possible Commissioners; the Students named Sir William Page Wood and Edward Twisleton. The five elected Longley as their chairman; Twisleton became secretary. They heard evidence in June and completed their Award in December 1866. The Referees were not a youthful body: Coleridge and Longley were well over seventy, Coleridge was older than the oldest Canon (Ogilvie), all were older than Prout, and all save Twisleton were older than the Dean. Their dispatch was both commendable and necessary.

There can be no doubt that this was a very strong body of Referees indeed. Four of them were lawyers: Page Wood had been one of the Vice-Chancellors since 1853, and was later to be Lord Chancellor; Palmer was at the time Attorney-General in Russell's ministry, and was later to succeed Page Wood as Lord Chancellor; Coleridge had edited Blackstone and been Justice of the Queen's Bench; Twisleton was a barrister and had sat on numerous Commissions. Coleridge, Longley, and Twisleton represented continuity with the changes of the 1850s, for all had been Commissioners under the Act of 1854, and so responsible for the Ordinance of 1858. Longley was the only Christ Church Referee, but he had had fifteen years' experience of the old system as Student and Censor from 1812 to 1827—had he been a trifle less distinguished he might well have become a Canon of Christ Church himself.[1] The Archbishop was soon to give signal proof of his skill as a chairman at the first Lambeth Conference of 1867, his wise conduct of which

[1] Longley knew Dodgson and his family well: he was Dodgson's most photographed male subject (H. Gernsheim, *Lewis Carroll, Photographer* (1949), p. 86 (pl. 41 shows Longley at Lambeth in 1864); cf. also the references in *Carroll Diaries*). The Archbishop's son Henry was Dodgson's contemporary at Rugby and Christ Church.

ARCHBISHOP LONGLEY in 1864
(aged 70)

has only recently received its due.[1] Longley's sons and Twisleton's nephew had been at the House. Palmer was Deputy Steward of the University. Three Referees had been Fellows of Oxford colleges (Coleridge—by virtue of local connection—at Exeter, Twisleton at Balliol, and Palmer at Magdalen, the first and last after migration from the colleges at which they had been undergraduates[2]); they could thus recall a system other than the anomalous Christ Church one. Page Wood, the only Referee who was not an Oxford man, had been at the largest Cambridge college, Trinity, with its strong Westminster connection; he had also been a member of the Cathedrals Commission set up in 1852, a body which had had to take special note of the anomalous position of Christ Church.

In politics the Referees were decidedly Liberal: Palmer was, and Page Wood was soon to be, a member of a Liberal Ministry, Longley usually voted on the Liberal side, and Twisleton had unsuccessfully fought the Cambridge by-election of 1859 in the Liberal interest. The lay Referees were all sound Anglicans: Palmer's papers leave on one the impression of a religious sincerity so complete as to be painful. Coleridge (later the biographer of Keble) was a leading lay High Churchman.

The Referees, being with one exception lawyers, were naturally well known to each other. Palmer was on fairly close terms with Coleridge; he thought very well of Wood, and until the Irish Church question arose found himself in agreement with him on every topic save one referred to them many years before. Twisleton was one of Palmer's oldest friends—he had been Palmer's senior at Winchester.[3] Palmer found Twisleton a curious mixture:

> Twisleton was a cadet of a noble family of some note in English history, to the honours of which his eldest brother succeeded.

[1] A. M. G. Stephenson, *The First Lambeth Conference 1867* (1967), esp. chap. 5.

[2] Palmer had matriculated at the House but then won a scholarship at Trinity.

[3] R. Palmer, *Memorials, Part I . . . 1766–1865* (1896), i. 388, 463–4; ii. 78; ii. 363–4.

He was of a quick, impulsive temperament, enthusiastic; his taste was excellent, his bearing and manners refined and attractive. When a boy at Winchester, he had been distinguished for the purity and religious tone of his character. His politics were, like those of his ancestors, Liberal. At Oxford, or soon after leaving it, he became a student of German philosophy and theology, and he imbibed the spirit of German Rationalism. His mind was disturbed by questions as to the possibility of divine revelation, and others not less fundamentally touching the conditions of human existence; he found no way of escape from difficulties, which to me seemed unreal.[1]

Twisleton's surviving correspondence[2] shows him to have been conscientious, earnest, and hardworking in the extreme throughout the period of thirty years during which he sat on a succession of committees of various kinds.

Little evidence has been found of the proceedings of the Referees; it is clear that they received communications and recorded evidence, but nothing of these survives in the papers of Longley, Twisleton, or Palmer, and there is no reference to the proceedings of the Referees in their surviving correspondence, or in the memoirs of Palmer or Page Wood. The Referees may have held some preliminary meetings; at all events, it was not until late in May that Twisleton set about seeking evidence. He injudiciously included in a letter to the Dean an intimation that the Referees were ready to hear the evidence of Senior Students on 16 or 18 June. The resident Senior Students, at a meeting on 31 May insisted on direct communication between Students and

[1] R. Palmer, *Memorials, Part I . . . 1766–1865*, i. 226–7; cf. also the following description in Goldwin Smith, *Reminiscences*, p. 109: 'Edward Twisleton was a man of leisure, very learned, among other things a Hebrew scholar, an unusual accomplishment for a layman. He was expected to turn out some great work. In the end he turned out nothing but a dissertation on the ecclesiastical miracle of the 'African Confessors,' who talked when their tongues had been cut out, and a preface to an inquiry by an expert in handwriting into the authorship of Junius, which concluded, like all the other evidence, in favour of Francis.'

[2] Consulted at Broughton Castle, Banbury, by the kindness of Lord Saye and Sele.

Referees. Sandford suggested to Twisleton the names of several former college officers whom it would be advisable to examine (W. E. Jelf, Osborne Gordon, George Marshall, and G. W. Kitchin, all recent Censors). Twisleton's reply outlined the Referees' programme: they planned to see the Dean and the Treasurer (Dr. Shirley) at Lambeth Palace on 13 June, Dr. Pusey and any other Canons who wished to give evidence on the 14th, and on subsequent days the Senior Students. After another meeting of Students on 4 June Sandford replied that Prout, himself, Harcourt, and Giffard certainly ought to give evidence, and probably Faussett (the new Steward) and H. L. Thompson also. Twisleton had incautiously written: 'I believe that there are different shades of opinion among the Senior Students. It would facilitate matters, if you agreed among yourselves as to those who should be in the first instance examined as representing such shades of opinion.' On this point Sandford felt bound to undeceive him: 'We shall not appear as representing different shades of opinion, for as regards the defects of our present constitution we are all of one mind.' There were times when the Students appear to have been unnecessarily prickly on such points: after all, Sandford's rejoinder was only half an answer. The Senior Students were unanimous on 'the defects of our present constitution'; but were they unanimous on the shape of a future constitution?

After taking evidence from Prout and others the Referees took the evidence of H. A. Giffard, who was by this time a non-resident. Giffard's account of this, sent to Prout on 22 June, is the only knowledge[1] we have of any examination before the Referees:

My examination before the Referees occupied a little more than an hour & a quarter. I did not say half I wished to say; but I feel pretty confident that what I left unsaid, and indeed much that I did say, had already been supplied by you and the others who

[1] According to the *Carroll Diaries*, i. 243–4, Dodgson did not give evidence; nor did Liddon. Dodgson sent suggestions to Longley.

preceded me. They first asked me about the Electoral body; and asked me if I could *from experience* say that it worked badly. This was exactly what I could not say. But I pointed out some of the obvious defects of the board, which nothing but a miracle could save from working badly. And the form which my opinion as to the future constitution of the Electoral body took was that it shd. be composed of the 'Dean & all the Students with or without the Chapter.' They went pretty closely into the question of how far non-resident Students were desirable as Electors. I answered as best I could, but felt a little hampered by the consideration that I was a non-resident and was speaking in my own interest.

The question of finance next turned up. The Archbp. asked me which of two systems I preferred, a division of estates, or the handing over of a portion of the revenues to be disposed of by the Students. I answered that of *the two* systems, I preferred the former. He then asked if there was any third course. I felt tempted to say that the most satisfactory plan would be management by us & the handing over of a sufficient revenue to the Chapter. But I could not quite venture so far. I stated that a satisfactory plan to me would be 'joint management and fixed revenues.' With that I should be quite contented.

In the matter of government, generally, I do not think I had any thing new to say. Indeed I referred them as much as possible to our written statement.

I was finally asked if I had any other defect to notice in the constitution. I immediately said that one of the most glaring defects was the immense amount of floating unappropriated power that the present constitution left open to the strongest hand: and showed how it enabled the Dean, if he wished it, to judge arbitrarily the kind of questions which in other places would necessarily be referred to a College meeting. The Referees, with the exception of Sir Page Wood, showed, I thought, some reluctance to receive any matter militating against the Dean's authority. They said (Sir J. Coleridge was the principal objector) that the Dean had not been put on his defence, and the question had not been raised in the correspondence. I submitted that the whole constitution was well understood by the Dean, Chapter & Students to be under consideration & that it was not a matter of personal complaint—but of a constitutional weakness which admitted of abuses that I wished to complain. I gained my point, and then they let me in & I had a grand campaign on the room-rent question. They all seemed (as far as I could judge) to listen very attentively to the instances I adduced—and Wood especially seemed interested in the question. I think I made them understand the kind of grievance which we felt in having no appeal from a decision of the Dean's except to the authority of the Visitor, a course which few of us, unless very hard pressed, would care to adopt. Wood asked some very pertinent questions as to the method in which such a question as the 'rooms' would have been decided if brought before the whole body of Students. Might I not then have been deprived? I said, yes, but I should have been much more ready to acquiesce in an adverse decision of a large body in the same interest as myself, than in that of a single chief, who would not necessarily fully understand those interests.

Before leaving I took up the ordinance, and went through several of the clauses. There is little for me to say about this part of my evidence, except that I pointed out how it was possible for petitions to be presented affecting the interests of the students, & for clauses of the ordinance repealed, and trusts imposed by the ordinance repudiated not only without the intervention but without the knowledge of the Students. V. C. Wood stopped me to ask Sir J. Coleridge how the hearing of these petitions was conducted; and let fall some rather severe remarks as to the course pursued. But of course I was not supposed to hear the conversation, though my tongue itched to join in it.

My evidence has not been sent me for correction. I think Martin's letter, and indeed all communications from Senior Students would do good. We all have the same cause: and the more is known the better. I am writing to Martin to-night. Will you kindly show this letter to Harcourt, Sandford, Faussett, Thompson and any one who may care to see it[1] . . .

This reads very much as though Giffard lectured the Referees; his attack on the Dean on a question of room-rents which had arisen between them may well have struck a false note, and the details, as usual with such trivia,

[1] Ch. Ch. Archives, MS. Estates 117, ff. 197–200.

remain far from clear.[1] But Giffard's account does show the Referees' concentration on the two main points at issue, elections and finance; it shows too that they clearly saw the possible courses open to them in the field of finance. There could be either a division of estates, i.e. the Dean and Chapter and the Dean and Students could each manage a body of estates specifically assigned to each; or the Dean and Chapter could manage the whole of the estates, out of which a stated revenue could be assigned to the body of Students and expended by them. The Referees had doubtless realized for themselves that there were other possibilities, though they preferred to hear them from Giffard rather than state them to him: there was the method which Giffard advocated, joint management of the estates by Dean, Canons, and Students, and the assignment of fixed revenues to the ecclesiastical and the educational sides of Christ Church; and there was the method which Giffard thought it prudent to suppress, management by the Students and the assignment of a 'sufficient revenue' to the Dean and Chapter.

No record has been found of the Referees' deliberations after the hearing of evidence, nor is their length known.[2] They appear to have begun by drawing up seventeen general recommendations.[3] Early in December 1866 these recommendations were sent to Mountague Bernard, now Professor of International Law at Oxford, and Assessor to Palmer as Deputy Steward, who had drawn up the Christ Church Ordinance of 1858 and was the most skilled practi-

[1] Sir Roundell Palmer was requested to give an opinion on this issue in 1871 (note by Bayne in his copy of the 1867 Ordinances, Ch. Ch. Library MS. 513, opp. p. 30).

[2] An article on Christ Church appeared at this time: 'An M.A. of the House' published 'Christ Church, Oxford: its Past, Present and Prospective Changes', in *The St. James's Magazine*, xvii (July–Dec. 1866), 366–83. Its author has not been identified, but it adds little to our knowledge. The same author also published 'A Royal Year at Oxford' (an account of the Prince of Wales's residence at Christ Church in 1859–60) in ibid. xiii (Jan.–July 1865), 493–502.

[3] Bodleian Library, G.A. Oxon, c. 258, no. 6. (Printed as Appendix VII.)

tioner of this specialist art then available, with a request that he would draw up new statutes for Christ Church on the basis of the seventeen points. Bernard's draft underwent some further amendment after its return to the Referees,[1] and on 22 December the Referees signed their Award, in the form of 'Recommendations and proposed Statutes'.[2] The following day Francis Fulford preached in Christ Church a sermon which played a vital part in the genesis of the first Lambeth Conference of 1867, in which the chairman of the Referees was to play so distinguished a part;[3] on the 27th R. M. Benson founded the Society of St. John the Evangelist.

The seventeen general recommendations and the Award based on them constituted a complete acceptance by the Referees of the Students' case. Twisleton wrote to Bernard: 'It is intended that the new Governing Body shall be a little Republic, with the amplest powers, subject only to the double vote, and the casting vote, of the Dean, and the reserved rights of the ecclesiastical Corporation.'[4] The scheme was one for that 'joint government' by Dean, Canons, and Senior Students which Sir John Awdry had thought impracticable, but which Prout had wanted from the outset: there was to be a single Governing Body, of all the Canons and all the appropriate Students, under the Dean's presidency, which (except in Cathedral matters) was to be omnicompetent; on this body the Students would, from the outset, be in a majority, indeed in an increasing majority as more Senior Studentships were created and

[1] Ibid., nos. 1 and 5. (No. 5 has marginal comments by Bernard, with extensive notes in Coleridge's neat minute hand and Palmer's round larger one. Two manuscript drafts by Palmer on 'The College Seal' are bound ibid., nos. 2 and 3.)

[2] Ibid., no. 4; other copies at Christ Church. Payne Smith offered Bernard a fee of thirty guineas 'for having performed a disagreeable operation on the Chapter in such a dexterous and delicate manner'; Bernard would have preferred no fee at all (Bodleian Library, MS. Top. Oxon. c. 309, ff. 16^{v}, 22–3).

[3] Stephenson, *First Lambeth Conference*, p. 167.

[4] Bodleian Library, MS. Top. Oxon. c. 309, f. 6^{v}.

one further Canonry was suppressed. The total number of Senior Studentships (twenty-eight), and the proportion of nine to nineteen clerical Senior Studentships was maintained, so that the new Governing Body of thirty-five would ultimately contain as many as twenty-six men in Anglican orders. (The Dean was given two votes apart from his casting vote.) However, although the Award created a new Governing Body, it did not create a new corporation; this was the result of some skilful drafting by Roundell Palmer.[1] As a result the corporate designation of Christ Church, whether as Cathedral or college, remains 'The Dean and Chapter of the Cathedral Church of Christ in Oxford of the Foundation of King Henry the Eighth'—although invitations are always issued in the name of 'The Dean, Canons and Students'—and it is still the Dean and Canons who seal documents. The solution to the problem of financial management was a compromise between the course which Giffard had advocated and the course which he had not dared to mention, i.e. management on behalf of the Governing Body as a whole but the assignment of a fixed revenue (£17,000, which was to become £15,500 on the death of Dr. Jelf) to the Dean and Chapter only, the balance being devoted to the educational purposes of the House. The sum of £17,000 was arrived at without reference to the financial needs of Christ Church as a college but by adding to the salaries of the Dean and seven Canons a further sum of £3,500 for the salaries of the chaplains, choir, organist, and other Cathedral officers, and for 'other incidental expenses' of the Cathedral, including the schoolmaster (for the choir), alms, and pensions. In the late 1860s £17,000 was nearly two-fifths of the net income of the House.[2] An

[1] Twisleton wrote to Bernard on 22 Dec. 1866: 'Palmer expressly wishes to avoid constituting a new Corporation; and he meets difficulties by a new Clause [III] respecting the College Seal' (ibid., f. 13). The Senior Students made no demur.

[2] College Accounts are full of pitfalls for the unwary: probably the Referees did not fall into them because until 1867 no Consolidated Account was available. During 1867 itself, according to the *Report of the Oxford and*

anomaly in the position created by the Ordinance was removed by the stipulation that the Governing Body should include not only the existing Senior Students but also Students on the Old Foundation who were 'resident in the University' (i.e. members of Congregation) or held any office within the House; thus Chamberlain, Benson, and Liddon under the first qualification, and Faussett and H. L. Thompson under the second, became members of the Governing Body. So too did the Lee Readers in Anatomy and Chemistry. Senior Students' salaries were raised to £300.[1] All powers previously exercised by the Dean and Canons over the Cathedral and its staff were reserved to the Dean and Canons. Provision was made for the use of the Cathedral as a college chapel between 9 a.m. and 1 p.m. on Sundays and Holy Days during Full Term; this point (though it became Clause V of the new Ordinances) was covered by the very first clause of the seventeen outline recommendations and was clearly seen as of great importance. According to the latter document, it was to be 'subject, during those hours, to the regulations of the Governing Body of the College'; according to the proposed new Ordinance, the new Governing Body was to 'have the same exclusive control over the use of the said Church during the hours aforesaid as the Governing Body of a College ordinarily has over the Chapel of such College'.

Cambridge Commissioners, i (1874), 669, 679, 681, the net external and internal income of the House was as follows:

net external income from Corporate property	£23,156
net external income from Trusts	£8,052
net internal income	£13,410
	£44,618

(During the next four years this total did not fall below £44,428, or rise above £45,746.) Of the Trusts' income, Dr. Lee provided nearly £3,000.

The history of the Chapter Fund from 1869 to 1944 was outlined by the late Dr. Danby in a lucid private pamphlet. The moment when this Fund became inadequate for its stated purposes was delayed by profitable vacancies, by sales of stock, and by various economies; but from 1919 onwards Governing Body subsidies were required for the Choir School.

[1] Bernard left this (maximum) figure blank; the Referees supplied it.

Palmer was responsible for the anodyne provision at the end of Clause V that the Cathedral should continue to be used as a college chapel on weekdays 'as has been heretofore accustomed'. Coleridge noted that 'no complaint was made as to the daily Chapel services'. Presentations to benefices were vested in the Governing Body; and provision made for the establishment of a Cathedral Fabric Fund. The Chapter Fund and the Cathedral Fabric Fund were prior charges on the revenues; the surplus was at the disposal of the new Governing Body for the payment of Senior and Junior Students 'and for other College purposes'. The Dean retained his alleged existing powers 'in respect of the general government and superintendence of the House, the enforcement of order and discipline, the appointment and removal of College Officers and Tutors and otherwise', except where repugnant to the new statutes. The short-lived proposals of 1857 concerning the Treasurer and Sub-Dean were not resurrected; but a proposal made by the Students in 1857 was. Their call then for a Student as deputy to the Dean was met by a clause empowering (but not requiring) the Dean to 'appoint from among the resident Senior Students a "Censor Theologiae", who shall perform the functions and possess the powers hitherto performed and possessed by the Sub-Dean in relation to the discipline of the House, but without prejudice to the precedence and authority enjoyed by the Sub-Dean at meetings of the Governing Body'.[1] This must be seen as an attempt to meet the Students' complaint that non-gremial Canons were given a say in the education and discipline of the House. Detailed provisions followed for the regulation of Senior Studentships, Honorary Studentships, and Junior Studentships, for appeals to the Visitor, for the abolition of distinctions in respect of academical dress, designation,[2] college

[1] At the end of 1865 Archdeacon Clerke, the Sub-Dean, had wished to resign the office of Censor Theologiae—on condition that it was not filled up (Chapter Act Book, 23 Nov. 1865).

[2] The word 'designation' was inserted at Palmer's instance.

charges and payments among undergraduate members of the House other than Junior Students or Exhibitioners within the House. As in the Ordinance of 1858, there was an attempt[1] to retain the traditional number of 101 Students, by a provision that 12 further Senior Studentships might be created in addition to the 28, and that 9 further Junior Studentships might be created in addition to the 52, thus producing 40 Senior and 61 Junior Studentships, or 101 in all. But, as before, the necessary funds were not likely to be available; nevertheless, Bayne for one welcomed the provision as a sign of respect for the old Constitution of the House.[2] (The possibility of a return to the traditional number of 101 was soon seen to be so remote that as early as 1871 there was a move to alter terminology, to call the Senior Students simply 'Students' and the Junior Students 'Scholars'; this was defeated, but such a change was effected by the next statutes, of 1882, and with it disappeared the last remote possibility of a return to this part of the old constitution—of which the one remaining vestige is the 101 strokes rung nightly from Tom Tower.) Various temporary provisions, notably that for the voidance at the next vacancy of the Canonry held by Dr. Jelf, concluded the proposed new statutes. These constituted a fairly lengthy document, but their essence was clear: the Students had won power over everything except Cathedral matters.[3]

In coming to these conclusions the Referees were entirely unanimous. Twisleton told Bernard that 'the decision in this case has been absolutely unanimous. Even in the preliminary discussions I have never known such little difference of opinion . . . as in this Refereeship'; a letter from

[1] Also at Palmer's instance.

[2] He wrote opposite these provisions in his copy of the 1867 Ordinances 'so that only want of money prevents the whole no. being raised to 101, as of old' (Ch. Ch. Library MS. 513).

[3] A provision for 'Privileged Senior Students' on the lines of the one which the Dean had thought of little 'practical utility' ten years before (above, pp. 59–60, 63, 79), did not find its way into the final document. Persons in this category are now termed Ordinary Students.

Page Wood to Bernard later in December confirms this: 'on all points in controversy we were well agreed'.[1] The Students' case for change was, surely, overwhelming; but it is notable that the Referees came down so firmly for a 'joint government', and (as far as we can tell in the absence of their minutes) gave no serious thought to the question of a 'seniority' of Students or of a joint equal representation of Students and Canons on the new Governing Body, or to the question of a division of estates, or to that of a division of powers as to elections and other matters. Instead they went the whole way, made all the Students members of the new Governing Body, with suitable safeguards for the powers of the Dean and Canons over the Cathedral, and kept the estates in the hands of the enlarged body without diminution. If the Archbishop of Canterbury, nobbled long before by Prout, thought the proposed safeguards for the Cathedral adequate, the lay referees (Liberals to a man) were not likely to hesitate.[2]

The attitudes of individual Referees cannot now be distinguished; but to one of them at least the Christ Church award gave a unique opportunity to put into effect his views on one important subject: Professors. The importance of Professorial instruction was an article of faith to liberals, as evidence before the Royal Commission shows; but in fact they had done relatively little about it in the Act of 1854. The Christ Church Award gave an opportunity: the Students' case could be met without demoting the Canon-Professors. Edward Twisleton's correspondence enables his attitude to be recovered with some precision. He had once been a great friend of Halford Vaughan, the former Regius Professor of Modern History;[3] but in 1860 the two had moved apart. Vaughan appears to have become unbalanced,

[1] Bodleian Library, MS. Top. Oxon. c. 309, ff. 7, 19.

[2] There is no evidence as to Bishop Wilberforce's attitude: but in any event he had no control over the cathedral of his diocese.

[3] In a letter of 1 Jan. 1848 to his sister-in-law Caroline, Twisleton described Vaughan as 'one of my most intimate friends' (Broughton Castle MSS.).

and it was with difficulty that Twisleton could correspond with him at all. Vaughan sought Twisleton's support in his bid to become non-resident; but Twisleton refused to sign a Memorial got up on Vaughan's behalf, and made amply clear his firm belief that residence would double a Professor's usefulness, and that 'as a prima facie rule' Professors ought to reside. As a Commissioner, Twisleton had thought that Professors should be paid £1,000–£1,200 yearly, to put them on something like an equality with Heads of Houses.[1]

The situation in Christ Church might have been specially designed to implement such views as these: here were adequately salaried and comfortably housed Professors who, because of their duties in the University and the Cathedral, could hardly not reside. From a liberal point of view it would have been foolish to sever them from the College. Among the reasons for the Referees' adoption of a 'joint government', this must surely be rated high.

(*g*) THE AMENDMENT AND ACCEPTANCE OF THE AWARD, 1867

There were signs in summer 1866 that a settlement was highly desirable; and also that it would not be easy. There is relatively little evidence from the Canons' side in the dispute; and their views deserve study. On 25 June (i.e. after both had given evidence to the Referees) Pusey wrote to Payne Smith a letter which suggests some deterioration of relations between Canons and Students, and shows that it was not only the older Canons who found the Students difficult:

> The Students do, as you say, take offence at everything. Some grounds of offence are really childish, viz. that we lent the Hall portraits to the Paris Exhibition without asking them, that they had not been asked about continuing the series of portraits of Students, that we were improving the condition of the library without consulting the librarians (which I thought we had

[1] Copy, Twisleton to Vaughan, 5 Dec. 1859, 3 Feb. 1860 (ibid.).

intended to do). It seems to me that the upshot was that they would be satisfied with nothing except having a vote as to every thing which should be done.[1]

These seem trivial matters; though, as to the first, since the Students regularly dined in Hall whereas the Canons rarely did, it was the Students who would miss the portraits. Pusey's last point must refer to the plans for 'altering and heating the Library' which the Chapter had four months earlier authorized the Dean to produce[2]—though if those plans involved the maltreatment of part of the ground floor of Christ Church Library effected in 1869, it was the enlarged Governing Body itself which failed to stop this unfortunate act of destruction.[3]

However, in the same letter Pusey expressed his forebodings on an issue of much greater importance: the control of the Cathedral. Hitherto this point has required no notice here; in the end it nearly upset the whole negotiation. To some extent the point was disciplinary, the enforcement of undergraduate attendance at college services in the Cathedral. In 1861 Pusey denounced the behaviour of Christ Church undergraduates on Sunday mornings, which they spent in eating and drinking 'and, I suppose, smoking', to the detriment of their attendance at college services; and Archdeacon Clerke went so far as to suppose that Christ Church men 'seem to require a different treatment from those of all other colleges, especially with regard to employment of their Sunday mornings'.[4] Before 1858 the Dean (or the Sub-Dean) and the two Censors had dealt with non-attendance at college services in the Cathedral; and the Canons took the view that enforcement of attendance was not one of the disciplinary matters entrusted to Chapter and Senior Students by the Ordinance of 1858. (Nor had Dean

[1] Christ Church Archives. [2] Chapter Act Book, 7 Feb. 1866.

[3] For details see Hiscock, *Ch. Ch. Miscellany*, pp. 103–4. By the time they were removed in 1963 certain of Dean Liddell's Library heating appliances were of fine antiquity but deplorable performance.

[4] Christ Church Archives.

a. DR. PUSEY in Tom Quad

b. ARCHDEACON CLERKE

c. DR. HEURTLEY in about 1856 (aged 50)

CANONS OF CHRIST CHURCH

Liddell in 1857 felt that it should be.)[1] Pusey was strongly opposed to any powers of excusing attendance at Cathedral being given to the Students; but during the hearings before the Referees he must have become painfully aware that not only dispensation from attendance but also nomination of preachers was now at stake. He told Payne Smith on 25 June 1866 that if the Chapter was deprived of complete control of its services, it would not only cease to be a Cathedral body and become a 'mere college', but, far worse, 'Stanley, Jowett and Co. may be our cathedral preachers and the cathedral may become an organ of undermining faith'. It would be unfair to Pusey to see in this outburst yet one more proof that personalities, rather than principles, provoke opposition to change; Pusey was simply taking his normal view. It has been well said of him that 'in every educational question the interests of religion must in his view be supreme'.[2] After six years' acquaintance with Stanley and his sermons in Christ Church, Pusey's mind was clear on the needs of 'the interests of religion'.

There had for some time been attempts to change the arrangements for college services in the Cathedral, and the whole matter of University and college services was a cause of much controversy during the period of the Award. In December 1861, when Sandford was Senior Censor and Kitchin about to become Junior Censor, the college Tutors, exercised by the same problem which troubled Archdeacon Clerke, requested the Dean to change the hour of Morning Prayer on Sundays;[3] this was presumably designed to make possible sermons at college services in the Cathedral, at a time when the only sermons which were required to be given were the two University Sermons preached at the University church each Sunday in Term at 10.30 p.m. and 2 p.m.[4] by Select Preachers nominated by

1 Above, p. 63.
2 C. E. Mallet, *A History of the University of Oxford*, iii (1927), 319.
3 Chapter Act Book, 19 Dec. 1861.
4 See E. M. Goulburn, *John William Burgon* (1892), ii. 17 ff.

the University, except when those sermons were preached in the Cathedral itself by those Canons who were on the list of Select Preachers. (The Statute requiring undergraduate attendance could not be enforced: for neither St. Mary's nor Christ Church could hold all the undergraduates.) There was a long discussion in a nearly full Chapter, and the Chapter, apparently divided on an issue which it had already discussed more than once, found itself 'unable to come to any satisfactory conclusion with regard to it at present'; but one change did follow, for Dean Liddell promptly abolished the use of Latin at (daily) college prayers.[1] At these services, subsequently held in English at 8 a.m. and 5.45 p.m., the question of sermons did not arise as it did in connection with Sunday services. In May 1865 a Memorial from the undergraduates, requesting more frequent celebration of Holy Communion, led to the institution of Communion at 7.30 a.m. and Morning Prayer (with Litany) at 9 a.m. on Sundays, except on the first Sunday in the month when Morning Prayer with Communion was held at 8 a.m.[2] Morning prayer at 9 a.m. was not only too early for undergraduates but also too early for a sermon. The Referees' provision for college services in the Cathedral between 9 a.m. and 1 p.m. on Sundays changed all this: if the college service was later than 9 a.m. was it to contain a sermon? If it did contain a sermon, what persons were to name the preacher? A phrase used in the summary of Pusey's evidence to the Heads of Houses in 1853 comes irresistibly to mind: 'Proposed plan—perilous.' For Pusey, if the Dean and Chapter lost control of the nomination of preachers in their own Cathedral, the floodgates would once

[1] Liddon gives the date of the first English weekday service as Monday, 27 Jan. 1862 in a note in his copy of *Liber Precum Ecclesiae Christi Cathedralis Oxon.* (1726), given by Sandford to Liddon the next day, and after Liddon's death by Dr. Lock to T. V. Bayne, whose executors gave it to Christ Church Library.

[2] Chapter Act Book, 10 May 1865; Pusey's letter to Liddon in Pusey Papers (Pusey to Liddon, vol. i, f. 135) probably refers. Choral Communion was first held at Christmas 1892 (second Bayne scrapbook, p. 110).

more be open. The fact that they had already been so often opened in his lifetime without total calamity never weighed with him; and perhaps it is a principle not altogether devoid of merit that the Dean and Chapter of a Cathedral should indeed nominate those who preach within their Cathedral walls, no matter to whom.

Before the completion of the Award the Senior Students held two meetings, on 24 November and 18 December 1866, to discuss the position of the Steward, Faussett, who wished to marry. The Referees were asked to make this possible by the Award, but in the event did not do so.[1]

In November 1866 the Treasurership again changed hands: for on 20 November Shirley died, aged thirty-eight. (Liddon took it ill that Heurtley, with his extreme views, made 'no sort of allusion' to Shirley in his Cathedral sermon on the 25th.)[2] Payne Smith became Treasurer on 30 November; he had had even less experience of Christ Church than Shirley the previous year. One possible Christ Church candidate for the now vacant Chair of Ecclesiastical History was already provided for: William Stubbs had accepted the Regius Chair of Modern History in August. Liddon was Bright's candidate for the succession, and Bright was Liddon's;[3] but Lord Derby appointed H. L. Mansel, a Conservative metaphysician from Magdalen. (J. R. Green thought 'the promotion of a popular novelist to the historical chair at Cambridge, the elevation of a leading metaphysician to the chair of Ecclesiastical History at Oxford' evidence of 'the singular conception which the

[1] At the second of these meetings Faussett was given permission to hold the living of Cassington with the Stewardship; but in fact he did not become incumbent there until 1875. It was as a result of the connection of Cassington with the House that the old Cathedral stalls were moved to Cassington church, where they still are, after Scott's restoration.

[2] Liddon Diary, 25 Nov. 1866.

[3] Johnston, *Liddon*, p. 87. Pusey supported Bright (Pusey Papers). Bishop Wilberforce told Liddon that he himself was pressing Liddon, Claughton, Milman, and Bright (in that order); Curteis and Kitchin were also candidates. Liddon Diary, 24 Nov. 1866.

powers that be seem to entertain as to what history is'.)[1] Mansel was installed on 29 January 1867; he took little part in the closing stages of the dispute, and departed for the Deanery of St. Paul's next year.

The Referees' Award was dated 22 December; the Archbishop sent copies to the parties on the 31st. When he saw it, Dr. Pusey was quite clear that on two points it would not do; and though pessimistic as to the outcome, he did not intend to give up without a fight. He opened his mind on the Award in a letter to Liddon on 11 January 1867:

It exceeds the powers which we gave or meant to give. [1.] We strictly limited our reference as to the election to Studentships to the alternative, that we should remain as we are or be excluded altogether. They have chosen neither; but have merged us in the Governing Body. I think, by its terms, that you, Chamberlain and Benson will be members of the Governing Body.

2. They have made the Cathedral a College Chapel from 9 to 1 on Sunday. This does not properly come under the word 'discipline'. Discipline surely is regulation as to the individuals; and, as regard to public worship, as to their attendance upon it, consequences of neglect so to do etc. This regulation, of course, could give Sandford, Kitchin [*sic*] etc. power to establish the 11 o'clock sermon which they have so long wished to do despite the University Statutes, and to appoint what preachers they will e.g. Stanley. So there will be plenty of discussion. I have written to Sir J. T. Coleridge to remonstrate individually; but it will, of course, be of no use.[2]

The later careers of Sandford as Bishop of Gibraltar and of his friend Kitchin as Dean of Winchester and then of Durham are not usually reckoned among the more revolutionary ones of their day; and of the two it was only Sandford whom Pusey had to fear within Christ Church, for Kitchin had

[1] J. R. Green, *Stray Studies: Second Series* (1903), p. 195 (originally in *Saturday Review*, 2 Mar. 1867).

[2] Pusey to Liddon, 11 Jan. 1867 (Pusey Papers). *The Churchman* of 13 Feb. mentioned the likelihood of opposition to the Award; this may refer to Pusey's efforts.

ceased to be a Student in 1863. Sandford, however, aided by Kitchin, had recently been very active in the then controversial matter of the University Sermon. He had sent the Vice-Chancellor a numerously signed Memorial on the subject in November 1865 and followed it with letters which were printed. It must be confessed that Sandford actually advocated, not a morning sermon at Christ Church or any other college, but a 10 a.m. service of Morning Prayer only, a morning University Sermon at noon, and college sermons 'of a practical character' in the afternoon, with an Evening University Sermon in Christ Church instead of St. Mary's.[1]

At all events, Coleridge refused to accept an individual remonstrance from Pusey; on the 12th he forwarded his letter to the Archbishop, and answered Pusey only to point out the latter's lack of standing. Did Pusey write for himself, or for all or any of the parties in the dispute? Did he want the Reference reopened, and if so did his request have the consent of all the parties? The Referees were now *functi officio* and could only act as a body.[2]

Pusey also wrote to Longley direct; but again he received small comfort. As to the Cathedral the Archbishop wrote: 'It is indeed to be lamented that the terms of the Reference were not distinctly stated, for if there was one point above all on which we believed that our arbitration [*sic*] was especially invited, it was that of the sermon for the Undergraduates of Christ Church in the Cathedral.' If this point was not to be settled by the Referees, it should have been expressly excluded. As to the matter of elections, Longley went on: 'I do not think we could any of us have consented

[1] C. W. Sandford, *The University and College Services. A letter addressed to the Vice-Chancellor* (1865), and *The University Sermon and College Services. A letter addressed to the Vicar of St. Mary-the-Virgin's* (1866). (The latter is dated 19 Jan.) In both Sandford felt bound to meet the criticism that his proposals were 'a plan to sacrifice the interests of the University to the special interests of Christ Church'. Sandford's colleague Bayne disapproved of sermons, though he would go to listen to Liddell, Liddon, or Heurtley (Strong, *H. P. Liddon*, p. 14).

[2] J. T. Coleridge to Pusey, 12 Jan. 1867, Pusey Papers.

to publish it as our deliberate opinion that the Canons ought to be excluded from the Election altogether'; all were 'fully satisfied' that they were acting in conformity with their instructions.[1]

Despite these rebuffs, Pusey and his colleagues continued their efforts. On 1 February he could report to Liddon:

> The Canons have sent an ultimatum to the Students on the ground of the decision of Referees being ultra vires, 1) as to the making the Cathedral a College Chapel on Sunday Mornings, 2) as to the election to Studentships. The first they require to be struck out as the condition of their not being free to oppose the Bill; on the second they have proposed a modification.
>
> The Dean has summoned a meeting of Students and Canons for Tuesday. Whether we attend, depends I suppose, on the answer to our proposals which is to be given I suppose on Tuesday. You are now an inchoate member of the G.B.; so I suppose you will be there. . . .[2]

The Students had already met in 31 January to discuss amendments to the award; two days later they met again to receive the Canons' objections, and on the 4th to appoint a Committee (of Faussett, Sandford, and Harcourt) to draft the Students' answer to the Canons.

The crucial meetings were held in the present S.C.R. of Christ Church, endowed by Dr. Busby of Westminster almost exactly 200 years before, on Tuesday and Wednesday, 5 and 6 February 1867; the first meeting on the 5th lasted from 11 in the morning until 3.15 p.m., the second from 8 p.m. to 10.30 p.m. At 11 a.m. on the 5th there assembled the Dean, two Canons (Heurtley and Payne Smith), and twenty-one Students, thirteen Senior Students and eight Students on the Old Foundation. These were Page, Chamberlain, Harvey, Faussett, Ingram, Collyns, Benson, and Thompson.

[1] C. T. Longley to Pusey, 16 Jan. 1867, Pusey Papers.

[2] Pusey to Liddon, 1 Feb. 1867, Pusey Papers. Pusey wrote no more to Liddon on this subject.

Bigg had recently left Christ Church for Cheltenham College, but the Senior Students had been reinforced by the election on 18 December of two newcomers; only one Studentship had been advertised, but there were eight candidates and by a majority it was agreed to elect two. These were E. S. Talbot, Junior Student of the House, who won a First in Literae Humaniores in 1865 and in Modern History in 1866, and Francis de Paravicini, a Marlburian and Scholar of Balliol who secured a First in Classical Moderations and the Hertford Scholarship in 1864, and a Second in Literae Humaniores and the Gaisford Prose Prize in 1866; Talbot attended the meeting. The Canons withdrew after presenting a letter in which (as Pusey foreshadowed) they stated their acquiescence in the Award 'so far as it corresponds with the points which they submitted to arbitration', but thought it 'at variance with the terms of their reference in two respects', the use of the Cathedral and the Electoral Body; as to the first, they had not intended to submit the question of the use of the Cathedral to the Referees, and felt that they would not be justified in surrendering any part of the powers ordinarily vested in the Dean and Chapter of a Cathedral church. On the second point, the Canons sought to limit the power of election to Senior Studentships to the Dean, Canons, and resident Senior Students. The Canons accordingly wanted the clause concerning the use of the Cathedral omitted, and the election of Senior Students limited to the Dean, Canons, and 'the *resident* Students, who are members of the Governing Body', i.e. to exclude non-resident Senior Students. The Canons were unanimous on the first point, but not on the second; they achieved their object on the former, but not on the latter.

The ensuing lengthy discussion, under the Dean's chairmanship, revealed a general anxiety (expressed, for instance, by Dodgson) to reach a settlement acceptable to all, and produced from Collyns the memorable statement that he 'would not degrade Christ Church to the level of a College'.

Page and Collyns, both Students on the Old Foundation, wanted to drop the clause concerning the use of the Cathedral; Harcourt, Faussett, Ingram, and Thompson were unwilling to weaken the Award, Sandford was ready to wait a year if necessary to achieve a harmonious settlement, Dodgson too wanted a harmonious conclusion, and Chamberlain (who at these last meetings emerged as a sensible conciliator) 'could well understand the Canons not wishing to be inferior to the Canons of other Cathedrals, yet there have been just grounds of dissatisfaction given to the Tutors'. The Students were almost evenly split (irrespective of status), but amendments to the original motion to drop the clause were carried by eleven to nine and eleven to seven, and an answer sent to the Canons.

Various amendments were then discussed, some of them on points of detail. Sandford's amendments showed a good deal of acumen; Bayne noticed that the Award gave the Dean a power to remove college officers which he had very certainly not previously possessed, and this was duly struck out. Prout himself raised two extremely important if obvious points. Bernard's draft statutes said nothing of the properties of trust funds; this was an extraordinary omission, considering the importance of trusts at Christ Church, and clearly required rectification. Prout's other point concerned the allotment of £17,000 to the Chapter: the draft statutes left unclear the number of Canons which was to receive this sum.

At 8 p.m. the Dean and sixteen Students met again (dinner at this time was at 6 p.m. except on Sundays); of those present earlier in the day, Benson, Bayne, Harcourt, Blore, and Shadwell were absent. The Canons had been considering their answer to the Students' letter of earlier that day; their reply, which did not lack ingenuity, was read out by the Dean:

The Canons, as they stated in their communication of Feb[y] 1st, had no intention of submitting the question of the services in the Cath: to arbitration; and they wd not have consented to any arbitration had they supposed this question to be included. They cannot therefore consider themselves bound to accept the Recommendation on this point as it now stands. They have no objection however to submit to the Referees any alterations in the proposed Ordinance, wh. may be agreed upon by the parties concerned; but with the understanding that shd. the Referees decline to act, or shd. they reject such proposed alterations, the freedom of action wh. the Canons at present claim shall not be in any way prejudiced.

The Students tabled motions on the two points at issue, the use of the Cathedral and the Electoral Board. On the first issue the Canons, led by Pusey, had an easy victory, for on the question of Cathedral services Sandford very readily abandoned the objectives which Pusey had attributed to him. Before the Canons joined this meeting Chamberlain and Sandford had proposed a resolution which maintained the Governing Body's power to arrange services for undergraduates and college servants, omitted any mention of the hours during which services should be held, and provided that they should not interfere with the ordinary Cathedral services; the resolution added a curious provision that if the Chapter, or two-thirds of it, thought the arrangements made by the Governing Body 'detrimental to the Cathedral Body', there should be a right of appeal to the Archbishop of Canterbury. This had already been accepted *nem. con.* by the Dean and Students when four Canons (the Sub-Dean, Pusey, Heurtley, and Payne Smith) joined the meeting, followed a little later by Mansel. The ensuing discussions were the first held by Canons and Students together in the Christ Church Senior Common Room under the chairmanship of the Dean.

After further debate concerning the nomination of preachers the Canons withdrew for half an hour to consider Chamberlain's motion; when they returned Pusey put forward a proviso that if the Chapter accepted the services at issue as Cathedral services, the Dean and Chapter should have power to nominate the preachers; and the issue was settled.[1] There was no time to vote on the other outstanding issues that night; and at 10.30 the meeting was adjourned until 4 p.m. the next day.

The next meeting was the last at which non-resident Students were present: the Dean and sixteen Students attended, Harvey and Ingram as non-resident and Faussett and Thompson as resident Students on the Old Foundation, and twelve Senior Students. (Paravicini was present for the first time.) The Dean, surely seizing the right moment, began by asking whether the Canons should attend: Bayne's own minute notes that 'Mr Bayne thought that, when they came to the meeting on Tuesday, matters were much facilitated, and hoped they would be willing to be present now.' If the Canons and all the Students were soon to sit together as one Governing Body, it was clearly time they began to get accustomed to one another. Payne Smith joined the meeting as the Canons' spokesman, expressed the Canons' consent to all the alterations to the Award made the day before, and read a paper explaining the Canons' reasons for wanting the clause setting up a 'Benefices Augmentation Fund' omitted altogether; the meeting accepted unanimously a clause vesting in the new Governing Body 'all trust estates and property now vested in the Dean and Chapter', and a further clause deleting the provision for a Small Benefices Augmentation Fund. It was much to the Canons' credit that the formal move for the vesting of all trust funds in the new Governing Body came from them.

The meeting then discussed the single remaining vexed question of the Election of Students; oddly enough this was nearly to cause a breakdown of the whole negotiation. Prout, seconded by Dodgson, attempted to meet the Canons' objections by proposing that the electors to Studentships should be the Dean, the resident Canons, resident Students

[1] The outcome (in 1869) was a service at 10 a.m. (Cathedral time) on Sundays which was an admired feature of the Oxford Sunday during term until its unfortunate decease in the face of various pressures ninety-nine years later.

who were members of the Governing Body, and such non-resident Senior Students who were asked by the electors to examine at any particular election. During the ensuing discussion, Clerke, Pusey, and Mansel joined the meeting. Pusey expressed the Canons' point of view: they 'had made it clear that the question must be decided, as far as they were concerned, in one of two ways, so that it is rather hard now to find that the very thing they guarded against is forced upon them.' After further discussion the vote was taken, and Prout's motion, the last of many, was (untypically) lost by three votes to ten.[1]

One important question still remained: would Roundell Palmer, to whom the Dean now wrote, pilot the necessary Bill through the House of Commons? The next meeting of Students was held on 15 February; eleven residents were present, and the Dean as chairman. The Canons, however, did not attend, but sent instead the following letter:

> The Canons feel bound to cooperate with the Students in promoting a Bill to give legal effect to the Recommendations as agreed to at the meeting of Tuesday, February 5th; except that they are under the necessity of reserving to themselves the right of opposing the clause concerning the Election of Students, to which they objected as beyond the terms of their reference, and on which the Canons and Students have been unable to agree.

This was signed by Clerke, Pusey, Jelf, Ogilvie, Heurtley, and Payne Smith; but the remaining Canon, Mansel, preferred not to sign, 'on the ground that I was not concerned in the proceedings which led to the Arbitration'. Palmer had agreed to introduce the Bill, provided the Dean could gain 'the consent and acquiescence of Canons as well as Students'; this, in view of the Canons' letter, obviously remained in doubt so far as the Canons were concerned, and it was agreed to submit the necessary papers to Palmer. The

[1] The next day (7 Feb.) a short summary of the Award appeared in *The Churchman* (p. 85; reproduced in *The Guardian* on the 13th), with the comment: 'Whether all its provisions will be suffered to pass unchallenged [through Parliament] remains to be seen.'

meeting also accepted without any opposition a number of amendments (made necessary in part by the amateur efforts of the Students) put forward by Mountague Bernard or by C. W. Lawrence, the Chapter Clerk of Christ Church;[1] four of these were merely verbal, but three were of some importance. Chamberlain's clause for a right of appeal to the Archbishop of Canterbury 'was struck out by veto of the Dean formally, with the consent of the mover (Mr. Chamberlain) and of the Canons'. The disappearance of a provision so calculated to cause future trouble was surely pure gain. Another amendment made it clear that when Jelf's Canonry was voided, the portion of the Chapter Fund assigned to its upkeep should thereafter be at the disposal of the Governing Body. An amendment put forward the previous morning by Collyns to enable the election as Senior Students without examination of Students on the Old Foundation who were qualified to be members of Congregation was 'struck out formally by the veto of the Dean'. The Dean doubtless knew the identities of possible beneficiaries under the amendment; however, a somewhat similar clause was enacted.

On the 19th the Dean and twelve resident Students met to conclude the business. The Dean had explained to Palmer the position of the Canons in the matter of elections to Studentships; Palmer had received this news 'with much regret' for the Canons' opposition to the proposed Bill in part was tantamount to opposition to the whole. It would be his duty to ascertain whether he could introduce the Bill as a public Bill, and whether 'without unanimity (or at least consent), on the part of the Canons', the Crown's consent was at all likely to be obtained. If he had to proceed by a Private Bill, the absence of the Canons' consent would

[1] Charles William Lawrence (nephew of Sir William Lawrence, 1st Bart., the surgeon) was Fellow of New College 1840–50, Chapter Clerk of Christ Church 1857–80; he died in 1883 (*ex inf.* Dr. Penry Williams). In 1870, at a time of financial stringency, the new Governing Body refused to increase his salary, but paid him a £50 'donation' 'for his trouble at the time of the change in the Governing Body'.

be fatal at the outset. The Dean, on receiving Palmer's reply, had called the Canons together, and read Palmer's letter to them. The Canons had then met separately, and drew up the following waiver:

> The Canons, having been led by a communication from the Dean, made to them on this day, to reconsider the Resolution, adopted on Thursday last and signed by the SubDean, Dr Pusey, Dr Jelf, Dr Ogilvie, Dr Heurtley, and Dr Payne Smith, are prepared to withdraw and hereby withdraw that portion of the above mentioned Resolution, which concerns the reservation of a right to oppose one clause of the intended Bill, on the ground that the Referees are now understood by the Canons to have interpreted the language of the original Reference in a sense different from that of both the Students and themselves; and, further, that the present crisis of the affairs of the House demands agreement in action between the two parties within the walls of Christ Church.
>
> (Signed) Charles C. Clerke Sub-Dean
>
> Mr. Mansel, not having signed the Resolution of Thursday last, declined to vote on this occasion.

Two more meetings of Students were held, each in vacation, and each attended by a mere six Students, one on 20 March 1867 to consider a suggestion by the Sub-Dean (the Archdeacon of Oxford) that the Archdeacons of Buckingham and Berkshire become members of the new Chapter (though not of course of the new Governing Body), and one on 10 December 1868 to resolve upon an application to the Visitor (for whom Page Wood, now Lord Chancellor, would act) for a ruling concerning the repairs of the Canons' houses. Clerke himself dropped the first proposal in view of objections from the Dean and other Canons, and nothing happened as a result of the second. The work on the draft statutes was completed with the Canons' final surrender on 19 February.

(*h*) THE CHRIST CHURCH, OXFORD, ACT OF 1867

The Christ Church Ordinances (Oxford) Bill, as it was called during its passage through Parliament, recited the history of the original Ordinances and the recent Reference, repealed the Ordinances of 1858, and (while saving certain vested interests) substituted the Ordinances set forth in the Schedule to the Act. These Ordinances (i.e. the Referees' 'Proposed Statutes' of December 1866, duly numbered, and as amended at Christ Church in February 1867) were to take effect from 11 October 1867 (Old Michaelmas Day), with the exception of clause 28 ('Certain Distinctions abolished'). The Governing Body was given powers to make orders on any matter contained in this clause. The Bill passed through Parliament in June and July 1867 as a public Bill, without incident or material amendment:[1] it was introduced in the Commons by Roundell Palmer, Chichester Fortescue, and W. H. Gladstone, and in the Lords by Archbishop Longley, who was able, at this safe distance from Dr. Pusey, to state as a positive disadvantage under which the Students of Christ Church suffered that 'sermons could not be preached in the chapel for the benefit of the undergraduates'. The only debate occurred on the Second Reading in the Lords on 12 July; it did not, perhaps, concern the most vital matters raised by the Bill—but this is a common fate of well-considered schemes, and one sometimes welcomed, perhaps even organized, by their designers. A trio of Christ Church peers directed their earnest attention to clause 28, with its provisions for the abolition of distinctions of dress, designation, and so on. Lord Stanhope (an

[1] *Parliamentary Debates*, 3rd ser., clxxxvii. 1652, 1776; clxxxviii. 15, 603, 653, 1425–6, 1660, 1708, 1774; clxxxix. 85. Prout had once more sought Ward Hunt's good offices; Hunt replied (13 June 1867) that he would help all he could, but that he foresaw difficulty in Faussett's (the Treasurer's) wish to amend the Bill to allow himself and certain others to marry (Hunt Papers at Northants Record Office; I owe this reference to the kindness of Mr. P. I. King). Faussett's suggestion was not pursued, and the issue was deferred.

Honorary Student) approved the clause; Derby entirely approved the general scope and tenor of the Bill, but thought clause 28 was in effect 'permissive'; Carnarvon disliked the clause because the provision in the Act itself deprived the Dean of a power with reference to the admission of Noblemen and Gentlemen Commoners which he had in the past possessed, and placed him in a position inferior to that of any other Head of a House. Carnarvon did not press his opposition.[1]

One other Christ Church peer had been exercised by clause 28: on 28 February Lord Bute had written to Lord Sandon:

> Respecting a matter about wh. we spoke in London, I believe that the 'arbitrators' appointed to decide upon the differences between the Canons and 'dons' of Ch. Ch. have prepared a bill to be passed in Parliament for the better regulation of the House, wh. has as one of it's proposals that 'all distinctions among the Undergraduates should be abolished' i.e. no more Tufts received. You will view this with as much disgust as I do. Can you not think of some means of defeating this project?[2]

Bute of course exaggerated: it was by no means intended to deny the British peerage admission to Christ Church.[3] In any case Bute was under age, and so unable to take his seat in the Lords: he was indeed still an undergraduate at Christ Church, a status not incompatible with the fact that he wrote to Sandon in Full Term from a Torquay hotel. (To judge from his Battels, Bute seems to have gone down, somewhat early, the previous day.)

The Bill received the Royal Assent on 12 August; the Ordinances annexed to it took effect from 11 October.[4]

[1] *Parliamentary Debates*, 3rd ser., clxxxviii. 1425–7.

[2] Harrowby MSS. xliv, f. 15. (Lord Harrowby kindly provided me with this extract.)

[3] The clause did not operate until 1869; accordingly, although the last Noblemen (Lord Dalmeny, Viscount Petersham, and the Earl of Ilchester) had been admitted in 1866, the last Gentleman Commoner, (Sir) George Chetwynd, was admitted in Jan. 1868.

[4] 30 & 31 Vict, Cap. LXXVI (Shadwell, iii. 355–79).

The first meeting of the enlarged Governing Body took place on 16 October 1867. Dodgson did not record the event in his Diary:[1] the agenda was, undeniably, dull.

[1] i.e. in the summary which covers the period between his return from Russia on 14 Sept. 1867 and the resumption of the Diary proper on 24 Nov. 1867.

VI

The New Christ Church

IT is usually presumptuous to attempt any assessment of the state and well-being of an Oxford college at some particular period; still more so to attempt to assess the effects of any particular constitutional change upon a college's general development. As David Hume once said, human affairs are determined by a great mixture of accident and a small amount of wisdom and foresight. Even to limit a study of the effects of the Act of 1867 upon Christ Church to the period of Dean Liddell's own rule, which ended in 1891, presents its own difficulties: for there were further new statutes in 1882, which prepared the way for the end of the clerical majority upon the Governing Body. As usual, outside critics—notably Mark Pattison, who in 1883 thought little of the House[1]—were not lacking during these years; and those outside critics had an enjoyable field-day a mere three years after the Act, for there then took place the most notorious case of indiscipline in the annals of Christ Church, in the great library riot of 1870.[2] (One by-product of this was the attack on 'Roughs' of the 'University Division' in a moralizing and mediocre later novel of Wilkie Collins.)[3] There is indeed some contrast between the crass vandalism of this riot and the engaging ingenuity of earlier exploits such as the walling-up of the passage under Fell Tower with snow effected by John Astley and his friends in the winter of 1846–7.[4] It is easy to give the facts, to show that the level of

[1] Pattison, *Memoirs*, p. 67.

[2] Hiscock, *Ch. Ch. Miscellany*, pp. 97–101. In view of earlier fears that discipline would suffer if Tutors continued to be excluded from the Governing Body (cf. above, p. 77), it is ironic that this incident took place soon after their admission.

[3] Wilkie Collins, *Man and Wife* (1870), Preface and Appendix.

[4] Sir J. D. Astley, *Fifty Years of my Life* (1894), i. 31.

admissions was rising (at a time when it was rising in all other colleges) and that the performance in the Final Honour Schools, to Dean Liddell's great disappointment, remained patchy; it is harder to assign causes. (For instance, the whole question of teaching methods requires greater attention than it can receive here.) Sir Keith Feiling has reminded us that mutual arrangements among schoolboys, not the fame of any particular college, may determine the nature of a college's entry.[1] There was certainly one parent who deliberately did not send his sons to Christ Church—but this was from dissatisfaction with the reputation of one particular Tutor: the third Marquess of Salisbury objected to the theological views of R. W. Macan, and sent his brilliant sons not to the House but to University College—where in due course Macan himself arrived! That the Governing Body was itself distinguished cannot be doubted, as the names of Harcourt, Baynes, Paget, Hassall, York Powell, and Haverfield are enough to show; the fears of Prout and others[2] that the ablest Christ Church men would obtain Fellowships elsewhere thus became irrelevant, and in any case had lacked substance.[3] That the House continued to produce politicians goes without saying; if no future Prime Minister came up between 1867 and 1919 this was not the fault of the college, but of the Conservatives who did not make Walter Long leader in 1911. It is clear that the country gentlemen were not kept at their books: Dean Liddell had not the gift of Fell or Jackson for this difficult operation. Walter Long looking back on the mid 1870s thought Liddell an 'ideal Dean', but admitted that

[1] K. G. Feiling, *In Christ Church Hall* (1960), p. 161.

[2] cf. above p. 129.

[3] Fellowships at All Souls, taken up between 1855 and 1865 by four men from Christ Church (G. A. J. Scott, Edward Stanhope, C. H. Robarts, and R. C. E. Abbott), were highly valued by the colleges which supplied their winners, as Balliol and Christ Church (in proportions increasingly favourable to the former) so often did. Fellowships elsewhere were taken up from Christ Church at this time by C. L. Shadwell (Oriel), R. Williams (Merton), R. G. Archibald and H. McNeile (St. John's), and J. A. Owen (University College)—but not until 1864 and thereafter.

amusements should have been curtailed, for 'we were subject to no control', and there was too much drinking and gambling.[1] (On the other hand, the Dean and Censors had ejected Rosebery for what was thought excessive addiction to the Turf; and there are striking examples of peers who did work at their books.) In one respect, however, the products of the House did change. It can hardly be claimed that Christ Church suddenly began, as in Elizabethan days, to produce literary men, for Stanley Weyman (1874) is but a modest addition to the attenuated list of such nineteenth-century Christ Church literary figures as Martin Tupper;[2] but it did produce scientists. The list given by A. E. Gunther,[3] of Sir William Thiselton-Dyer and others, is a most distinguished one, and a great tribute to the teaching of Harcourt and of Baynes, the Lee's Reader in Physics from 1872 onwards. The creation of the two new Lee's Readerships under the Ordinances of 1858 and 1867 respectively was a most fruitful step.

The importance of the Act of 1867 lay not only in what it achieved but also in what was avoided in the agitation for it. By and large little bitterness was created. This account may conjure up visions of a Christ Church which for nearly three years was hopelessly riven by internecine feuds, with

[1] Viscount Long, *Memories* (1923), pp. 38–43 (his portrait of Vere Bayne is full of affection); contrast Lord Redesdale's criticisms of Liddell in the later 1850s in *Memories* (1915), i. 100. On Liddell's rule, cf. Feiling, *In Christ Church Hall*, p. 130: 'To "work like a tiger", Dean Jackson's recipe for Peel, had lost its appeal for the sons of the country houses, and the college place in the class lists steadily declined. Liddell's sway was benevolent, majestic, but in its social consequences selective, and many survivors would deplore the class discrimination which weakened that fine facade.' After all, the Dean was under conflicting pressures: had not his former pupil, Lord Elcho, expressed to him on his appointment his confidence 'that in your hands Christ Church will hold out every possible inducement to us to send our sons there, in the full confidence that you will turn them into *gentlemen* and useful members of society'? (Thompson, *H. G. Liddell*, p. 132).

[2] The subject cannot be gone into here; but Mr. Bill considers that evidence from Christ Church suggests that those who framed the new Honours School of Law and Modern History in the hope that it would interest and profit the aristocracy and gentry were in fact justified by events.

[3] A. E. Gunther, *Early Science in Oxford*, xi. 225.

open meetings and secret conciliabula of Students, and no doubt of Canons too, taking place in stray corners of the college. In fact this was not the case at all. The tolerance normally characteristic of the place prevailed. Ordinary business went on, and meetings of the Dean and Chapter and of the Electoral Board took their accustomed course and discussed the business appropriate to each. Moreover the usual civilities continued: there is no hint in Dodgson's or Liddon's diary that social relations ceased.[1] There is no sign that this new and temporary division of opinion among colleagues divided Christ Church into two permanently hostile camps. It is, after all, a saving virtue of the increased activity of University and colleges since 1850 that the multiplication of possible subjects of difference normally prevents any one subject of difference from determining personal friendship and enmity to the exclusion of others: ranks break and re-form with great rapidity.

The Christ Church dispute certainly cut across all other lines. It was not a dispute of Liberal against Conservative: most Students and some Canons supported Gladstone in the University election of 1865 in which Clerke and Jacobson chaired Hardy's and Gladstone's Committees respectively. It was not a quarrel of High Church against Low Church, for Canons and Students numbered some of each persuasion within their ranks: Pusey and Heurtley, Chamberlain and Dodgson, were very far apart. It was not a dispute of clerics against anti-clericals, but one of some clerics with a few laymen against other clerics. The dispute did not, thanks to the moderation of all concerned and the good sense of the Referees, involve the question of the endowments of the Church of England. It was obviously not a contest of gremial members of the House against 'foreigners'. It did not concern the nature of education

[1] For instance, on 5 Dec. 1866, during the last stages of the Reference, Dodgson dined at the Deanery and had 'one of the pleasantest evenings I have had there for a very long time' (*Carroll Diaries*, i. 249). Perhaps Alice was present?

within Christ Church, though to some extent it did concern the selection of undergraduates for Christ Church, in that the Students wished to deprive the Canons of the share in that process which they had recently acquired. To some extent the battle was one of old against young: older canons were unlikely to accept change, while the arrival of younger ones was bound to stimulate the Students' desire for change. In the main the struggle was a special version, in a unique context, of the well-known wider struggle of Tutors against Professors; but the Professors at Christ Church were not only, as most Professors in the University were, in Anglican Orders but also the holders of Canonical stalls. It was unusual, as yet, for Professors to be Fellows of colleges; the presence of so many at Christ Church was unique. The tussle was one for academic power and for a more equitable distribution of endowments. Once it was over, fresh issues supervened to occupy the members of the new Governing Body. The Canons accepted their altered position, and the Dean, 'pre-eminently good as a Chairman',[1] guided the new body with skill.

It follows that the lengthiest printed explanation of the Students' motives is inadequate. In 1935 E. W. Watson, Regius Professor of Ecclesiastical History from 1908 to 1934, summed up the story as he saw it thus:

> It will be remembered that they [i.e. the Canons] had no control of the College as an educational institution, with Dean, Censors and Tutors. Still, there was a reason why the students should desire that the system should continue. By an unwritten but strictly observed rule vacancies in six canonries—those to which the ancient professorships of Divinity and Hebrew were not attached—should be filled from the ranks of those who were, or had been, Students. In any individual case the prospect may not have been bright, but it was valued as a collective possibility. But in 1842 two more professorships were endowed with canonries, and a few years later a third, while in 1854 two canonries were ordered to be suppressed on the next avoidance, and the one

[1] Thompson, *H. G. Liddell*, p. 194.

remaining was annexed to the Archdeaconry of Oxford. There was deep resentment among the Students at the deprivation of their hope, and a most clerical body plunged into anti-clerical agitation.[1]

This account, which omits to mention the Ordinance of 1858, needs amplification in three particulars. Whatever the hopes of earlier Students, hopes amply realized in the cases of Bull and Barnes, the Senior Students under the Ordinance wanted to be not Canons, but Students with the powers of Fellows of other colleges; and while the Canons (except the Sub-Dean) had indeed had 'no control of the College as an educational institution' in former times, after 1858 they did, under the Ordinance, come to have some such control, and this at a time when the Canons themselves were to a steadily decreasing extent Christ Church men. Finally the Students' conduct over the control of the Cathedral services should suffice to show that their agitation was not 'anti-clerical'. If a single adjective is required, the agitation was above all anti-professorial.

The credit for the swift and conclusive outcome of the dispute belongs to several men. Dean Liddell certainly did not take the initiative;[2] but had he chosen, or wished, to exert himself he could doubtless have held matters up; and during the final meetings he was not afraid to employ a decanal veto when circumstances required it. (H. L. Thompson, a former pupil of the Dean quotes Sandford's tribute to his 'impartial and conciliatory attitude . . . throughout'[3].) During the last stages Payne Smith exerted a moderating influence. The Censors' conduct, Sandford as chairman, Bayne as secretary with his impeccable minutes, played its part; but the main credit undoubtedly must go to Prout. He was over-optimistic at times, but combined a perception of

[1] E. W. Watson, *The Cathedral Church of Christ in Oxford* (1935), pp. 68–9.

[2] The positive nature of the Dean's role is probably exaggerated by C. E. Mallet, *A History of the University of Oxford*, iii. 382–3, in his summary of these changes at Christ Church.

[3] Thompson, *H. G. Liddell*, p. 145.

the main needs of the situation with a clear notion that good causes only triumph when furthered by sound organization and correct procedure; and (unlike Dr. Pusey on a famous earlier occasion), when he wanted something done, he went to those who could do it. Few Third Class men can have exercised greater influence on the development of their college than T. J. Prout.

All things considered, the whole affair was settled remarkably quickly and efficiently, as so often in such cases. Probably the Students' victory could not in any case have been long delayed: Payne Smith's moderate position, and Mansel's aloof one, suggest that as vacancies among the Canon-Professors occurred, resistance by the Chapter would have been less and less effective. However, had the Act not come when it did, well before the appointment of the Commission of 1872, change at Christ Church might, as Prout feared, have come in a very altered form. There was much of the old Christ Church (such as the non-professorial Canonries or the 101 Students) which Prout could not possibly hope to restore; but he did want to retain the Cathedral connection in its existing form. The new Statutes which came into force in 1882 ensured the ultimate disappearance of the clerical majority on the Governing Body; and in December 1879, when this outcome was seen to be inevitable,[1] Liddon wanted the Chapter 'at least to *consider* the advisability of separating the Cathedral and Chapter of

1 The balance on the Governing Body was narrow: the draft Statutes, submitted by it to the Commission in June 1878, provided for at least eight 'Prize Studentships' and an unstated number of 'Educational Studentships'. Of the latter, one-third were to be in Holy Orders at the time of election; but this had only been carried by fifteen to fourteen, and would have been rejected (in favour, apparently, of a lower proportion) by seventeen to sixteen had all been present. However, the new Statutes as 'partly settled' by the Commissioners in Nov. 1879, laid down that not less than six 'Educational Students' should be in Orders, thus making it probable that the remaining (? ten) such Students, and all or most of the 'prize Students' would be laymen and that the Governing Body would thus contain up to about twenty-seven laymen (including the Lee's Readers) and not more than thirteen ordained members. (Documents in Ch. Ch. Library MS. 514.)

the Diocese of Oxford from Christ Church as it is to be', for then 'the unbelieving elements' could, as he thought, no longer be kept sufficiently 'at bay', and he would want 'a separation, not in the interests of Christ Church, but in the interests of the Church of Christ'.[1] Liddon's fears of the lay majority were misplaced;[2] but the changed conditions after 1882 (quite unforeseen by the Chapter in 1867, when there was no thought of a lay majority), together with one or two particular incidents, did at times lead to greater tension; this in turn may have created a tradition of constant previous tension under the old system and at its end which anti-clericals were glad to foster but which has little basis in fact.

C. M. Blagden had left attractive pictures of the three survivors of the agitation as they were some thirty years later; of the five senior Senior Students of 1865, Pickard and Sandford had both long ceased to be members of the Governing Body, but Dodgson, Bayne, and Prout were all still resident, Dodgson increasingly remote from his colleagues and the world, and Bayne as friendly, courteous, and devoted to the House as ever. Bayne and Prout seemed to Blagden equally reactionary.[3] His portrait of Prout deserves quotation:

> It is interesting to note how the revolutionaries of one generation become the diehards of the next. Prout's fame lingered on

[1] Johnston, *Liddon*, pp. 249–50. The whole section (pp. 249–53) is extremely interesting.

[2] He may have been disturbed by the fact that the Committee appointed by the 'Teaching Staff' in Dec. 1877 to submit new statutes had recommended that the appointment of Cathedral preachers at collegiate services during Full Term should be vested alternately in the Dean and Chapter and the Governing Body, on which there would ultimately be a lay majority. This must have caused in Pusey (though no record of his views has been found) and in Liddon the same fears which Pusey had expressed in 1867. (After all, Dean Stanley and Dr. Jowett were still alive.) But the proposal was rejected by the Governing Body. Unhappily, Bayne's minutes as Secretary of the G.B. during these years are less informative and more reticent than those which he had kept as Secretary to the Students in 1865–7.

[3] The obituary in *The Oxford Magazine*, xxvi (1907–8), 355, said of Bayne, understandably but incorrectly, 'What changes he had witnessed in his

when I joined Christ Church as that of 'the man who slew the Canons', for in the middle of last century he had been one of those who helped to disestablish the old regime, and to secure the rightful place of the Students in the government of the House. But there was not much of the revolutionary left in 1896. He was then a little old man, living by himself, separated by increasing deafness from the society of his fellows, watching from afar the things which he so much disliked. He did not like the clothes of the modern undergraduate. He hated to see them smoke in the quadrangle. . . . He had reduced starvation to a fine art, but he was a poor advertisement of it, for all the winter through he suffered agonies from chilblains, and try as he would could find no remedy. But he was never surly or sullen or anything but the prince of courtesy to us all, and we who laughed at his funny old-fashioned ways had a deep regard for him and, when he went, felt that Christ Church was the poorer for his going.[1]

Prout outlived Dodgson by eleven years, Sandford by six, Pickard by four, and Bayne and Faussett by one; he died in 1909 as the last survivor of the Senior Students named in 1858. (Benson, the last Student on the Old Foundation, died in 1915, having been a Student for over sixty-eight years; E. S. Talbot, the last survivor of the Senior Students elected between 1858 and 1867, died in 1934.) It is hard to see in the chilblain-ridden octogenarian described by Blagden the brisk athletic leader of the Senior Students of forty years before; and to Prout's sole surviving colleague he seems the last man likely to be an agitator.[2] But Prout has been proved right; thanks to the co-operation of the victors and the vanquished of 1867 and their successors, the 'joint government', though anomalous, indeed unique, has passed the greatest test. No one would create it *de novo*; but it has worked.

sixty years of academic life. He regretted them all'; but it was quite right to say that Bayne 'had, indeed, a large toleration for the aberrations of a Christ Church man'.

[1] C. M. Blagden, *Well Remembered* (1953), pp. 111–12.

[2] The Revd. R. F. McNeile (Student, 1902–8) who also confirms the complete reliability of Blagden's recollections.

APPENDIX I

'The Fourteen Points'

The Oxford University Commissioners to the Dean of Christ Church, 10 December 1856:

Very Reverend Sir,

The Oxford University Commissioners direct me to communicate to you, and to request that you will lay before the Chapter the Scheme which they have framed in order to carry out the objects of the Act in relation to your House.

In framing this Scheme the Commissioners have been guided by the conviction that, to enable Ch. Ch. henceforth to maintain its position in the University, it is desirable to employ all the available resources of the House in sustaining its efficiency and attractiveness as a place of Education. With this view the Commissioners propose

1. That, in place of the Hundred and One Permanent Studentships, there shall henceforth be in the House *sixteen* Senior Studentships and sixty one Junior Studentships.

2. That the Senior Students shall furnish the Educational Staff of the College, and shall be elected out of the whole University, with special reference to the interests of the House as a place of Education.

3. That the Value of the Senior Studentships shall be at least £200 a year. It is calculated that the Tuition Fee being added to the Studentship, might raise the Incomes of eight Tutors to Sums ranging from £450 to £800.

4. That the Senior Students shall be required to reside for ten years from the date of their Election. The excess of the number of Senior Students over the number required as Tutors will probably give a sufficient margin for Superannuation after ten years service as Tutors.

5. That of the Sixty One Junior Studentships Forty, including

the Vernon, shall be open to general competition; and that the remaining Twenty One shall be appropriated to Westminster School.

6. That the Open Junior Studentships shall be of the annual value of *£80* and tenable for five years, the period generally adopted for the tenure of Scholarships in other Colleges.

7. That the Westminster Students shall receive *£46* per annum from the Funds of the House in addition to the Lee Exhibitions. It is calculated that the Lee Estate might afford twenty one Exhibitions of *£74* which would make the total value of the Studentships, with the Exhibitions attached, *£120* per annum. It is proposed that these Studentships shall be tenable for seven years, on account of Dr Carey's benefaction, which will be enjoyable by Graduates only.

8. That of the eight Open Studentships, which will be vacant each year, three shall be appropriated to the encouragement of Mathematics and the Physical Sciences. But that this appropriation shall terminate at the end of twenty years.

9. That the Students, Senior and Junior, shall be elected by the Dean, Canons, and Senior Students.

10. That the Direction of the Instruction & Discipline of the House be vested in the Dean, SubDean, and Senior Students.

11. That the power of depriving Students shall remain vested in the Dean & Chapter.

12. That two Canonries shall be suppressed, if needful to carry out the Scheme. That half the Income of one of these Canonries shall be appropriated to the Domus Fund, which appears to stand in need of assistance. That the other half of this Canonry and the whole of the other Canonry shall be applied, with the revenues of the present Studentships and the Bostock Exhibitions, in giving effect to the objects of this Scheme.

13. That the Fell, Boulter, Pauncefort, Gardiner, Frampton, Cotton, and Paul Exhibitions shall form a Fund to be applied partly to Prizes and Exhibitions open to competition among the Members of the House, and partly to the institution of Exhibitions to be assigned to poor Students by the Dean, without competition.

14. Enclosed is a copy of a Memorial addressed by the Chaplains to the Commissioners. It does not appear to the Commissioners that the position of the Chaplains is, at present, a satisfactory one;

and they would suggest for the consideration of the Chapter the expediency of diminishing the number in order to increase the Incomes.[1]

The Commissioners will be happy to receive any Observations which the Governing Body of your House may have to make on the foregoing Scheme.

I have the honour to be

&c. &c. &c.

(Ch. Ch. Archives, MS. Estates 117, ff. 32–8)

[1] The number was reduced to six in 1860. It is now (1968) two.

APPENDIX II

Ordinances Concerning Christ Church, 1858

GENERAL ORDINANCE, FRAMED BY THE COMMISSIONERS

We, the Commissioners appointed for the purposes of an Act passed in the seventeenth and eighteenth years of the reign of Her Majesty Queen Victoria, intituled 'An Act to make further Provision for the good Government and Extension of the University of Oxford, of the Colleges therein, and of the College of Saint Mary Winchester,' ordain as follows in relation to the Cathedral or House of Christ Church in Oxford:—

1. The first and second Canonries in the said Cathedral or House, which shall become vacant after the approval of this Ordinance by Her Majesty in Council, not being Canonries annexed by law or custom to any Professorship or Archdeaconry, shall not be filled up.

2. In place of the hundred and one Studentships now existing within the said House, there shall be established and maintained within the House twenty-eight Senior Studentships and fifty-two Junior Studentships, twenty-one of which shall be called Westminster Junior Studentships, and the remaining thirty-one are herein-after referred to as open Junior Studentships. Of the open Junior Studentships there shall be seven which shall be called the Fell Studentships, two which shall be called the Bostock Studentships, and two which shall be called respectively the Vernon and the Boulter Studentships.

3. Two of the said twenty-eight Senior Students shall be maintained out of the income of the lands and tenements now held by the Dean and Chapter under the will of Dr. Matthew Lee, with emoluments not less than Two hundred pounds each *per annum*, exclusive of rooms, but inclusive of all other allowances. Such two Senior Students shall be called respectively Dr. Lee's Reader in Anatomy, and Dr. Lee's Reader in Chemistry. The

former of the said two Studentships shall be established as speedily as possible after the approval of this Ordinance by Her Majesty in Council if the Readership in Anatomy founded by the said Dr. Matthew Lee shall then be vacant, or, if not, immediately after the first vacancy therein, in substitution for that Readership, which shall not hereafter be filled up. The emoluments of the other Senior Studentships shall be Two hundred pounds each *per annum*, exclusive of rooms, but inclusive of all other allowances, or as near thereto as the funds available for the time being will permit. The emoluments of the open Junior Studentships shall be Seventy-five pounds each *per annum*, exclusive of rooms, but inclusive of all other allowances; those of the Westminster Junior Studentships shall at the first establishment thereof respectively be not less than Seventy-five pounds each *per annum*, and shall be raised as speedily as may be to such amount, not less than One hundred and fifteen pounds nor more than One hundred and twenty-five pounds each *per annum*, as the Dean and Chapter shall determine. There shall be applied towards the maintenance of the Senior Studentships (other than those held by the said Dr. Lee's Readers), and of the said fifty-two Junior Studentships, the emoluments of the existing hundred and one Studentships as the same shall become vacant, and the emoluments of the aforesaid two Canonries (subject to a deduction out of the gross emoluments of each Canonry of all payments now usually made out of such emoluments): Provided that the emoluments of the said Canonries shall be applicable to the maintenance of such of the Senior Studentships as are herein-after termed Clerical Studentships, yet not so as to raise the emoluments of any Clerical Studentship above those of any Lay Studentship, or to increase the number of Clerical Studentships beyond the amount herein-after mentioned. The emoluments of the Exhibitions of the foundations of Bishop Fell, of Archbishop Boulter for Commoners, and of Mrs. Bostock, shall be applied towards the maintenance of the said thirty-one open Junior Studentships. An annual sum of One thousand two hundred and sixty pounds out of the income of the said lands and tenements, together with the emoluments of the Exhibitions of the foundations of Dr. South, Dr. Frewin, and Canon Hill, shall be applied towards the maintenance of the twenty-one Westminster Junior Studentships. The provisions of this Ordinance shall not be construed to extend to or include the estate held under the will of Bishop Wood for the benefit of the Senior Masters of the House, being Students, or any payments or allowances which may be made thereout pursuant to the said will, except that holders of Senior Studentships shall, and holders of Junior Studentships shall not, be deemed Students of the House within the meaning of the said will.

4. If after the whole number of the aforesaid twenty-eight and fifty-two Studentships shall have been completed, with the full emoluments specified in the next preceding clause, the Dean and Chapter shall have at their disposal, from the sources hereinbefore made applicable to the maintenance of the Senior Studentships (other than those held by the Lee's Readers) and of the fifty-two Junior Studentships, means sufficient for the purpose, it shall be lawful for them to establish and maintain within the house, besides the said twenty-eight and fifty-two Studentships, any number of additional Senior Studentships not exceeding twelve, and any number of additional Junior Studentships not exceeding nine. It shall also be lawful for the Dean and Chapter, at any time, to establish and maintain, out of any funds at their disposal not appropriated by this and the next preceding clause, any number of additional Senior and Junior Studentships which they may think fit. The electors, mode and conditions of election, emoluments, and conditions of tenure, to and of the additional Senior and Junior Studentships, shall be the same as are herein prescribed with respect to the said twenty-eight Senior and thirty-one open Junior Studentships (other than the Vernon Studentship) respectively.

5. The election of Senior Students (including the Lee's Readers) shall be vested in the Dean, the Canons, the two Censors, and the four Senior Tutors of the House, and shall be held on a stated day or stated days in each year, to be appointed by the electors, subject to the provision for postponement herein-after contained; and notice of such intended election, and of the conditions of election, shall be given by the Dean, in such manner as he shall deem best adapted to secure publicity, thirty days at least before the day of election. It shall be lawful for the electors whenever they shall think fit, having regard to the subjects of examination, to appoint an assessor or assessors, not being more than two in number, to assist them in examining candidates for Senior and Junior Studentships.

6. The Senior Students shall be persons of unblemished character, conforming to the Liturgy of the United Church of England and Ireland as by law established, who shall have passed all the examinations required by the University for the degree of Bachelor of Arts, unmarried, and not disqualified by the possession of any such property, benefice, pension, or office, as herein-after mentioned. The candidates shall be examined in such subjects connected with the studies of the University as the electors shall determine; provided that the system of examinations shall be such as shall render Senior Studentships accessible from time to time to excellence in every branch of knowledge for the time being recognized in the Schools of the University; and the electors shall choose that candidate who after such examination shall appear to them to be of the greatest merit and most fit to be a Senior Student of the House as a place of religion, learning, and education. That candidate for whom the greatest number of votes shall have been given shall be deemed elected. In case of an equality of votes, the Dean, or in his absence the Sub-Dean, or in the absence of both, the senior Canon present, shall give an additional casting vote.

7. Of the said twenty-eight Senior Studentships, nine (including the Lee's Readerships) shall be Lay and nineteen shall be Clerical Studentships. The holders of the Lay Studentships shall not be required, as a condition of retaining their Studentships, to take Holy Orders; but if any Lay Student should do so, then upon the next vacancy in a Clerical Studentship a Lay Student shall be elected, so that the aforesaid proportion between Lay and Clerical Studentships shall always be preserved as nearly as may be. No person shall be eligible to a Clerical Studentship who shall not either be a Priest or Deacon of the United Church of England and Ireland, or declare that he intends to take Holy Orders in the said Church. Every person who shall have made such declaration, or who, at the time of his election, shall be in Deacon's Orders, shall be required to take Priest's Orders within four years after the time at which he shall be of sufficient standing, according to the Statutes of the University, to take the degree of Master of Arts, and in default thereof shall vacate his Studentship: Provided that it shall be lawful for the Dean and Chapter, in case of sickness, or for any other very urgent cause, to grant a delay for a period not exceeding six months. The said twelve additional

Senior Studentships mentioned in clause 4, or so many of them as may be established under that clause, shall likewise be divided into Clerical and Lay Studentships, one at least in every three being a Lay Studentship. Any other additional Senior Studentships, which the Dean and Chapter may establish under the same clause out of funds not appropriated as aforesaid, may also be divided in the same or any other proportion, or may be exclusively Lay or Clerical, as the Dean and Chapter may think fit. The Lee's Readers in Anatomy and Chemistry shall be persons qualified to teach those sciences respectively, and shall be bound to lecture or otherwise give instruction therein as the Dean and Chapter may direct. No person in Holy Orders shall be eligible to either of the said Readerships, and any Reader who shall take Holy Orders shall thereupon vacate his Studentship.

8. Every person elected to a Senior Studentship shall undergo probation for twelve calendar months from the day of his election inclusive, and at the end of such twelve calendar months shall be admitted an actual Senior Student, if found fit in the judgment of the then electors to Senior Studentships. Every person admitted to probation shall receive during the period of probation the same emoluments as if he had been admitted an actual Senior Student, but shall not be entitled to vote on any occasion.

9. Every Senior Student who shall marry shall thereupon vacate his Studentship.

10. Every Senior Student who shall be instituted to an ecclesiastical benefice, or shall become entitled either by descent or devolution, or by virtue of any testamentary or other gift or settlement, to property, or to any government pension, or be admitted to any office tenable for life or during good behaviour (not being an academical office within the University of Oxford), and who shall retain such benefice, property, pension, or office, for twelve calendar months from the day of his institution, accession, or admission thereto, shall, if such ecclesiastical benefice be a benefice with cure of souls, (except in certain cases to be specified as herein-after mentioned,) or if the annual income derivable by him from such property, pension, or office, or from any ecclesiastical benefice without cure of souls, or from any two or more of the above-mentioned sources (including or not including a benefice with cure of souls), clear of deductions (except for property or

income tax), shall exceed Five hundred pounds, vacate his Studentship at the expiration of such twelve calendar months; and for this purpose the income which the estimated value of any property would produce, if invested in Three pounds per centum Consolidated Annuities, at the price current at the time of the acquisition thereof, shall, in case of doubt, be considered to be the income derivable from such property. It shall be lawful for the Dean, Canons, two Censors, and four Senior Tutors to declare, by a bye-law or bye-laws, in what cases a benefice with cure of souls may be tenable with a Senior Studentship. The word 'property' shall in this clause include any estate or interest in possession in any property real or personal. In any case in which the property or sources of income may have been acquired at several times, the latest time at which any part of such property, or any of such sources of income, shall have been acquired shall, in construing this clause, be considered as the time of the acquisition of the whole thereof. It shall be lawful for the Dean and Chapter to require from any Senior Student any information which they may deem necessary for enabling them to enforce the provisions of this clause.

11. It shall be lawful for the electors to Senior Studentships to elect distinguished persons to Honorary Studentships within the House. Persons so elected shall be termed Honorary Students, and shall not be entitled to vote on any occasion as Students, or to receive any emolument whatever, but shall be entitled to enjoy such other privileges and advantages as the said electors shall by resolution from time to time determine. The conditions of eligibility to and tenure of Honorary Studentships, and the mode of election thereto, may also be determined by the electors from time to time. Honorary Students shall not, in the construction of this Ordinance, be counted among the Students of the House, nor Honorary Studentships among the Studentships of the House.

12. Every Senior Student who shall be appointed to a Canonry in the House (whether annexed to a Professorship or not), or shall be elected to and accept a Headship or Fellowship in any College within the University, shall thereupon vacate his Studentship.

13. The Dean, Canons, two Censors, and four Senior Tutors shall, within six calendar months after the approval of this Ordinance by Her Majesty in Council, and from time to time thereafter,

make such regulations respecting the residence of Senior Students within the University, and respecting the mode in which and the conditions under which leave of absence may be granted to any Senior Student, as they may deem expedient for the interests of the House as a place of learning and education, and may vary such regulations from time to time, and may enforce such regulations, if they shall think fit, by pecuniary penalties, and, in case of contumacious non-compliance, by deprivation.

14. Every holder of a Clerical Studentship shall be required to take the degree of Master of Arts within one year after the time at which he shall be of sufficient standing to take that degree by the Statutes of the University; and every holder of a Lay Studentship shall be required to take either the degree of Master of Arts, or the degrees of Bachelor and Doctor of Civil Law, or those of Bachelor and Doctor of Medicine, within one year after the times at which he shall be of sufficient standing to take those degrees respectively by the Statutes of the University. Any Student failing to comply with the foregoing provisions shall vacate his Studentship; provided that the Dean, Canons, two Censors, and four Senior Tutors may, whenever they shall deem it just on special grounds to do so, allow the taking of any such degree to be postponed for a period not exceeding, except in case of unsoundness of mind or disability of body, one year.

15. Any Senior Student who shall, in the judgment of the Dean, Canons, two Censors, and four Senior Tutors, or the greater part of them, have been proved guilty of grave immorality, or of contumaciously ceasing to conform to the Liturgy of the United Church of England and Ireland as by law established, shall cease to be a Student of the House; and every Senior Student who shall in like manner have been judged guilty of conduct bringing dishonour upon the House, of gross negligence or misconduct in any office within the same, or of contumacious non-observance of the Statutes or Bye-laws of the House, or of grossly offensive behaviour towards any member thereof, may be deprived of his Studentship by the Dean, Canons, two Censors, and four Senior Tutors, if, in the judgment of them or the greater part of them, the gravity of the offence shall so require.

16. The Westminster Junior Studentships shall be filled up at Westminster School, on the Wednesday in Rogation Week in each year, by election from those boys on the Royal Foundation

of the Collegiate Church of Westminster who shall have been presented as candidates by the Head Master of the said school. The electors shall be those who, if this Ordinance had not been made, would have been entitled to elect to Studentships under the Statutes of the said Collegiate Church. The candidates shall be examined in such subjects as shall have been previously selected by the Head Master with the approval of the Dean of the said Collegiate Church, and in such manner as the electors shall determine; and those candidates shall be elected who, after such examination, shall appear to the electors to be of the greatest merit and who shall desire to proceed to Christ Church, and shall, in the judgment of the Dean of Christ Church, or his duly appointed representative, present at the election, be in all respects fit to be admitted Students of the House. Whenever there shall be no duly qualified candidate for a Westminster Junior Studentship of sufficient merit for election in the judgment of the majority of the electors, and fit as aforesaid to be admitted a Student of the House, the election to such Studentship shall be postponed to the next annual election day; but if there shall then be no duly qualified candidate of sufficient merit for election, and fit as aforesaid, such Studentship shall be thrown open for that turn to general competition as an open Junior Studentship, and the election thereto shall be held at Christ Church by the same persons, after public notice for the same time, and after an examination conducted in the same manner as an ordinary election to an open Junior Studentship.

17. The Patron of the Vernon Studentship shall be the same as of the Vernon Studentship existing within the House at the time of the date of this Ordinance. The election to the remaining thirty open Junior Studentships shall be vested in the electors to the Senior Studentships. The election to open Junior Studentships, other than the Vernon Studentship, shall be held on a stated day or stated days in each year to be appointed by the electors, subject to the provision for postponement herein-after contained; and notice of such intended election, and of the conditions of election, shall be given by the Dean, in such manner as he shall deem best adapted to ensure publicity, thirty days at least before the day of election. The candidates shall be examined in such subjects as the electors shall determine; and that candidate shall be elected who, after such examination, shall

appear to the electors to be of the greatest merit and most fit to be a Student of the House; provided that in elections to one in every three open Junior Studentships the subjects of competitive examination shall be alternately Mathematics and Physical Science. On each vacancy occurring in the Vernon Studentship, the Patron shall be required to appoint an election thereto at the next ensuing election to open Junior Studentships. The candidates shall be examined by such persons and in such manner as the Patron shall appoint; and that candidate shall be chosen who after such examination shall appear to the Patron to be of the greatest merit. If the Patron shall decline or neglect to appoint an election and examiners, thirty days' previous notice at least having been given to him by the Dean, the election to the Vernon Studentship shall be held for that turn by the same persons and in the same manner as to the other open Junior Studentships; provided that no candidate for the Vernon Studentship, or for any of the Studentships appropriated to the encouragement of Mathematics and Physical Science as aforesaid, shall be entitled to be admitted to a Studentship if in the judgment of the electors to open Junior Studentships he shall not be in all respects fit to be a Student of the House.

18. No person shall be admissible as a candidate for any open Junior Studentship who shall have completed the eighth Term inclusive from the date of his matriculation, or who shall not have produced a certificate of baptism and testimonials of his moral character satisfactory to the Dean: Provided that the foregoing regulation, so far as it relates to the University standing of the candidates, shall not take effect until after the first election shall have been held to open Junior Studentships, if such first election shall be held within six months after the approval of this Ordinance by Her Majesty in Council.

19. Each Westminster Junior Studentship shall be tenable until the Tuesday in Rogation Week in the seventh year from the day of election inclusive, and no longer. Any Junior Studentship which shall be filled up at Westminster School at an election postponed under the foregoing provisions shall be tenable until the Teusday in Rogation Week in the sixth year from the day of election inclusive, and no longer. Any Westminster Junior Studentship which shall be thrown open to general competition shall be tenable until the expiration of the period for which it

would have been tenable if the election thereto had not been postponed, and no longer. Each open Junior Studentship shall be tenable for five years from the day of election inclusive, and no longer. The electors to the Junior Studentships shall not be required to fill up in any one year more than three Westminster Junior Studentships (exclusive of any Studentship the election to which may have been postponed under the foregoing provisions,) nor (until the said nine additional open Junior Studentships shall have been established) more than six open Junior Studentships.

20. The whole number of the said twenty-eight Senior and fifty-two Junior Studentships shall be completed as speedily as the amount of the funds gradually becoming available will permit. The relative rate at which the whole number of Senior and Junior Studentships shall be established shall be in the discretion of the Dean and Chapter; provided that three Westminster Junior Studentships of the value of at least Seventy-five pounds each *per annum*, exclusive of rooms, (to be raised with all convenient speed to One hundred and fifteen pounds *per annum* at least, exclusive of rooms), shall be established in every year in which the Dean and Chapter shall have in their hands sufficient means for the purpose, arising from the funds herein-before made available thereto, other than the emoluments of either of the said two Canonries; and it shall be lawful for the Dean and Chapter, in order to enable themselves to establish such three Studentships yearly, to apply to that purpose from time to time, and so long as it may be necessary, in addition to the said sum of One thousand two hundred and sixty pounds, any portion of the income of the estates and funds held under the will of Dr. M. Lee which shall not be required for carrying into effect the provisions of this Ordinance and the other regulations for the time being in force respecting the application of the said income. The present Censors, Readers, Tutors, and Lecturers of the House shall, without election or admission, be Senior Students of the House, and their emoluments in respect of their Studentships shall be increased to the annual sum of Two hundred pounds previous to the establishment of any other Senior Studentships. One Lay Studentship shall, as nearly as may be, be established for every two Clerical Studentships, until the whole number of nine Lay Studentships shall have been completed.

21. Every Junior Student, and every member of the House under the degree of Master of Arts, shall be subject to such general regulations as to residence, discipline, and attendance on Divine Worship, as the Dean, Canons, the two Censors, and the four Senior Tutors of the House shall from time to time determine; and any Junior Student may be deprived of his Studentship by the same persons, or the greater part of them, for any misconduct which in their judgment shall merit deprivation, subject to such appeal to the Visitor as is herein-after provided. Every Junior Student who shall marry, be elected to a Senior Studentship, or to a place on the foundation of any other Collegiate Body within the University, shall thereby vacate his Studentship.

22. Whenever there shall be no duly qualified candidate for a vacant Senior or open Junior Studentship whom the electors or the Patron, as the case may be, shall judge of sufficient merit for election, and whenever a Senior or open Junior Studentship shall fall vacant, and there shall not be time to give the notice herein-before directed before the day of election, the election shall be postponed to some other day, to be fixed by the electors or the Patron for the purpose, not later than the next ensuing stated day of election, in the case of a Senior Studentship, to Senior Studentships, and in the case of an open Junior Studentship, to open Junior Studentships; and every such postponed election shall be held and conducted in the same manner, and after the same previous notice, as if there had been no postponement. In the case of any open Junior Studentship, the election to which shall have been postponed under the provisions of this Ordinance, the term of five years shall be computed from the day on which the election would have been held if there had been no postponement.

23. Bye-laws binding on the Senior Students (not being repugnant to any of the Statutes of the House in force for the time being) may be made by the Dean, Canons, and Senior Students; and such Bye-laws may be enforced by pecuniary penalties.

24. Every question which may arise at any meeting of the Dean, Canons, Censors, and four Senior Tutors, or of the Dean, Canons, and Senior Students of the House, held under this Ordinance, or for the doing of anything hereby authorized or

permitted to be done, shall be decided by a majority of the votes of those present; whenever the votes shall be equal, the Dean, or in his absence the Sub-Dean, or in the absence of both the Senior Canon present, shall have a casting vote in addition to his own.

25. It shall be lawful for the Dean and Chapter, if they shall think fit, to reduce the number of Chaplaincies to any number not less than four, by not filling up vacancies; the emoluments of the Chaplaincies which shall not be filled up being equally distributed among the remaining Chaplains. The provisions of this Ordinance shall be without prejudice to the Dean's power of appointing and removing Chaplains, and of making rules for their residence within the House.

26. It shall be lawful for the Dean and Chapter to alter, in such manner as they shall think fit, the designation of the Servitors, and to apply the Exhibitions of the foundation of Archbishop Boulter for Servitors, Mr. Pauncefort, Dr. Gardiner, Bishop Frampton, Dr. Cotton, and Mrs. Paul, to the support of the persons bearing such altered designation.

27. If in any case it shall appear to the Lord Chancellor that by reason of any change in the value of money any specific sum fixed by this Ordinance has become insufficient or excessive, and that such insufficiency or excess is productive of injustice or hardship, or is injurious to the general interests of the House, it shall be lawful for the Lord Chancellor from time to time, for the purpose of correcting or obviating such injustice, hardship, or injury, to direct that such annual sum shall be increased or diminished as he shall think fit, and the increased or diminished sum shall thenceforth be substituted for and stand in the place of the sum originally fixed as aforesaid.

28. The Dean and Chapter, or the Dean, Canons, Censors, and four Senior Tutors, as the case may be, shall, as often as they may be required to do so, answer in writing touching any matter as to which the Visitor may deem it expedient to inquire, for the purpose of satisfying himself whether the Statutes in force for the time being are duly observed.

29. It shall be lawful for the Dean, or for any Canon, Senior Student, or Chaplain, if he shall conceive himself aggrieved by any act, decision, or sentence of the Dean, or of the Dean and Chapter, or of the Dean, Canons, Censors, and four Senior Tutors, or of the Dean, Canons, and Senior Students, as the case

may be, and for any Junior Student or Exhibitioner who may have been deprived of his Studentship or Exhibition, to appeal against such act or decision or sentence to the Visitor; and it shall be lawful for the Visitor to adjudicate on such appeal, and to disallow or annul such act or decision, and to reverse or vary such sentence, as he shall deem just.

30. It shall be lawful for the Lord Chancellor, on the complaint of the Dean or of any one of the Canons or Senior Students, to disallow and annul any Bye-law which shall, in his judgment, be repugnant to any of the Statutes of the House in force for the time being.

31. In the construction of this Ordinance, the words 'Lord Chancellor' shall mean the Lord High Chancellor of Great Britain, and shall include the Lord Keeper and Lords Commissioners for the custody of the Great Seal of Great Britain for the time being; and the word 'Tutor' shall mean a Tutor who is a Senior Student of the House.

32. This Ordinance shall not be construed to diminish or affect the interest of any member of the House elected before the approval thereof by Her Majesty in Council; but, subject to the provisions of clauses 20 and 25, no existing member of the House shall be entitled by virtue of anything herein contained to receive larger emoluments than he would have been entitled to receive if this Ordinance had not been made. This Ordinance shall be construed to speak and take effect as if framed immediately before the said approval.

Given under our Common Seal this Ninth day of January one thousand eight hundred and fifty-eight.

ORDINANCE CONCERNING THE EXHIBITIONS OF DAME ELIZABETH HOLFORD'S FOUNDATION, FRAMED BY THE COMMISSIONERS

WE, the Commissioners appointed for the purposes of an Act passed in the seventeenth and eighteenth years of the reign of Her Majesty Queen Victoria, intituled 'An Act to make further Provision for the good Government and Extension of the University of Oxford, of the Colleges therein, and of the College of Saint Mary Winchester,' hereby ordain as follows in relation to the five Exhibitions of Dame Elizabeth Holford's foundation within the Cathedral or House of Christ Church in the said University.

The said five Exhibitions shall be consolidated, as vacancies occur therein, into two Exhibitions, the holders of which shall receive yearly one half of the total amount of the emoluments which would have been payable to the holders of the said five Exhibitions. The consolidated Exhibitions shall respectively be tenable for five years from the day of election inclusive, and no longer. The Exhibitioners shall be elected, after a competitive examination of the candidates, from among persons educated at the Charterhouse School for two years at least last preceding the day of election, or last preceding their matriculation in the University. No person shall be entitled to preference by reason of his being an Exhibitioner or Pensioner of Sutton's Hospital. No person shall be admissible as a candidate who shall have completed the fourth Term inclusive from the date of his matriculation. The Dean of Christ Church shall give thirty days' notice at least of every intended election to the Head Master of the Charterhouse School, and shall also give public notice thereof for the same period. Whenever there shall be no candidate whom the electors shall judge of sufficient merit for election, the Exhibition shall be thrown open for that turn to general competition, and the election shall be postponed to a day to be appointed by the electors, not later than the next ensuing stated day of election to open Junior Studentships. It shall be lawful for the Dean and Chapter of Christ Church, with the consent of the Governors of the Charterhouse, to increase the number of the

Exhibitions, if there shall be sufficient funds for the purpose, but so that the emoluments of each Exhibition shall not fall short of Sixty pounds *per annum*.

Given under our Common Seal this Sixteenth day of April 1858.

L.S.

(Printed, 1863)

APPENDIX III

Christ Church, Oxford, 1865

At a Meeting held in Christ Church on March 21st, 1865, to which were invited all Senior Students, together with the Students on the Old Foundation who were in residence, it was resolved to print for private circulation the following statement.

In venturing to reopen a question which might be supposed to have been finally settled by the late University Commissioners, the Students of Christ Church beg to call attention at the outset to the following considerations:—

1. The case of Christ Church, owing to its twofold character as a College and a Cathedral, was not thoroughly dealt with by the University Commission. The Commissioners had no power to enter on the questions which lay at the root of all real reform; they could not remove the defects and anomalies peculiar to the constitution of Christ Church. They were authorized to suppress two Canonries, but they had no power to touch or inquire into the capitular revenues or incomes. Moreover, they were compelled to leave in the hands of the Dean and Chapter the supreme government of the College as well as of the Cathedral, the administration of all revenues and property of the House, and the settlement of the amount to be set aside for the incomes of the Dean and Canons, and of that to be devoted to educational and other College purposes.

2. The Chapter alone, as the governing body of the House, were consulted by the late Commissioners, and as the Chapter did not communicate with the Students, nor in any way take them into their counsels, the Students had no opportunity of making known to the Commissioners their views as to the alterations required in Christ Church until the Commissioners had completed the scheme which eventually, with a very few alterations, passed into law.

The system thus established has now been tested by the experience of nearly seven years, and the Senior Students are unanimous in desiring that such further changes should be effected as would remedy the evils of which they are sensible. In the following pages the Students have endeavoured to set forth the principal defects of the present constitution and to indicate the changes which in their opinion are required.

The present constitution of Christ Church differs from the constitution of other Colleges in Oxford in many material respects. In other Colleges the governing body consists of the Head of the College and the Fellows, in whom the estates and other property of the College are vested. The management of the estates and revenue of the College is usually delegated to one or more officers, chosen by the Fellows out of their own body and styled Bursars, who have to account to the Head and Fellows for their receipts and disbursements of the College funds. Out of these funds the emoluments of the Head, Fellows, and Scholars of the College, (which are in most cases limited by Statute,) the salaries of the College officers, and the wages of some of the servants (which are fixed from time to time by the governing body,) are paid,—the surplus being applied to the extension of the educational staff, the improvement of the estates and buildings of the College, or otherwise as the governing body may direct.

Many of the Colleges are bound by statute to pay out of their revenues certain sums for the support of one or more University Professors, who on their appointment become in some cases *ex officio* members of the College which provides their income, but have no share in its government.

The Head of a College is not expected to take any active part in the education of the Undergraduates. This duty devolves on the Tutors, who are usually selected by the Head of the College from the Fellows, unless it so happens that there is no one among the Fellows qualified and willing to undertake the duty. It is the object of every College to provide itself with a competent body of Fellows from whom the Tutors may be selected, and this is effected by opening the Fellowships to competition.

When a vacancy occurs in the Headship of a College, or in any College Living or Preferment, the Fellows usually elect to fill the vacancy some one who is or has been a member of their own body.

The right of electing to vacant Fellowships is vested in the Head and Fellows (the former having usually a casting vote), who are bound by the ordinances framed or accepted by the late Commissioners to guide themselves in their choice by the result of an open competitive examination held before each election in subjects connected with the studies of the University. The result is that the candidates for Fellowships are usually men who have distinguished themselves in their University career, and a Fellowship is looked upon both as a reward for past exertions, and as a guarantee that the holder is intellectually fitted to become a College Tutor. The right of electing to Scholarships is also vested in the Head and Fellows. The emoluments of a Fellow vary in the different Colleges from £200 to £300 a year.

CHRIST CHURCH is at once a College and a Cathedral. The Head of the College is also the Dean of the Cathedral, and is appointed by the Crown. The body most nearly corresponding to the Fellows of a College are the Senior Students. The Junior Students correspond to the Scholars. But between the Dean and the Students come the Canons of the Cathedral, and it is the existence of this body which constitutes the chief difference between Christ Church and the other Colleges.

The Dean and Chapter are the governing body. In them all the estates and other property of the House are vested. They occupy as private residences a large portion of the buildings. They are the sole receivers of the revenue, and are accountable to no one for their receipts or their expenditure. The emoluments of the Senior and Junior Students are fixed by statute, but the emoluments of the Dean and Chapter are left to their own discretion; no account is given of the surplus revenue; it is not known to any but themselves whether a surplus revenue ever exists, or if so, what is its amount.

The Canonries, with one exception, are attached to University Professorships; and just as certain Professors become *ex officio* members of the College, from whose revenues they are endowed, so certain other Professors become *ex officio* members of Christ Church; but there is this material difference, that while Professors become at other Colleges, at most, merely honorary Fellows, at Christ Church they become Canons, and as such they constitute the chief portion of the governing body. The Canons are usually men of eminence in theological learning. Their services are due to the University as Professors, and as in other cases it is found inexpedient to hamper the Professors in the discharge of their public duties by imposing on them a share in the educational work of a College, so at Christ Church the Canons take no part in College work, which falls entirely upon the Tutors and Lecturers. Moreover the Canons, being chosen neither from nor by the Members of the House, and being necessarily men of more advanced age than those who become Senior Students, have not an equal opportunity with the Senior Students, from whom the staff of Tutors and Lecturers is recruited, of becoming intimately acquainted with the wants, or keenly interested in the academical success of the Undergraduates of the House.

The Censors, besides being Tutors, perform the duties which devolve on the Deans and Junior Bursars of Colleges. They present for degrees, and superintend the discipline and attendance at Divine worship of the Junior Members of the House. They receive any complaints that the Undergraduates may have to make concerning the conduct of the College Servants or the provisions supplied by the Butler, Cook, or Manciple. The Senior Censor has, subject to the Dean's approval, the assignment of rooms and the nomination of Scouts and some other College Servants. He receives the valuation of rooms, but has no power to order any repairs. The Junior Censor is Curator of Hall. But, while the Censors have the duties and responsibilities of governing, they have little real power. They have no control over any portion of the revenues set apart for domestic administration. The principal servants of the House have not fixed salaries, as at other Colleges, but are allowed to exercise monopolies, and to make very large profits at the expense of the members of the House. Neither the Students as a body, nor the Censors, have any power to remedy a grievance, which presses most heavily on the Undergraduates and their parents.

Except on Sundays and Saints' Days the College Services are distinct from those of the Cathedral. On Sundays and Saints' Days they coincide. In the regulation therefore of the Services on these days it might be expected that the Censors should have a voice; and it is specially enacted by clause 21 of the Ordinances that 'every Member of the House under the degree of M.A., shall be subject to such general regulations as to residence, discipline, and attendance on Divine Worship, as the Dean, Canons, two Censors, and four Senior Tutors shall from time to time determine,' yet the Censors have no share in determining either the character or the time of the Services which the Junior Members of the House attend.

The election of Senior and Junior Students is vested in a body consisting of the Dean, the Canons, two Censors, and four Senior Tutors. The Senior Students, as such, have no voice in elections. Of the electoral body the Dean and Canons form a majority, and, if combined, may carry an election against the votes of the Censors and Tutors; although, with regard to the election of Senior Students, it is the Censors and Tutors who, from their more intimate acquaintance with the Undergraduates, are most competent to decide which of the candidates are best qualified to become Tutors of the House, and are most likely to be acceptable to the general body of Students with whom, as members of the same Common Room, they will be brought into daily contact.

The Dean and Chapter present to College Livings and Preferments, but by custom the option of Livings is given to Students in Holy Orders successively according to seniority.

The emoluments of the Senior Students are fixed at £200 a year exclusive of Rooms.

It must be remembered that the Senior Students are all chosen from the same ranks, for the same qualifications, and by the same tests, as Fellows of Colleges. On their fitness for conducting the educational business of the House its academical success mainly depends, and they would be held responsible for its failure. It would seem only fair that they should enjoy the same privileges as the Fellows of a College, and the same freedom in the choice and application of means to their end.

It has been seen that from several of the chief privileges exercised by Fellows of Colleges—the election of a Head, the Presentation to Livings, the management and control of the finances, and the superintendence of domestic and economical arrangements—the Senior Students of Christ Church are altogether excluded; in the right to vote at elections they have but an indirect and insignificant share, and their emoluments are fixed at a standard considerably below that to which the Fellows of a College may attain.

It is to be feared that the inferiority of the position of Senior Students to that of Fellows in these respects will exercise a pernicious influence in deterring the best men in the University from competing for Senior Studentships, when they can obtain Fellowships elsewhere. This evil has not been felt hitherto because the true position of Senior Students of Christ Church is not generally known. But it will undoubtedly be felt as the facts become more notorious, and so Christ Church will have, in comparison with other Colleges, a less competent body of men from whom to select its staff of working Tutors, and will lay itself open to the accusation (which the Senior Students have no power to avert) that in proportion to its numbers and endowment it gains fewer academical honours than other Colleges.

The Students, being convinced that these defects in the present constitution of Christ Church must, if allowed to continue, go far to prevent its holding in the University and country at large the position to which, from its wealth and numbers, it is entitled, as well as seriously impair its usefulness as a place of religion, education, and learning, have attempted to secure the co-operation of the Chapter in effecting such changes as shall enable the House to compete at least on equal terms with other Colleges in the University. The Chapter, however, have declined to take steps towards promoting constitutional changes of the kind desired. The Students, therefore, find themselves compelled to make an independent appeal to higher authority.

The Students will welcome, as the best constitution for Christ Church, that which will best enable it to fulfil the purposes of its foundation. They consider that to this end two things are essential—(1) the best available staff of duly qualified Tutors and Lecturers, (2) an equitable application of the vast resources of the House.

To secure the former, Christ Church ought to be able to offer in its Senior Studentships prizes which shall be as attractive as Fellowships to the best men in the University.

To secure the latter, it seems indispensable that the present financial system—a system which gives an unlimited portion of the revenue to a small body incapable of growth or extension, and a limited and insignificant portion to a body whose growth and extension are unrestricted, and which leaves the control of the finances to a Chapter chiefly composed of University Professors who have little or no acquaintance with the working and wants of the College to which they only accidentally belong, and treats as mere stipendiaries the Students, who from their position and pursuits can best appreciate the wants, and are most anxious for the success of the College,—should be entirely remodelled.

The following suggestions as to the kind of constitution required are appended for consideration:—

The Students shall be included in the Corporation of the House, and as member of that Corporation they shall share with the Chapter the government of the House, and the administration of its revenues, and also enjoy such other rights and privileges as commonly attach to the Fellows of a College.

The corporate property of the House shall be vested in the Dean, Canons, and Students.

On the subject of the governing body, two schemes are suggested:—

I. The governing body shall consist of the Dean, Canons, and Students, who shall administer the revenues and also elect to Studentships.

II. The governing body shall consist of the Dean, and an equal number of Canons and Students. The electoral body shall consist of the Dean, the Canons, the three Censors, the two Senior Tutors, the Mathematical Lecturer, the Lee's Readers, and two other Students to be appointed from time to time by the Students.

The person next in authority to the Dean in the House as a place of education shall be a Student holding the office of Censor Theologiæ.

A Student Bursar shall be appointed to superintend the College Servants and to control the general economy of the House.

The governing body shall appoint the College Officers, and regulate their duties and emoluments, and shall have power to institute such other offices and lectureships as they shall deem expedient for the better management of the affairs of the House, and the instruction and discipline of its members.

The income of the Dean, Canons, and Senior Students shall be fixed within certain limits.

The presentation to livings shall be vested in the governing body, the option remaining as at present.

The admission of the Students to share with the Dean and Canons the government of the House shall be without prejudice to the independent exercise by the Dean and Canons of their functions as a Chapter in purely Cathedral matters.

Throughout this statement reference has generally been made to the body of Students, as reconstituted by the University Commissioners; but inasmuch as there still exists a considerable number of Students on the Old Foundation, it is wished that their interests should be consulted equally with those of the Students on the New Foundation, in any change that may be made in the constitution of the House.

(Copies in: Christ Church Library; Bodleian Library, G.A. Oxon. 4°. 430 (9)).

APPENDIX IV

Account of Negotiations, 1865–1866[1]

[PRIVATE]

A FEELING of dissatisfaction has long existed among the Students of Christ Church with regard to the constitution of the House and their relations to the Chapter, and at the beginning of last year they were of opinion that a revision of the Ordinance framed by the late University Commissioners was required. It had been resolved that an effort should be made for a reform of the constitution, when on Feb. 18, 1865, a meeting of the Students in residence was summoned by the Senior Censor in order to lay before them a proposal of the Chapter communicated to the College Officers by the Dean, (in conformity with what the Chapter understood to be the wish of some at least among the Students,) to the effect that the Students should appoint a certain number of their body to confer with three members of the Chapter on matters affecting the general interests of the House. In accordance with this proposal a conference took place between three members of the Chapter on the one hand, and three Delegates from the Students on the other, under the presidency of the Dean. At this conference the Delegates from the Students were instructed to state that the Students considered the interests of the House to require the following changes:—

1. 'That the Students be included in the Corporation of the House, and that as members of that Corporation they be

[1] There were apparently three forms of this statement. The first, circulated to all Senior Students and Students on the Old Foundation early in January 1866 began: 'The following statement will explain the circumstances under which it has been thought advisable to convene a meeting of Students on the 18th of January next. It is well known that a feeling of dissatisfaction has long existed among the Students of Christ Church. . . .' In the second, drawn up after 25 January, the first sentence was naturally omitted, but the words 'It is well known that' were retained. However, these were apparently felt to be provocative, and were removed from the final form of the statement, here printed.

admitted to a due share in the Government and administration of the revenues of the House, and to the enjoyment of such other rights and privileges as commonly attach to the Fellows of a College.'

2. 'That one of such rights be the right to vote at the election of Students.'

After a conference, in which the deputies of the Chapter inquired what was meant by 'a *due* share in the government and administration of the revenues of the House,' and whether the right of voting was claimed on behalf of all the Senior Students, the Chapter, being dissatisfied with the answers given, replied in the following terms:

'In reference to the propositions submitted to the Dean and Chapter by the Students, the Dean and Chapter are sorry to find themselves in opposition to the wishes of the Students. They are not prepared to take steps towards promoting constitutional changes of the kind desired.'

On receiving this answer the Students determined to proceed independently, and, in the month of November, it was decided to present a Memorial to the Prime Minister, to which were to be attached the names of the Senior Students and the names of as many present and former Students on the Old Foundation as could be obtained. A form of Memorial had been drawn up, and copies were on the point of being circulated for signature, when the Canons, understanding that some at least of the Students would prefer an amicable settlement, made a proposal in the following terms:—

Christ Church, Tuesday, Dec. 12, 1865

MY DEAR SANDFORD,

The Canons have arrived at the following conclusions.

That it is desirable that certain matters in dispute between the Canons and Students be submitted to arbitration.

That the points to be submitted to arbitration be

1. Whether it be desirable that the Canons retain their present share in the Election of Senior Students, or be excluded from all share in such Elections.

2. Whether it be desirable that the Canons retain their present share in the Election of Junior Students, or be excluded from all share in such Elections.

3. Whether it be desirable that the Canons should retain that share in the Government of the House as a Collegiate Body, which the

Ordinance assigns to them in conjunction with the Dean, the two Censors, and the four Senior Tutors.

4. Whether it be desirable to make any change in the (1) management, and (2) application of the revenues of the College.

The Canons are of opinion that the number of Arbitrators should be three.

I remain,
Very sincerely yours,
(*Signed*) CHARLES C. CLERKE,
SUB-DEAN

In consequence of this proposal the Students deferred proceeding with their memorial until the question of arbitration should have been fully considered.

The following is the answer made by them to the proposals of the Chapter:—

Christ Church, Thursday, Dec. 14, 1865

MY DEAR MR. SUB-DEAN,

I am requested to inform you that the Students have arrived at the following conclusions:—

The Students entertain the hope that the proposal of arbitration now made by the Canons signifies their willingness to join with the Students in determining what changes are desirable in the constitution of the House, and in obtaining for such changes the requisite legal sanction. In order however to avoid fruitless negociations, and to ascertain how far joint action between the Dean, the Canons, and the Students is possible, the Students think it advisable again to state generally the end which they have in view, and the attainment of which they consider indispensable to the welfare and good government of the House, viz. that the position of Senior Students be assimilated to that of Fellows in other Societies with reference to the Finance, the Government of the College, and the Elections.

The Students having suspended, in consequence of the proposal for arbitration, the course of independent action in which they were engaged, respectfully request the Dean and Canons to decide at their next meeting whether they will consent to the above-mentioned principle being taken as a basis for cooperation with the Students in obtaining a settlement of the questions at issue.

In the case of a favourable reply being received from the Dean and Canons, they are willing to accept the proposal of arbitration on the following conditions:—

1. That the Arbitrators shall have every facility afforded them for enquiring into the existing government and revenues of the House,

and shall be empowered to recommend such alterations in the late Ordinance, as they may deem expedient.

2. That the Dean and Canons and Students shall combine in obtaining legal authority for the carrying out of such alterations as the Arbitrators shall recommend.

Believe me to be,
Yours very sincerely,
(*Signed*) CHARLES W. SANDFORD

THE VEN. THE SUB-DEAN

The Canons rejoined in these terms:—

Christ Church, Thursday, Dec. 14, 1865

MY DEAR CENSOR,

I am requested by the Canons to communicate to you the following reply to the statement of the Students received from you this morning:—

The Canons, as far as they are concerned, and without answering for the Dean, who will exercise his own judgment, have considered the answer of the Students to their proposal for arbitration, and beg through the Sub-Dean to communicate the following reply:—

They concur in the two conditions of arbitration laid down at the close of the Student's letter, viz.:

1. That the Arbitrators shall have every facility afforded them for enquiring into the existing government and revenues of the House, and shall be empowered to recommend such alterations in the late Ordinance as they may deem expedient.

2. That the Dean and Canons and Students shall combine in obtaining legal authority for the carrying out of such alterations as the Arbitrators shall recommend.

With regard to the principle which the Students have proposed as a basis for the arbitration, viz.: 'That the position of Senior Students be assimilated to that of Fellows in other Societies, with reference to the Finance, the Government of the College, and the Elections,' the Canons consider the absolute freedom of the Arbitrators to decide without restriction upon the questions submitted to them, to be an essential condition of arbitration; and they hope that the Students will be willing to submit the questions at issue to arbitration as unreservedly as the Canons themselves have done.

I remain,
My dear Censor,
Very sincerely yours,
(*Signed*) CHARLES C. CLERKE

From the Dean was received the following letter:

Dec. 15, 1865

DEAR MR. SANDFORD,

A copy of the correspondence between the Canons and Students during Dec. 12–14 has been put into my hands.

It appears to me that the principles laid down in the last communication from the Canons,—bearing date Thursday, Dec. 14th—are very reasonable, viz.;—that the conditions cited from the close of the Students' Letter should be taken as the conditions of arbitration, but that the Arbitrators should be left free to decide without restriction upon the questions submitted to their judgment. I am perfectly ready, on my part, to abide by those conditions.

Yours very truly,
(*Signed*) H. G. LIDDELL

The Students replied in the morning of Dec. 15:

Christ Church, Dec. 15, 1865

MY DEAR MR. SUB-DEAN,

I am requested to communicate to you the conclusions arrived at by the Students; and to express a hope that, as many of the Students are leaving Oxford for the Vacation, they may receive an answer as early as may be convenient.

The Students desire to express their appreciation of the spirit in which both the Dean and the Canons have met their propositions, and they are desirous if possible of agreeing to the terms of arbitration, which would satisfy the Dean and Canons.

They feel, however, that no arbitration would result in a way satisfactory to themselves, which did not start upon the principle that the Students, either as a body, or by representatives, be admitted to a due share in the Government of the College, not only as regards discipline, but also in relation to the elections and to the administration of the revenues. If this principle were admitted, the Students would be willing to leave it unreservedly to the Arbitrators to decide in what mode and to what extent it should be carried into effect.

The Students adopt the proposal of the Canons that there should be three Arbitrators, and they would suggest that the Dean and Chapter appoint one, that the Students appoint one, that these two Arbitrators appoint a third.

Believe me to be,
Yours very sincerely,
(*Signed*) CHARLES W. SANDFORD.

The following answer was received from the Canons in the evening of the same day, Dec. 15:—

Christ Church, Friday, Dec. 15

MY DEAR CENSOR,

I am requested to send to you the following reply from the Canons to the letter sent to me by you this morning.

In answer to the communication of the Students dated this day, the Canons are anxious to renew their offer of submitting the questions, which they believe to be at issue, unreservedly to arbitration, to facilitate all inquiries, and to abide absolutely by the result.

But they still feel that arbitration can only be satisfactory to all parties, if the Arbitrators are entirely free to follow their own judgment, unfettered by any instructions, as to the line which they are expected to take.

The Dean, the Canons, and the Students will of course severally present their own views of the case, and the Arbitrators should be free to decide.

If the Students concur in what has been said, it will remain only to agree upon the Arbitrators. The Canons have felt that the position of the Dean, in some important points, is so essentially different from their own, that he ought not, in their judgment, to be left without a substantive voice in the choice of the Arbitrators.

* * * *

Believe me to be,
Yours very sincerely,
(*Signed*) CHARLES C. CLERKE,
SUB-DEAN

THE REV. THE CENSOR

And at the same time this letter came from the Dean:—

Dec. 15, 1865

MY DEAR MR. SANDFORD,

I have seen the reply of the Canons to the last communication from the Students. It appears to me to contain a fair and temperate expression of opinion; and I sincerely trust that Arbitrators may be found so far above all suspicion of partiality, that we may all readily concur in referring the whole case to their judgment, without any instructions to embarrass them.

With regard to the persons to be applied to, I have no sort of wish to press any opinion of my own. The Canons have consulted me, and I have named one who I should think would do his part admirably, if only he would consent to act. But I am perfectly ready to concur in the names of *any* three persons, who by their station, their character, and their perfect impartiality may command respect. I care not who suggests their names.

I beg leave to remain
Yours very truly,
(*Signed*) H. G. LIDDELL.

On the receipt of this communication it was thought right to summon all the Students on both Foundations, in order to give every one an opportunity of expressing his opinion on the subject.[1]

The Students met on Jan. 18th, 1866, and agreed upon the resolutions contained in the following letter:—

Christ Church, Jan. 18, 1866

MY DEAR MR. SUB-DEAN,

I am empowered to communicate to the Canons the following resolutions, which have been adopted by the Students, and to request the favour of an answer from the Canons at their earliest convenience.

The Students are advised that, the Chapter having declined to accept as a basis of arbitration the principle which the Students consider essential, no arbitration in the ordinary sense of the word is possible.

But being desirous to obtain the cooperation of the Dean and Canons in promoting changes which seem necessary to the welfare of the House, the Students are ready to refer the whole question of the Elections to Studentships, the Finance, and the Government of the College, to Private Commissioners, who shall be nominated by the Dean, the Canons, and the Students.

The Commissioners thus appointed shall be desired, after making full enquiry, to frame such a scheme for the future government of the House and the management and application of its revenues as they may deem most likely to conduce to the welfare and usefulness of Christ Church.

[1] The first form of this statement naturally ended with this paragraph, which then ran: 'As it appeared that this communication must be considered as containing the ultimatum of the Dean and Chapter, it was thought right before returning a definite reply on so important a point to send notice of the next meeting to all the Students on both Foundations, in order to give every one an opportunity of expressing his opinion on the subject.' In the second and final forms of the statement the reference to the capitular 'ultimatum' was wisely dropped.

The Students desire to express their readiness to cooperate with the Dean and Canons in obtaining legal authority for the scheme which the Commissioners shall recommend.

The Students would suggest that the number of Commissioners be five, of whom three shall form a quorum; and that two be appointed by the Dean and Chapter, two by the Students, and one by the Dean.

* * * *

With regard to the cost arising from such a private enquiry, the Students suppose that it will be defrayed by Domus.

Believe me to be,
Yours very sincerely,
(*Signed*) CHARLES W. SANDFORD

THE VEN. THE SUB-DEAN

A similar letter was also sent to the Dean.

The following answers were received from the Dean and Canons:—

Christ Church, Oxford, Jan. 20, 1866

DEAR MR. CENSOR,

I beg leave to acknowledge the receipt of your letter, dated the 18th inst., containing Resolutions agreed to at a meeting of Students.

I wish to express my entire concurrence in those Resolutions, understanding that all parties agree to abide by the decision of the Commissioners, or by whatever name they are to be called.

* * * *

I have the honour to be,
Dear Mr. Censor,
Yours very truly,
(*Signed*) H. G. LIDDELL

THE REV. C. W. SANDFORD

Christ Church, Oxford, Jan. 19, 1866

MY DEAR CENSOR,

The Canons have requested me to transmit to you in their name the following reply to the paper which I have received from you, and which I read to them this morning.

The Canons beg to acknowledge the receipt of the letter of the Students dated January 18.

They believe that they may consider it as substantially accepting the proposal contained in their letter of Dec. 12. In this sense they accept it.

With regard, however, to the alterations proposed,

1. They consider that the name of Commissioner, as implying the delegation of authority, is at least as liable to objection as that of Arbitrator; and without pressing a point which seems purely verbal, they would venture to suggest the name of Referee.

2. They are willing, for themselves, to accept the suggestion of the Students that the number of the Referees should be five instead of three.

* * * *

The expense attending the enquiry will be borne by Domus.

I remain, my dear Censor,
Very sincerely yours,
(*Signed*) CHARLES C. CLERKE,

SUB-DEAN OF CHRIST CHURCH

The Students replied to the Canons' letter in these terms:—

Christ Church, Jan. 22, 1866

MY DEAR MR. SUB-DEAN,

I am requested to communicate to the Canons the resolutions at which the Students have arrived.

The Students fear that confusion may arise from considering the resolutions of Jan. 18 as a substantial acceptance of the proposition of the Canons dated Dec. 12, 1865, and therefore beg once more to express their readiness to unite with the Dean and Canons in the appointment of Referees, provided it be distinctly understood, that their functions be not limited to giving a simple affirmative or negative answer to the questions specified in the letter of the Canons dated Dec. 12, 1865, but that the whole question of the Finance, the Government of the College, and the Elections to Studentships be submitted without reserve of any kind to their judgment; and further, that the Referees, after making full enquiry into all these points, shall be desired to frame such a scheme for the future Government of the House, and the management and application of its revenues as they may deem most likely to conduce to the welfare and usefulness of Christ Church.

* * * *

Believe me to be,
Yours very sincerely,
(*Signed*) CHARLES W. SANDFORD

THE VEN. THE SUB-DEAN

The Canons sent the following explanation:—

Christ Church, Jan. 23, 1866

MY DEAR CENSOR,

In answer to the letter of the Students dated Jan. 22, 1866, the Canons wish to explain that, in the reference to their letter of the 12th of December last, they intended to leave all questions as to the government and finance of the College unreservedly to the judgment of the Referees: only, in regard to the election of Students they wished matters to be decided in one of two ways, which they originally proposed; either that the Board of Electors should remain constituted as it was by the Ordinance, or that they should be themselves altogether excluded.

* * * *

If the Canons learn that this statement is satisfactory to the Students, they will be prepared to join with them in making communications to the Referees, whether by each party separately making application to the respective Referees, or—which the Canons would prefer—by letters written by the Dean on the part of the whole Society.

I remain, my dear Censor,
Very sincerely yours,
(*Signed*) CHARLES C. CLERKE,
SUB-DEAN OF CHRIST CHURCH

The Students finally answered:—

Christ Church, Jan. 25, 1866

MY DEAR MR. SUB-DEAN,

I have great pleasure in forwarding to you the following answer. The Students accept with satisfaction the explanation of the Canons dated Jan. 23, 1866; and they are quite prepared to concur with the proposal of the Canons that the Dean should write letters to the Referees on the part of the whole Society.

Believe me to be,
Yours very sincerely,
(*Signed*) CHARLES WALDEGRAVE SANDFORD

THE VEN. THE SUB-DEAN

(Copies in Christ Church Library)

APPENDIX V

Dean Liddell to Archbishop Longley, February 1866

My Lord Archbishop,

For some time past the Students of Ch. Ch. have been dissatisfied with the position assigned to them in relation to the Chapter:

The points in wh. they wish changes to be made relate (1) to Elections to Studentships, (2) to the Government of the House as a Collegiate Body, (3) to the Revenues.

The Chapter & Students have consented to leave decision on these points to five Referees.

All parties agree to abide by the decision of the Referees, & to do their best to procure Legislative sanction (if necessary) for their Recommendations.

I beg leave to ask whether your Grace's engagements will allow you to undertake the Office of Referee. The persons asked to serve with you are Sir J. Coleridge, Sir W. Page Wood, the Hon. E. Twisleton, & the Attorney General (Sir Roundell Palmer).

The enquiry into the subjects of the Elections to Studentships and the Government of the House is not likely to involve much difficulty.

The enquiry into the Revenues, wh. are in a transition state, will be more complicated—But the Treasurer could easily put the Referees in possession of the facts, so that it need not occupy much time to adjudicate in regard to them.

I beg to enclose a copy of the correspondence that has taken place on this subject, and have the honour to be my Lord Archbishop, etc.

(Ch. Ch. Library, MS. 449, f. 34^{v})

APPENDIX VI

Statement for the Use of the Referees [*March 1866*]

[PRIVATE]

The following account of the Foundation has been agreed to by all Parties

I. CHRIST CHURCH, as is well known, originated in the foundation of CARDINAL COLLEGE, erected by Wolsey in 1526 out of the lands and revenues of monasteries suppressed by a Papal Bull.

In one point of view this College had, from the beginning, a more ecclesiastical air than other Colleges. The Head of the College was entitled *Dean*; the Fellows were represented by sixty *Major Canons*; the Scholars by forty *Petty Canons*. But the extant Statutes of Cardinal College shew that the qualifications, duties, and ages of these persons were to be much the same as the qualifications, duties, and ages of the Head, Fellows, and Scholars of other Colleges. The Dean was to be above thirty years of age; in Holy Orders, but not a Bishop or a Monk; a B.D., or capable of becoming a B.D. within four months after his appointment. The sixty Major Canons were to be well advanced in the studies of Theology, Canon Law, Civil Law, Medicine, or Philosophy, according to the faculties which they represented, and were to be Bachelors in that faculty, or capable of becoming Bachelors within four months. The forty Petty Canons were to come from the schools which Wolsey proposed to found in fifteen dioceses designated by name; they were to be over fifteen and below twenty-one years of age.

The Dean was to be elected in this way. The thirty senior of the Major Canons in residence were to choose two out of their own number; and the twelve senior of the thirty were to choose one of these two.

The Major Canons were to be elected by themselves, in certain proportions from certain dioceses and faculties, being subject to a year of probation. They were not necessarily to be chosen from the Petty Canons.

The Petty Canons were to be elected by the Dean, Sub-Dean, and ten of the Major Canons (seven being College officers), after an examination held 'in cantu et litteris.' If under twenty, they were to have tutors. They were to be re-examined by the Dean and College officers at the end of two years, and were to be removed, if 'verisimiliter in studio non essent profecturi, aut pro ratione temporis quo in Collegio fuissent non profecissent.' If then approved, they were to hold their places for three years longer, or till they had completed the age of twenty-five.

There were to be FOUR PRIVATE PROFESSORS (chosen annually from the Major Canons) of Sophistic, Dialectic, Philosophy, and Literæ Humaniores. All the Petty Canons, and the Major Canons below a certain standing, were to attend their Lectures.

There were to be FOUR CENSORS (chosen annually from the Major Canons), who were to regulate the disputations, in which all the Canons were to take part; and to assist the Dean and Sub-Dean in maintaining discipline. There were to be THREE BURSARS (chosen from the same body), to manage the property and control the daily expenditure.

All these regulations point to a strictly collegiate foundation. Indeed, the Statutes are to a great extent borrowed from those of New College and other older Colleges.

Besides this, there were to be SIX PUBLIC PROFESSORS chosen by the Dean, Sub-Dean, certain of the Major Canons, the Professors of the University, and ten Heads of Colleges, without respect of family or county, solely for their learning, ability, and skill in teaching; three of Theology, Canon Law, and Philosophy, who were to live in College, and remain unmarried; three of Civil Law, Medicine, and Literæ Humaniores, who might marry and reside in the city. They were to lecture publicly for all the University, but within the College.

The Archbishop of York was to be Visitor.

II. This College fell with its founder in 1529. But in 1532 the King re-founded it under the name of KING HENRY THE EIGHTH'S COLLEGE. A draft form of Statutes remains, which shews that the foundation consisted of a Dean, with twelve Prebendaries or Canons, with certain Priests or Vicars, Clerks, and Choristers. But there is no mention of Students or Scholars. Either the draft of Statutes is wholly incomplete, or this foundation was not of an academical character.

III. In 1542 the Abbey of Osney had been converted into a Cathedral for the new Bishopric of Oxford, with a Dean and six Prebends. And in 1545 the King abolished his newly-founded College, and in the next year founded it anew in combination with the Cathedral establishment at Osney, under the title of THE CATHEDRAL CHURCH OF CHRIST IN OXFORD OF THE FOUNDATION OF KING HENRY VIII.

The foundation now first assumed its double character of a College and a Chapter. There were on this foundation a Dean, eight Canons, sixty Students of higher order, and forty of lower, but all with perpetual tenure of their places,—numbers which appear to have been borrowed from Wolsey's original foundation. Of the sixty, the twenty senior were called Theologi, and were all to be in Holy Orders. The other forty (of the sixty) were called Philosophi, and were all obliged to proceed to Holy Orders within a year of the time they passed into the first twenty, with the exception of four so-called Faculty Students, who could not rise into the first twenty. By an order from Queen Elizabeth, three at least of the Junior Students were to be chosen every year from the Royal College of St. Peter's, Westminster. One Studentship was afterwards added by private bequest, which raised the whole number to 101.

Some other traces of Wolsey's foundation appear in the creation of five Regius Professors, of Theology, Hebrew, Greek, Law, and Medicine, with a stipend of £40 each, payable from the Chapter revenues. In 1604 King James I. annexed one of the Canonries with the Rectory of Ewelme to the Professorship of Theology; and in 1630 King Charles I. annexed another of the Canonries to the Professorship of Hebrew. In 1840 the Margaret Professor of Divinity was endowed with a canonry in lieu of a stall of Worcester. And in 1842 Professorships of Ecclesiastical History and Pastoral Theology were created, and similarly endowed with Canonries. So that five Canonries were now annexed to Professorships, the annexations having been all confirmed by Acts of Parliament; as was also the rule that a sixth was to be held by the Archdeacon of Oxford, charged with an annual payment to the Archdeacon of Berks. Two Canonries were left unattached to any special offices.

The Dean was to be Head of the College and of the Cathedral. He was to be appointed by the Crown.

The Canons were at first all appointed by the Crown. Since 1857, the Canon holding the Margaret Professorship is to be elected by the Graduates of Divinity and Resident Members of Convocation who are in Holy Orders, and the Canonry attached to the Archdeaconry has been placed in the nomination of the Bishop of the Diocese.

The Students were partly elected from the Royal Scholars of Westminster, partly nominated by the Dean and Canons in order. But in 1854 the Dean and Chapter gave up their right of nomination, and the non-Westminster Students were elected, after examination, from Commoners of Christ Church who had been resident for a year.

The discipline was administered by the Dean, Sub-Dean, and College Officers,—such Officers being appointed by the Dean and Chapter, according to seniority, from the Tutors. Only in the case of Students did the Dean and Chapter as a body take any part in the discipline, and then only on extraordinary occasions, and always by reference from the Dean and College Officers. In all other respects the Dean and Chapter were the governing body. They formed the corporation; they had the entire administration of the revenues, paying the Students by dividends from the reserved rents of the estates, one-third of such dividend being estimated by the market-value of wheat and malt, according to the provisions of the Act of Elizabeth.

IV. We now come to the present state of the Foundation as modified by the Ordinance of the Parliamentary Commissioners in 1858. A copy of this Ordinance is enclosed for the use of each Referee.

Two Canonries were to be suppressed, when avoided, and their emoluments applied towards the endowment of Clerical Senior Studentships. One of these Canonries has been so applied.

The Students are divided into two bodies,—twenty-eight Senior Students, elected under the same conditions as the Fellows of Colleges, whereof nine are to be Laymen, and nineteen must proceed to Holy Orders; and fifty-two Junior Students, whereof twenty-one are to be elected from the royal foundation of Westminster, and the remaining thirty-one elected under the same conditions as the Scholars of other Colleges. Power is given to the

Dean and Chapter to increase the number of Senior Studentships to forty, and the number of Junior Studentships to sixty-one,—thus restoring the original number of one hundred and one (Ordinance, § 2).

The Senior Students receive a fixed annual sum of £200, and the Junior Students of £75 (in the case of Westminsters, to be increased to £115), in each case independent of rooms (§ 3). The tenure of the Senior Studentships is to be during good conduct, unless the holders marry or become possessed of property above a certain value (§ 10); the Westminster Junior Studentships are tenable for seven years, the rest for five years, from the day of election (§ 19).

The Dean and Chapter remain as the governing body, with the sole control of the corporate revenues, and with sole power to affix the corporate seal to deeds.

For the purposes of election both to Senior and Junior Studentships a new Board has been created. This Board will consist (when the two Canonries have lapsed) of the Dean, six Canons, and the two Censors and four Senior Tutors being Students (§ 5). To the same Board is committed the duty of making regulations for the residence, discipline, and attendance on Divine worship of the Junior Students (§ 21); they are also required to make bye-laws for the residence of Senior Students (§ 13), and have the power of removing Senior Students who shall have been found guilty of grave immorality, of contumaciously ceasing to conform to the Liturgy, of gross negligence or misconduct in any office, of contumacious non-observance of the statutes or bye-laws, or of grossly offensive behaviour to any member of the house (§ 15). A further power of making bye-laws binding on the Senior Students is conferred on the Dean, Canons, and Senior Students as a body (§ 23).

Practically, this power of making new regulations has not been called into exercise; and the Dean, Sub-Dean, and College Officers have administered the discipline as before the passing of the Ordinance.

Two of the Senior Lay Students are endowed from the funds held in trust by the Dean and Chapter under the will of Dr. Lee. They are entitled The Lee's Readers in Anatomy and Chemistry, and are bound to lecture or otherwise give instruction therein as the Dean and Chapter may direct (§ 7). The income of this trust-fund has largely increased; the Dean and Chapter have, under powers granted by the Court of Chancery, created a third Lee's Reader, of Law and History, (not a Senior Student,) with a salary fixed at a maximum of £300 a-year. They have also obtained further powers to apply the surplus funds to purposes of teaching within the House, in subjects (other than Classics) included in the University course.

The endowments of the Senior Students, other than the Lee's Readers, are provided out of part of the emoluments of the vacant Studentships of the old foundation, together with the proceeds of the two suppressed Canonries, when avoided; the endowments of the Westminster Students are provided from the trust-funds of Dr. South, Dr. Frewin, and Canon Hill, together with a large sum from Dr. Lee's estates (which were in great proportion to be devoted to the use of Westminster Students); the endowments of the thirty-one open Junior Studentships come partly from the emoluments of the vacant Studentships on the old foundation, partly from the bequests of Bishop Fell, Archbishop Boulter, and Mrs. Bostock (§ 3). The Dean and Chapter, believing that at a future time they will be able to avoid using these bequests for this purpose, are petitioning the Privy Council to allow these bequests to revert to their original purpose of providing Exhibitions for Commoners.

The Students on the old foundation will, in December next, be reduced to the number of thirty-five; of whom five are also Students on the new foundation under the provision of the Ordinance (§ 20). Of Senior Students on the new foundation there are now (including these five) fifteen; of Junior Students on the new foundation there will be, in June next, nineteen Westminsters and twenty-six open,—in all forty-five.

To this account may be added a brief statement from the Dean and Chapter respecting their corporate revenues, especially in relation to the collegiate establishment. This has been shewn to the Students, but cannot (of course), except in a few particulars, be within their knowledge.

Since 1859 the Dean and Chapter have restricted their incomes to a fixed sum; and out of their incomes, so restricted, they have raised the salary of the Regius Professor of Greek from £40 to £500.

They have also, out of the surplus occasioned by the above-mentioned restriction, voted a sum of £500 per annum to increase the tutorial fund and assist in the education of the Undergraduates. (It may not be out of place to mention, that ten or more so-called Servitors receive tutorial instruction without payment of fees.)

They have also raised the salaries of the Lay-clerks, in order to put the Choir on a more efficient footing; and first and last, the additional charges will amount to nearly £400 a-year.

The Dean and Chapter are the nominal patrons of a number of livings; but they never present any of their own body. The option of livings are offered, by seniority, to such Students as are in Holy Orders, and after them to the Chaplains in succession.

The Dean and Chapter have provided out of their corporate revenues an annual sum of about £5000 a-year, present and prospective, for the augmentation of the most needy of these livings. These augmentations have been in progress ever since the passing of Archbishop Howley's Enabling Act. They have also made grants to churches, schools, and parsonage-houses, amounting (on the average of the last three years) to about £1200 annually.

Recently it has been thought necessary to remodel the whole kitchen and buttery department, and to put all these matters, together with the management of the College servants, under a Steward, appointed by the Dean and Senior Students. Towards his salary the Dean and Chapter have voted £150 a-year, and have taken part in providing pensions for certain servants who were obliged to retire in order to give effect to the new arrangements.

On the subject of the revenues, as on all other subjects, the Dean and Chapter will be prepared to state particulars to the Referees. Generally, they may say that they have for some time past refused to renew beneficial leases on lives, and to renew leases of manors under any circumstances. Most of their estates and titles are now let on beneficial leases of twenty-one years, generally renewed every seven years. Several lessees have on their part declined to accept offers of renewal; and in a few special cases the Dean and Chapter have refused to renew. Consequently, the rack-rent income has increased of late, and may be expected eventually to increase largely. But the various calls which have been made recently, and which will be made in the course of the coming years, upon their funds, make it unlikely that for some time at least any considerable amount of surplus revenue will be at their disposal.

(Ch. Ch. Archives, MS. Estates 117, ff. 189–92).

APPENDIX VII

General recommendations of the Referees

1. That the Cathedral be regarded as a College Chapel on Sundays and Saints' Days, during Term, from Nine o'clock, A.M., to One o'clock, P.M.; and shall be subject, during those hours, to the regulations of the Governing Body of the College.

2. That the Governing Body of the College shall consist of the Dean, the Canons, and the Senior Students; and that, for the purposes of this scheme, Students on the Old Foundation, while in actual residence or holding office, shall be deemed Senior Students.

3. That all powers over the House of Christ Church, and the Possessions and Revenues thereof, which are now vested in the Dean and Chapter, or any other authority, shall hereafter, with the exceptions hereinafter mentioned, be vested in the Governing Body of the College.

4. That, subject to the first Recommendation, all powers over the Cathedral, its Fabric, Chapter House, and over the Officers and Services of the Cathedral, now vested in the Dean and Chapter, shall be reserved to them as an Ecclesiastical Corporation. The Dean and Chapter shall also retain all powers now vested in them, with reference to the occupation and appropriation of the Deanery and Canons' Houses.

5. That there shall be a Fund set apart annually for the repairs of the Cathedral and Chapter House: the disposal of which shall remain with the Dean and Chapter.

6. That with this view the Governing Body shall, once at least in every ten years, appoint a Surveyor, who shall lay before them a Report in writing of the probable average annual expenditure for the repairs of the Cathedral and Chapter House during the succeeding ten years; and thereupon the Governing Body shall order that during those years a sum, not less in amount than the sum so reported, shall be set apart for the purposes aforesaid.

7. That a sum not less than £1,200 a year, from the General Fund, be set apart as 'Contributions to Small Livings,' in every

year in which the Dean and Chapter shall signify their desire to have such appropriation made; without prejudice to the power of the Governing Body in any year, if they should think fit, to increase that sum.

8. That a sum not less than £17,000 be set apart for the payment of the Income of the Dean and Canons, the Chaplains, the Choir, the Organist, and other Officers, and for defraying the other incidental expenses of the Cathedral, including the Schoolmaster, and the Cathedral Alms and Pensions; and that this sum be at the disposal of the Dean and Chapter for the above purposes.

9. That £500 a year be set apart for the Greek Professor.

10. That a permissive power be given to the Governing Body to increase the emolument of the Senior Students engaged as Public Tutors of the College to any sum not exceeding £300 a year, exclusive of Rooms, during residence, but inclusive of all other allowances; and that a like permissive power be given to increase the Emoluments of the open Junior Studentships to any sum not exceeding £100 a year, exclusive of Rooms, but inclusive of all other allowances.

11. That after the death or resignation of the present Sub-Dean, the Dean be empowered to appoint from among the resident Senior Students a 'Censor Theologiae,' who shall exercise all the functions respecting the discipline of the College which are now exercised by the Sub-Dean. Nothing, however, herein provided shall affect the precedence or power of the Sub-Dean at any Meeting of the Governing Body of the College.

12. That the general powers given to the Governing Bodies of Colleges in the Ordinances of the late Oxford University Commissioners shall, mutatis mutandis, and subject to any special recommendations herein contained be given in this scheme to the Governing Body of Christ Church.

13. That in divisions of votes in the Governing Body, the vote of the Dean shall be computed as two votes, without prejudice to his having a casting vote.

14. That in all cases of Benefices in the gift of the College falling vacant, if within the space of [ ] months from the vacancy of the Benefice, the Governing Body of the College shall not nominate a Student or Chaplain of the House to be presented thereto, the right of presentation shall belong to the Dean and Chapter alone.

15. That no Student of the College not in actual residence (with the exception of any who, when this scheme takes effect, may be already in the receipt of room-rent)[1] shall be entitled to any room-rent.

16. That in regard to all Undergraduates who shall be hereafter admitted to residence, not being Junior Students, and not receiving any Exhibition of any Foundation in the House, there shall be no distinction in classification, dress, College charges, or College payments.

17. That all the provisions in the existing Christ Church Ordinance, not inconsistent with any recommendation herein made, shall, mutatis mutandis, be incorporated with the present scheme.

(Bodleian Library, G.A. Oxon. c. 258, no. 6)

[1] A reference to Giffard?

APPENDIX VIII

Ordinances Concerning Christ Church, 1867[1]

I. THE HOUSE OR COLLEGIATE FOUNDATION

THE House or Collegiate Foundation of the Cathedral Church of Christ, in Oxford, shall include the Dean, Six Canons, Twenty-eight Senior Students, and Fifty-two Junior Students, besides Chaplains and other Ministers and Servants of the said Cathedral Church.

The Six Canonries shall be those annexed respectively to the Regius Professorships of Divinity, Hebrew, Ecclesiastical History and Pastoral Theology, the Lady Margaret's Professorship of Divinity, and the Archdeaconry of Oxford.

It shall be lawful for the Governing Body herein-after mentioned, if and when they shall have at their disposal funds available for the purpose, to increase the number of Senior Studentships above Twenty-eight, and likewise to increase the number of Junior Studentships above Fifty-two by adding to the number of those which are herein-after called Open Junior Studentships. Provided that if, in the exercise of this power, Senior Studentships shall be created, not more than Twelve such Senior Studentships shall be added to the number of Twenty-eight, until Nine new Junior Studentships shall also have been created; and, if Junior Studentships shall be created, not more than Nine such Junior Studentships shall be added to the number of Fifty-two, until Twelve new Senior Studentships shall also have been created.

[1] At the beginning of Vere Bayne's copy of the 1872 revision of these Ordinances (Ch. Ch. Library MS. 513) are the cryptic words from Aeschylus, *Eumenides*, lines 490–1 (νῦν καταστροφαὶ νέων θεσμίων), which have long been a famous crux in Greek scholarship. Professor K. J. Dover, 'The Political Aspect of Aeschylus's *Eumenides*', *The Journal of Hellenic Studies*, lxxvii (1957), 230–1, argues that Aeschylus gave them their obvious meaning of 'Now new ordinances are overthrown'. Vere Bayne was probably referring with glee to the overthrow of the Ordinances of 1858: he inscribed the same words on his copy of the Referees' 'Recommendations and proposed Statutes' (Ch. Ch. Library MS. 354). For the reference to Professor Dover's note we are grateful to our colleague Mr. P. J. Parsons.

The number of Chaplains may, if the Dean and Canons shall think fit, be diminished by them as herein-after provided.

The Servitorships existing within the House shall be maintained, either under that designation or under such new designation as the Governing Body herein-after mentioned may determine; and the Exhibitions of the foundation of Archbishop Boulter for Servitors, Mr. Pauncefort, Dr. Gardiner, Bishop Frampton, Dr. Cotton, and Mrs. Paul may, in the latter case, be applied to the support of the persons bearing such altered designation.

II. THE GOVERNING BODY: ITS CONSTITUTION AND GENERAL POWERS

The Government of the Foundation, and the disposal and management of its Possessions and Revenues, including all Estates now vested in the Dean and Chapter, or in the Dean and Canons, or in the Dean and certain of the Canons, upon any Trust for purposes connected with the House, shall be vested in the Dean, Canons, and Senior Students; and all Powers and Authorities whatsoever heretofore exercised by the Dean and Canons alone, or by the Dean and Canons conjointly with any other person or persons within the House, shall henceforth be exercised by the Dean, Canons, and Senior Students, as the Governing Body of the House; except only certain powers and authorities which are herein-after expressly reserved to the Dean and Canons.

Students of the House elected before the day on which the Commissioners' Ordinance of the Ninth day of January 1858 was approved by Her Majesty in Council shall, if resident in the University, or holding any Office within the House, be entitled to act as members of the Governing Body. Those only shall for this purpose be considered resident in the University who shall, at the time when the privilege of Residence is claimed or exercised, be qualified as Residents to vote in the Congregation of the University under the Act 17th and 18th Victoria, chapter 81.

III. THE CORPORATE SEALS

Of the two Seals now in use by the Dean and Chapter, the one called 'the Small Seal' shall henceforth be 'the Chapter Seal,' and be retained for the exclusive use of the Dean and Chapter in the exercise of the powers herein reserved to them, and of other powers ordinarily vested in the Dean and Chapter of a Cathedral Church (except such as are herein specially conferred on the Governing Body hereby constituted); and the other Seal, called 'the Large Seal,' shall, with a duplicate thereof on a reduced scale, be 'the College Seal,' and be retained for the use of the Governing Body in the exercise of the powers herein conferred upon them. And the affixing of the College Seal shall be sufficient to pass all interest in real and personal Estate, the property of the House, or held in trust as aforesaid, the disposal and management whereof is hereby vested in the Governing Body.

IV. RESERVED POWERS OF THE DEAN AND CHAPTER

All Powers heretofore lawfully exercised by the Dean and Canons over and in respect of the Cathedral Church itself, its fabric and appurtenances, including the Chapter House, and over the Chaplains, Organist, Schoolmaster, Lay Clerks and Choristers, and other Ministers and Servants of the said Church, and over and in respect of the residentiary houses now occupied by the Dean and the six Canons herein-before referred to, shall be excepted out of the Powers assigned to the Governing Body, and shall be reserved to the Dean and Canons, as Dean and Chapter of the said Cathedral Church; and the Dean and Canons shall have, in respect of the things and persons aforesaid, all the powers now vested in them, or ordinarily vested in the Dean and Chapter of a Cathedral Church, subject only, as to the said Church, to the provision herein-after contained, under which it is, at certain times, to be used and regarded as a College Chapel for members of the House.

The Dean and Chapter may, if they shall think fit, diminish the number of Chaplains to not less than Four, by not filling up vacancies, and may assign to them such stipends, not less individually than the emoluments they have heretofore received, nor less in the aggregate than the emoluments heretofore received by the Six Chaplains, as the Dean and Chapter may think fit.

The Dean and Canons shall likewise have the exclusive disposal of the moneys to be annually set apart as herein-after directed, and to be called respectively the 'Cathedral Fabric Fund' and the 'Chapter Fund'.

In the exercise of the Powers herein reserved to them, and in the disposal of the said Funds, the Dean and Canons shall be free from all control or interference on the part of the Governing Body of the House, and subject only to the legal authority of the Visitor; and the Dean and Canons shall not on their part, otherwise than as individual members of the Governing Body, be entitled to control or interfere with the exercise of the powers herein assigned to the Governing Body.

V. USE OF THE CATHEDRAL

The Governing Body shall have power to arrange Services for the benefit of Undergraduate Members of the House, as well as for College servants, on Sundays and Holy Days, and to determine the time at which such Services shall be celebrated; provided always, that there be no interference with the ordinary Cathedral Service, and further that, in case the Canons should concur in adopting such Collegiate Service as the Cathedral Service also, the right of preaching Sermons or of appointing Preachers (if there should be Sermons) shall remain with the Dean and Chapter.

VI. RIGHT TO PRESENT TO LIVINGS

The right to present to vacant Benefices in the gift of the House, or held in Trust for any Members of the House as such, shall belong in the first instance to the Governing Body, but may be exercised by them only in favour of persons who shall be either Students or Chaplains of the House. If the Governing Body shall not within three calendar months after the avoidance of any Benefice have presented thereto a Student or Chaplain of the House, the right of Presentation shall pass to the Dean and Canons, who may exercise it in favour of any person whom they may think fit.

SEPARATE FUNDS

VII. *The Cathedral Fabric Fund*

The Governing Body shall, as soon as conveniently may be after these Recommendations shall come into force, and afterwards, once at least in every ten years, cause a Surveyor to report to them in writing what in his opinion will be the average annual expenditure required during the ensuing ten years for the repairs and proper sustentation of the Cathedral and its appurtenances, including the Chapter House. And the Governing Body shall thereupon order that a sum not less than the amount of such estimate shall be set apart in every year of such decennial period, or until a new estimate shall have been laid before them in the same manner. The annual sums so set apart shall form a separate Fund, which shall be called the 'Cathedral Fabric Fund,' and shall be applied to such repairs as aforesaid, under the exclusive control of the Dean and Chapter.

VIII. *The Chapter Fund*

The Governing Body shall further cause to be set apart in every year a sum not less than 17,000*l*., which shall be applicable, under the exclusive control of the Dean and Canons, to the following purposes, viz.:—

Payment of Stipends or Salaries to the Chaplains, Organist, Schoolmaster, Lay Clerks, Choristers, and other Ministers and Servants of the Cathedral Church, and of all outgoings and expenses whatever on account of or in relation to the said Church or the Celebration of Divine Service therein (other than those provided for by the Fabric Fund).

Payment of Cathedral Alms and Pensions.

Payment to the Dean and existing Canons of their respective Stipends or Emoluments in the accustomed proportions.

IX. *Regius Professor of Greek's Fund*

The Governing Body shall cause a yearly sum of 500*l*. to be set apart and paid out of the revenues of the House to the Regius Professor of Greek within the University for the time being, in addition to the two yearly sums of 40*l*. each now payable to the Regius Professor of Hebrew and the Regius Professor of Divinity.

X. APPLICATION OF REVENUES

The several sums herein-before directed to be set apart shall be considered as charges on the general revenues of the House, prior to all Studentships. The surplus revenue, after payment of all necessary charges and outgoings whatsoever, including the emoluments of the Senior and Junior Students, shall be at the disposal of the Governing Body, for the increase of the numbers of Senior and of Open Junior Studentships, and for other College purposes; with power, under the conditions and to the extent herein-after mentioned, to divide the same among the senior Students.

The income arising from the Canonry which has been suppressed in pursuance of the Commissioners' Ordinance, and that which will arise from the suppression of the seventh existing Canonry, shall always be applicable to such of the Senior Studentships as are herein-after called Clerical Studentships; yet not so as to raise the emoluments of any Clerical Studentships above those of any Lay Studentship, nor to increase the number of Clerical Studentships above that herein-after fixed.

XI. POWERS OF GOVERNING BODY AS TO COLLEGE OFFICERS AND BYELAWS

The Governing Body may from time to time regulate as they shall think fit the duties and emoluments of the officers of the House (not being such officers as are herein-before placed under the control of the Dean and Chapter), and the mode of their appointment or election, and may institute such new offices as they shall deem expedient for the better management of the property, revenue, and affairs of the House, and the instruction and discipline of its members, and may assign to such new offices such stipends or emoluments as the Governing Body shall think proper: Provided that it shall be lawful for the Visitor, upon the petition of any member of the Governing Body, or of any officer of the House whose stipend or emoluments may have been diminished in exercise of the foregoing power, to disallow such regulation or assignment if he shall think fit.

The Governing Body may from time to time make Bye-laws, binding on the Students, and on all members of the Governing Body, as such: Provided that such Byelaws be not repugnant to any Statute of the House.

XII. MEETINGS OF THE GOVERNING BODY

There shall be two stated General Meetings at least of the Governing Body in each year, on such days as the Governing Body shall appoint. Any stated General Meeting may be adjourned by resolution of the Meeting to a day to be specified in the resolution. The Governing Body may make from time to time such rules for regulating the proceedings at stated or special Meetings, and for determining what business shall be transacted thereat, and for fixing (if they shall think fit) the notice to be given before bringing forward any question, as they may deem expedient.

At all Meetings of the Governing Body (including Meetings for the Election or Deprivation of Senior or Junior Students) the Dean shall preside, and his vote shall be counted as two votes; and whenever the votes shall be equal he shall have an additional casting vote. Subject to the foregoing provision, and except in cases in which the concurrence of any specified proportion of the Governing Body is hereby made requisite, every question arising at any Meeting shall be determined by a majority of the votes of those present.

XIII. THE DEAN'S POWERS

All powers heretofore exercised by the Dean in respect of the general government and superintendence of the House, the enforcement of order and discipline, the appointment and removal of Tutors and otherwise, may be hereafter exercised by him, except so far as the exercise of such powers would be inconsistent with any provision herein contained. The Dean may, if he shall think fit, appoint from among the resident Senior Students a 'Censor Theologiæ,' who shall perform the functions and possess the powers hitherto performed and possessed by the Sub-Dean in relation to the Discipline of the House, but without prejudice to the precedence and authority enjoyed by the Sub-Dean at meetings of the Governing Body. The office of 'Censor Theologiæ,' if created, is, like other offices in the House, to be subject to the power of making Byelaws or Regulations possessed by the Governing Body.

XIV. THE SUB-DEAN

The authority heretofore possessed by the Sub-Dean to act in the place of the Dean in his absence shall be retained, subject to the operation of the Clause last preceding; and the Sub-Dean shall, at Meetings of the Governing Body, have the same precedence and power, if the Dean be absent, as the Dean would have had, if present.

XV. THE SENIOR STUDENTS

The election of Senior Students shall be held on a stated day or stated days in each year, to be appointed by the Governing Body (subject to the provision for postponement herein-after contained); and notice of such intended election and of the conditions of election shall be given by the Dean, in such manner as he shall deem best adapted to secure publicity, thirty days at least before the day of election.

The Senior Students shall be persons of unblemished character, conforming to the Liturgy of the United Church of England and Ireland as by law established, who shall have passed all the examinations required by the University for the Degree of Bachelor of Arts, unmarried, and not disqualified by the possession of any such property, benefice, pension, or office as herein-after mentioned. The Candidates shall be examined in such subjects connected with the studies of the University as the Governing Body shall from time to time determine; provided that the system of examinations shall be such as shall render Senior Studentships accessible from time to time to excellence in every branch of knowledge for the time being recognized in the Schools of the University; and the Governing Body shall choose that Candidate who after such examination shall appear to them to be of the greatest merit and most fit to be a Senior Student of the House as a place of religion, learning, and education. That Candidate for whom the greatest number of votes shall have been given shall be deemed elected. Whenever there shall be no duly qualified Candidate for a vacant Senior Studentship whom the Governing Body shall judge of sufficient merit for election, and whenever a Senior Studentship shall fall vacant and there shall not be time to give the notice herein-before directed before the day of election, the election shall be postponed to some other day, to be fixed by the Governing Body, not later than the next ensuing stated day of election to Senior Studentships; and every such postponed election shall be held and conducted in the same manner, and after the same previous notice, as if there had been no postponement.

Of the said twenty-eight Senior Studentships, nine (including the Lee's Readerships herein-after mentioned) shall be Lay, and nineteen shall be Clerical, Studentships. The holders of the Lay Studentships shall not be required, as a condition of retaining their Studentships, to take Holy Orders; but if any Lay Student should do so, then upon the next vacancy in a Clerical Studentship a Lay Student shall be elected, so that the aforesaid proportion between Lay and Clerical Studentships shall always be preserved as nearly as may be. No person shall be eligible to a Clerical Studentship who shall not either be a Priest or Deacon of the United Church of England and Ireland, or declare that he intends to take Holy Orders in the said Church. Every person who shall have made such declaration, or who at the time of his election shall be in Deacon's Orders, shall be required to take Priest's Orders within four years after the time at which he shall be of sufficient standing, according to the Statutes of the University, to take the Degree of Master of Arts, and in default thereof shall vacate his Studentship: Provided that it shall be lawful for the Governing Body, in case of sickness, or for any other very urgent cause, to grant a delay for a period not exceeding six months. Such additional Senior Studentships as the Governing Body may hereafter establish, to the number of Twelve or fewer, shall likewise be divided into Clerical and Lay Studentships, one at least in every three being a Lay Studentship. Any Senior Studentships which may be established after the number has been raised to Forty may also be divided in the same or any other proportion, or may be exclusively Lay or Clerical, as the Governing Body may think fit.

Every person elected to a Senior Studentship shall undergo probation for twelve calendar months from the day of his election inclusive, and at the end of such twelve calendar months shall be admitted an actual Senior Student, if found fit in the judgment of the Governing Body. Every person admitted to probation shall receive during the period of probation the same emoluments as if he had been admitted an actual Senior Student, but shall not be entitled to vote on any occasion.

Every Senior Student who shall marry shall thereupon vacate his Studentship.

Every Senior Student who shall be instituted to an ecclesiastical benefice, or shall become entitled, either by descent or devolution, or by virtue of any testamentary or other gift or settlement, to property, or to any government pension, or be admitted to any office tenable for life or during good behaviour (not being an academical office within the University of Oxford), and who shall retain such benefice, property, pension, or office for twelve calendar months from the day of his institution, accession, or admission thereto, shall, if such ecclesiastical benefice be a benefice with cure of souls (except in certain cases to be specified as herein-after mentioned), or if the annual income derivable by him from such property, pension, or office, or from any ecclesiastical benefice without cure of souls, or from any two or more of the above mentioned sources (including or not including a benefice with cure of souls), clear of deductions (except for property or income tax), shall exceed 500*l*., vacate his Studentship at the expiration of such twelve calendar months; and for this purpose the income which the estimated value of any property would produce, if invested in Three pounds per Centum Consolidated Annuities, at the price current at the time of the acquisition thereof, shall, in case of doubt, be considered to be the income derivable from such property. The Governing Body may, by a Byelaw or Byelaws, declare in what cases a benefice with cure of souls may be tenable with a Senior Studentship. The word 'property' shall in this clause include any estate or interest in possession in any property, real or personal. In any case in which the property or sources of income may have been acquired at several times, the latest time at which any part of such property or any of such sources of income shall have been acquired shall, in construing this clause, be considered as the time of the acquisition of the whole thereof. It shall be lawful for the Governing Body to require from any Senior Student any information which they may deem necessary for enabling them to enforce the provisions of this clause.

Every Senior Student who shall be appointed to a Canonry in the House (whether annexed to a Professorship or not), or shall be elected to and accept a Headship or Fellowship in any College within the University of Oxford, or any other University, shall thereupon vacate his Studentship.

The Governing Body may, from time to time, make such regulations respecting the residence of Senior Students within the University, and respecting the mode in which and the conditions under which leave of absence may be granted to any Senior Student, as they may deem expedient for the interests of the House as a place of learning and education, and may vary such regulations from time to time, and may enforce such regulations, if they shall think fit, by pecuniary penalties, and, in case of contumacious non-compliance, by deprivation. Present regulations respecting the residence of Senior Students shall be binding until altered by the Governing Body.

Every holder of a Clerical Studentship shall be required to take the Degree of Master of Arts within one year after the time at which he shall be of sufficient standing to take that Degree by the Statutes of the University; and every holder of a Lay Studentship shall be required to take either the Degree of Master of Arts, or the Degrees of Bachelor and Doctor of Civil Law, or those of Bachelor and Doctor of Medicine, within one year after the times at which he shall be of sufficient standing to take those Degrees respectively by the Statutes of the University. Any Student failing to comply with the foregoing provisions shall vacate his Studentship; provided that the Governing Body may, whenever they shall deem it just on special grounds to do so, allow the taking of any such degree to be postponed for a period not exceeding, except in case of unsoundness of mind or disability of body, one year.

Any Senior Student who shall, in the judgment of the Governing Body, or the major part of it, have been proved guilty of grave immorality, or of contumaciously ceasing to conform to the Liturgy of the United Church of England and Ireland as by law established, shall cease to be a Student of the House; and every Senior Student who shall in like manner have been judged guilty of conduct bringing dishonour upon the House, or gross negligence or misconduct in any office within the same, or of contumacious non-observance of the Statutes or Byelaws of the House, or of grossly offensive behaviour towards any member thereof, may be deprived of his Studentship by the Governing Body, if, in the judgment of the Governing Body, or the major part of it, the gravity of the offence shall so require.

The emoluments of each Senior Student shall be 200*l.* per annum, exclusive of rooms, but inclusive of all other allowances, or as near thereto as the funds available for the purpose will admit. If and when the number of Senior Studentships and that of Open Junior Studentships shall have been respectively raised to Forty, the surplus Revenues of the House, after all prior charges have been satisfied, may be divided among the Senior Students; but so that the emoluments of a Senior Studentship shall never exceed 300*l.* per annum, exclusive of rooms.

The Governing Body may nevertheless, if they shall think fit, at any time increase the emoluments of every Senior Student who shall be a College Officer, Tutor, Reader, or Lecturer within the House to an amount not exceeding 300*l.* per annum, exclusive of rooms, but inclusive of all other allowances.

XVI. *Dr. Lee's Readers*

Of the Senior Students, one shall always be a person qualified to give instruction in Anatomy, and another to give instruction in Chemistry. They shall be called respectively 'Dr. Lee's Reader in Anatomy,' and 'Dr. Lee's Reader in Chemistry,' and shall be bound to lecture or otherwise give instruction in those Sciences, as the Governing Body may direct. No person in Holy Orders shall be eligible to either of the said Readerships; and any Reader who shall take Holy Orders shall thereupon vacate his Studentship.

The emoluments of each Reader shall never be less than 200*l.* per annum, exclusive of rooms, but inclusive of all other allowances, and shall be a charge upon the income of the lands and tenements held under the Will of the said Dr. Matthew Lee, posterior to the annual charge or sum of 1,260*l.* herein-after appropriated to Westminster Junior Studentships; if such income shall not be sufficient, they shall be further charged upon the General Revenues of the House. The Lee's Readers shall, as to emoluments and otherwise, be on the same footing as other Senior Students, except that their emoluments are not to fall short of the minimum above specified.

XVII. *Honorary Students*

It shall be lawful for the Governing Body, at stated general meetings, to elect distinguished persons to Honorary Studentships within the House. Persons so elected shall be termed Honorary Students, and shall not be entitled to vote on any occasion as Students, or to receive any emolument whatever, but shall be entitled to enjoy such other privileges and advantages as the Governing Body shall by resolution from time to time determine. The conditions of eligibility to and tenure of Honorary Studentships, and the mode of election thereto, may also be determined by the Governing Body from time to time. Honorary Students shall not, in the construction of this Ordinance, be counted among the Students of the House, nor Honorary Studentships among the Studentships of the House.

XVIII. THE JUNIOR STUDENTS

Of the Fifty-two Junior Studentships, twenty-one shall be called Westminster Junior Studentships; the remaining thirty-one are herein-after referred to as Open Junior Studentships.

Of the Open Junior Studentships, there shall be seven called the Fell Studentships, two called the Bostock Studentships, and two called respectively the Vernon and the Boulter Studentships.

XIX. *The Westminster Junior Students*

The emoluments of the Westminster Junior Studentships shall be of such amount, not less than 115*l.* nor more than 125*l.* each per annum, as the Governing Body shall determine. An annual sum of 1,260*l.* out of the income of the lands and tenements held under the Will of Dr. Matthew Lee, together with the emoluments of the Exhibitions of the foundations of Dr. South, Dr. Frewin, and Canon Hill, shall be applied towards the maintenance of these Studentships.

The Westminster Junior Studentships shall be filled up at Westminster School on the Wednesday in Rogation Week in each year, or on such other day as the Electors shall from time to time determine, by election from those boys on the Royal Foundation of the Collegiate Church of St. Peter, Westminster, who shall have been presented as Candidates by the Head Master of the said School. The electors shall be those persons who, under the Statutes of the said Collegiate Church of Westminster, would have been entitled to elect to Studentships on the old Foundation. The Candidates shall be examined in such subjects as shall have been previously selected by the Head Master, with the approval of the Dean of the said Collegiate Church, and in such manner as the electors shall determine; and those candidates shall be elected whom, after such examination, the electors shall deem to be of the greatest merit, and who shall desire to proceed to Christ Church, and shall, in the judgment of the Dean of Christ Church or his duly appointed representative present at the election, be in all respects fit to be admitted Students of the House. Whenever there shall be no duly qualified Candidate for a Westminster Junior Studentship of sufficient merit for election in the judgment of the majority of the electors, and fit as aforesaid to be admitted a Student of the House, the election to such Studentship shall be postponed to the next annual election day; but if there shall then be no duly qualified Candidate of sufficient merit for election and fit as aforesaid, such Studentship shall be thrown open for that turn to general competition as an open Junior Studentship, and the election thereto shall be held at Christ Church by the same persons after public notice for the same time, and after an examination conducted in the same manner, as an ordinary election to an open Junior Studentship.

Each Westminster Junior Studentship shall be tenable until the Tuesday in Rogation Week in the seventh year from the day of election inclusive, and no longer. Any Junior Studentship which shall be filled up at Westminster School at an election postponed under the foregoing provisions shall be tenable until the Tuesday in Rogation Week in the sixth year from the day of election inclusive, and no longer. Any Westminster Junior Studentship which shall be thrown open to general competition shall be tenable until the expiration of the period for which it would have been tenable if the election thereto had not been postponed, and no longer. The Governing Body shall not be required to fill up in any one year more than three Westminster Junior Studentships (exclusive of any Studentship the election to which may have been postponed under the foregoing provisions).

XX. *Open Junior Studentships*

The emoluments of the Open Junior Studentships shall be not less than 75*l.* each per annum, exclusive of rooms, but inclusive of all other allowances; and may be raised if the Governing Board shall deem it expedient, and have sufficient funds at command, to 100*l.* per annum, exclusive of rooms.

The election to Open Junior Studentships, other than the Vernon Studentship, shall be held on a stated day or stated days in each year to be appointed by the Governing Body (subject to the provision for postponement herein-after contained); and notice of such intended election, and of the conditions of election, shall be given by the Dean, in such manner as he shall deem best adapted to ensure publicity, thirty days at least before the day of election. The Candidates shall be examined in such subjects and manner as the Governing Body shall determine; and that Candidate shall be elected who, after such examination, shall appear to the electors to be of the greatest merit and most fit to be a Student of the House; provided that in elections to one in every three Open Junior Studentships the subjects of competitive examination shall be alternately Mathematics and Physical Science. On each vacancy occurring in the Vernon Studentship, the Patron of that Studentship shall be required to appoint an election thereto at the next ensuing election to Open Junior Studentships. The Candidates shall be examined by such persons and in such manner as the Patron shall appoint; and that Candidate shall be chosen who, after such examination, shall appear to the Patron to be of the greatest merit. If the Patron shall decline or neglect to appoint an election and examiners, thirty days previous notice at least having been given to him by the Dean, the election to the Vernon Studentship shall be held for that turn by the same person and in the same manner as to the other Open Junior Studentships. No Candidate for the Vernon Studentships or for any of the Studentships appropriated to the encouragement of Mathematics and Physical Science as aforesaid, shall be entitled to be admitted to a Studentship if in the judgment of the electors to Open Junior Studentships he shall not be in all respects fit to be a Student of the House.

No person shall be admissible as a Candidate for any Open Junior Studentship who shall have exceeded the age of nineteen years on the first day of January last preceding (except in the case of Physical Science Studentships), or who shall not have produced a certificate of baptism and testimonials of his moral character satisfactory to the Dean. Persons shall be admissible as Candidates for Physical Science Studentships who shall not have exceeded the age of twenty years on the first day of January last preceding.

Each Open Junior Studentship shall be tenable for five years from the day of election inclusive, and no longer.

Whenever there shall be no duly qualified Candidate for a vacant Open Junior Studentship whom the electors or the Patron, as the case may be, shall judge of sufficient merit for election, and whenever an Open Junior Studentship shall fall vacant, and there shall not be time to give the notice hereinbefore directed before the day of election, the election shall be postponed to some other day, to be fixed by the Governing Body, or the Patron, not later than the next ensuing stated day of election to Open Junior Studentships; and every such postponed election shall be held and conducted in the same manner, and after the same previous notice, as if there had been no postponement. In the case of any Open Junior Studentship, the election to which shall have been postponed under the provisions of this Ordinance, the term of five years shall be computed from the day on which the election would have been held if there had been no postponement.

The Governing Body shall not be required to fill up more than six Open Junior Studentships in any one year, so long as the whole number of Open Junior Studentships shall be less than forty.

XXI. *Discipline and Causes of Deprivation of Junior Students*

Any Junior Student who shall marry, or be elected to a Senior Studentship, or to a place on the foundation of any other Collegiate Body within the University, shall thereby vacate his Studentship.

Any Junior Student may be deprived of his Studentship by the Governing Body for any misconduct which, in the judgment of the Governing Body, or the major part of them, shall merit deprivation.

Every Junior Student, and every Member of the House under the Degree of Master of Arts, shall be subject to such general regulations as to residence, discipline, and attendance on Divine Worship as may be made from time to time by the Governing Body.

XXII. THE VISITOR

If in any case it shall appear to the Visitor that by reason of any change in the value of money, or increase or diminution of the revenues of the House, any specific sum hereby fixed or which may be hereafter fixed, or any limitation of the amount of any stipend or emolument hereby fixed or which may hereafter be fixed, in exercise of any power hereby given, has become insufficient or excessive, and that such insufficiency or excess is productive of injustice or hardship, or is injurious to the general interests of the House, it shall be lawful for the Visitor, from time to time, for the purpose of correcting or obviating such injustice, hardship, or injury, to direct that such annual sum or limitation shall be increased or diminished as he shall think fit, and the increased or diminished sum or limitation shall thenceforth be substituted for and stand in the place of the sum originally fixed as aforesaid.

The Governing Body shall, as often as they may be required to do so, answer in writing touching any matter as to which the Visitor may deem it expedient to inquire, for the purpose of satisfying himself whether the Statutes in force for the time being are duly observed. The Dean and Chapter shall in like manner, and for the like purpose, be bound to answer any such inquiry as to themselves, the exercise of their Reserved Powers, and the persons and things under their control.

It shall be lawful for the Dean, or for any Canon or Senior Student, if he shall conceive himself aggrieved by any act, decision, or sentence of the Governing Body, and for any Chaplain who may deem himself aggrieved by any act or decision of the Dean or of the Dean and Chapter, and for any Junior Student or Exhibitioner who may have been deprived of his Studentship or Exhibition, to appeal against such act or decision or sentence to the Visitor; and it shall be lawful for the Visitor to adjudicate on such appeal, and to disallow or annul such act or decision, and to reverse or vary such sentence, as he shall deem just.

It shall be lawful for the Visitor, on the complaint of the Dean or of any member of the Governing Body, to disallow and annul any Byelaw which shall in his judgment be repugnant to any of the Statutes of the House in force for the time being.

As often as any question shall arise on which the Members of the Governing Body shall be unable to agree, depending wholly or in part on the construction of a Statute of the House, it shall be lawful for the Governing Body, or any three of them, to submit the same to the Visitor, and the Visitor may thereupon declare what is the true construction of such Statute with reference to the case submitted to him. Any like question which may arise between the Governing Body and the Dean and Chapter may be in like manner submitted to the Visitor by the Governing Body or the Dean and Chapter.

XXIII. POWER TO ALTER OR REPEAL

It shall be lawful for Her Majesty in Council, upon the application of the Governing Body of the House, such application having been agreed to at a stated General Meeting by a majority of not less than two thirds of the votes of those present, from time to time to repeal or to alter any clause or provision herein contained, or to add new clauses or provisions: Provided that no such repeal, alteration, or addition shall extend to or affect such of the provisions herein contained as reserve any special rights or powers to the Dean and Chapter: Provided also, that notice of every proposal to apply to Her Majesty for any such repeal, alteration, or addition shall have been given at the stated General Meeting next preceding that at which such proposal may be adopted.

MISCELLANEOUS

XXIV. *Holford Exhibitions*

The two consolidated Holford Exhibitions shall respectively be tenable for five years from the day of election inclusive, and no longer. The Exhibitioners shall be elected, after a competitive examination of the Candidates, from among persons educated at the Charterhouse School for two years at least last preceding the day of election, or last preceding their matriculation in the University. No person shall be entitled to preference by reason of his being an Exhibitioner or Pensioner of Sutton's Hospital. No person shall be admissible as a Candidate who shall have completed the fourth Term inclusive from the date of his matriculation. The Dean shall give thirty days notice at least of every intended election to the Head Master of the Charterhouse School, and shall also give public notice thereof for the same period.

Whenever there shall be no Candidate whom the electors shall judge of sufficient merit for election, the Exhibition shall be thrown open for that turn to general competition, and the election shall be postponed to a day to be appointed by the electors, not later than the next ensuing stated day of election to Open Junior Studentships. It shall be lawful for the Governing Body, with the consent of the Governors of the Charterhouse, to increase the number of the Exhibitions, if there shall be sufficient funds for that purpose, but so that the emoluments of each Exhibition shall not fall short of 60*l.* per annum.

XXV. *Exhibitions for Commoners*

The Governing Body may create Exhibitions for Commoners of the House out of the moneys left for that purpose by Bishop Fell, Archbishop Boulter, and Mrs. Bostock, when those moneys shall have ceased to be required for the temporary purpose of establishing Open Junior Studentships.

XXVI. *Bishop Wood's Estate*

No clause or provision herein contained shall extend to or include the estate held under the Will of Bishop Wood for the benefit of the Senior Masters of the House, being Students, or any payments or allowances which may be made thereout pursuant to the said Will, except that holders of Senior Studentships shall, and holders of Junior Studentships shall not, be deemed Students of the House within the meaning of the said Will.

XXVII. *Room-rents*

No Student of the House, not being actually resident, shall be entitled to receive any room-rent in respect of his rooms within the House.

XXVIII. *Certain Distinctions abolished*

There shall be no distinctions in respect of Academical dress, designation, College charges, or College payments, among Undergraduate Members of the House, not being Junior Students nor Exhibitioners within the House.

XXIX. TEMPORARY PROVISIONS

The Canonry now existing, not attached either to a Professorship or to the Archdeaconry of Oxford, shall not be filled up when it shall become vacant, and the portion of the Chapter Fund devoted to the support of this Canonry shall thereafter be at the disposal of the Governing Body. Meanwhile, the House or Collegiate Foundation shall be deemed to consist of the Dean and Seven Canons, and other Members, as provided in Clause I.

Studentships of the old Foundation, when they become vacant, are not to be filled up.

The whole number of the said twenty-eight Senior and fifty-two Junior Studentships shall be completed as speedily as the amount of the funds gradually becoming available will permit. The relative rate at which the whole number of Senior and Junior Studentships shall be established shall be in the discretion of the Governing Body; provided that three Westminster Junior Studentships shall be established in every year in which the Governing Body shall have in their hands sufficient means for the purpose; and it shall be lawful for the Governing Body, in order to enable themselves to establish such three Studentships yearly, to apply to that purpose from time to time, and so long as it may be necessary, in addition to the sum of 1,260*l.* above specified, any portion of the income of the estates and funds held under the Will of Dr. M. Lee which shall not be required for carrying into effect the provisions of this Ordinance and the other regulations for the time being in force respecting the application of the said income.

The emoluments of Westminster Junior Studentships may, at the first establishment thereof, be 75*l.* each per annum, exclusive of rooms; but they shall be raised, with all convenient speed, to the minimum amount, herein-before fixed, of 115*l.* per annum, exclusive of rooms.

One Lay Senior Studentship shall be established for every two Clerical Studentships until the whole number of nine Lay Studentships shall be completed.

The emoluments of the Exhibitions of the Foundations of Bishop Fell, of Archbishop Boulter, for Commoners, and of Mrs. Bostock, may be applied towards the maintenance of the Open Junior Studentships so long as it may be necessary; but, so soon as the funds necessary for the endowment of those Studentships shall have been provided from other sources, the Governing Body may create Exhibitions for Commoners of the House out of the moneys left by Bishop Fell, Archbishop Boulter, and Mrs. Bostock for that purpose.

The power of appointing a Censor Theologiæ herein-before given to the Dean shall not be exercised until after the next vacancy in the office of Sub-Dean.

The Governing Body may, if they think fit, increase the emoluments of any Student on the Old Foundation who shall be a College-officer, Tutor, Reader, or Lecturer, within the House, to an amount not exceeding 300*l.* per annum, exclusive of rooms but inclusive of all other allowances.

Nothing contained in the above provisions shall be taken to interfere with any of the emoluments heretofore enjoyed by Students on the Old Foundation.

The limitations of age above specified (Clause XX.) shall not apply to Candidates for Junior Studentships who may have matriculated before the 24th day of March 1866. Of such persons no one shall be admissible as a Candidate who on the day of election will have completed the eighth Term inclusive from the date of his matriculation. And the prohibition of distinctions in respect of dress, precedence, payments, and charges shall not apply to Undergraduate Members of the House who shall before that time have been admitted to residence.

C. T. CANTUAR
J. T. COLERIDGE
W. P. WOOD
ROUNDELL PALMER
EDWARD TWISLETON

APPENDIX IX

Canons of Christ Church, 1830–67

The Chapter in 1830	*Date of installation*	*No. of stall*	*Date of death or resignation*
*Edward Christopher Dowdeswell	13 Feb. 1808	IV	d. 1 Aug. 1849
*Frederick Barnes	17 Feb. 1810	VII	d. 19 Aug. 1859
*Henry Woodcock	19 Mar. 1824	II	d. 8 Aug. 1840
William Buckland (C.C.C.)	14 July 1825	I	r. 1845
†*Edward Bouverie Pusey	9 Dec. 1828	VI	d. 16 Sept. 1882
†*Edward Burton	1 Aug. 1829	V	d. 19 Jan. 1836
*Richard William Jelf	15 Mar. 1830	VIII	d. 19 Oct. 1871
*John Bull	15 Mar. 1830	III	d. 21 Feb. 1858
The succession of Canons, 1830–67			
†Renn Dickson Hampden (Oriel and St. Mary Hall) (*vice* †*Burton)	1 Mar. 1836	V	r. 1848
†Godfrey Faussett (Corpus and Magdalen) (*vice* *Woodcock)	19 Aug. 1840	II	d. July 1853
*Charles Carr Clerke (*vice* Buckland)	29 Mar. 1846	I	d. 24 Dec. 1877
†William Jacobson (S.E.H., Lincoln, Exeter, and Magdalen Hall) (*vice* †Hampden)	13 Apr. 1848	V	r. 1865
†Charles Atmore Ogilvie (Balliol) (*vice* *Dowdeswell)	10 Aug. 1849	IV	d. 17 Feb. 1873
†Charles Abel Heurtley (C.C.C.) (*vice* †Faussett)	8 July 1853	II	d. 30 Apr. 1895
†Arthur Penrhyn Stanley (Balliol and Univ.) (*vice* *Bull)	13 Mar. 1858	III	r. 1863
†Walter Waddington Shirley (Univ. and Wadham) (*vice* †Stanley)	13 Feb. 1864	III	d. 20 Nov. 1866
†Robert Payne Smith (Pembroke) (*vice* †Jacobson)	11 Oct. 1865	V	r. 1871
†Henry Longueville Mansel (St. John's and Magdalen) (*vice* †Shirley)	29 Jan. 1867	III	r. 1868

NOTE: The Canonries (i.e. the Seventh and Eighth Stalls) voided by the deaths of Barnes in 1859 and of Jelf in 1871 were not filled up.

* Gremial member of Christ Church.   d. Died.
† University Professor.   r. Resigned.

INDEX

Peers are indexed under their surnames

PRINTED IN GREAT BRITAIN
AT THE UNIVERSITY PRESS, OXFORD
BY VIVIAN RIDLER
PRINTER TO THE UNIVERSITY